Forensic Mental Health Practice and the Law

Forensic Mental Health Practice and the Law

A Primer for Clinicians, Researchers, and Consultants

DAVID DEMATTEO
DANIEL A. KRAUSS
SARAH FISHEL
KELLIE WILTSIE

OXFORD
UNIVERSITY PRESS

OXFORD
UNIVERSITY PRESS

Oxford University Press is a department of the University of Oxford.
It furthers the University's objective of excellence in research, scholarship,
and education by publishing worldwide. Oxford is a registered trade mark of
Oxford University Press in the UK and in certain other countries.

Published in the United States of America by Oxford University Press
198 Madison Avenue, New York, NY 10016, United States of America.

CIP data is on file at the Library of Congress

ISBN 9780197686560

DOI: 10.1093/9780197686591.001.0001

Printed by Marquis Book Printing, Canada

The manufacturer's authorized representative in the EU for product safety is
Oxford University Press España S.A., Parque Empresarial San Fernando de Henares,
Avenida de Castilla, 2 – 28830 Madrid (www.oup.es/en or product.safety@oup.com).
OUP España S.A. also acts as importer into Spain of products made by the manufacturer.

MIX
Paper | Supporting responsible forestry
FSC® C103567
FSC www.fsc.org

To Don Bersoff, my mentor, colleague, and friend, who trained generations of psychology-law scholars, researchers, and practitioners
Dave DeMatteo

To my family, who always stands by me
Daniel A. Krauss

To Jonah, whose unwavering support made my contributions to this book possible
Sarah Fishel

To my mother, for providing me with unending love and support in pursuing my passion
Kellie Wiltsie

Contents

Preface

It is axiomatic that mental health professionals working within the legal system should have a sufficient understanding of the laws applicable to their work. The work of forensic mental health professionals, regardless of whether they are clinicians, researchers, or consultants, takes place (and/or is important) in the legal system. As such, mental health professionals who work within the legal system must be familiar with relevant legal considerations.

Despite the foundational importance of understanding the law, most forensic mental health professionals do not have any formal legal training, which can make it challenging for them to develop a sufficient understanding of the legal cases, court rules, and statutes applicable to their work. Ideally, forensic mental health professionals would have knowledge of several key concepts, including the structure of the United States court system, standards and rules that govern the recognition of experts and the admissibility of expert testimony, the process of discovery, the legal bases of expert testimony, how expert reports and testimony may be affected by the rule against hearsay (and other rules regarding inadmissible evidence), laws governing interjurisdictional and telepsychology practice, and expert immunity. These can be complex issues, with a variety of nuances, intricacies, and jurisdictional differences in how courts and laws operate. There are also various sources of law, including state and federal constitutions, statutes, case law, and administrative regulations, that can be challenging to understand and apply, particularly when those laws are confusing or conflicting.

We wrote this book to provide forensic mental health professionals with relevant information about the legal system, particularly as it relates to the work of forensic clinicians, researchers, and consultants. Given the topics we cover and the associated chapter content, we believe this book is appropriate for students who are aspiring to work in the forensic mental health field, early career professionals who are already in the field or interested in pursuing forensic work, and experienced forensic professionals. The chapters provide both foundational and advanced knowledge that will be useful to students and professionals at all levels. To enhance the book's utility, we structured it so that it can be read in the traditional cover-to-cover way, or readers can focus on specific chapters of interest.

Two caveats are worth noting. First, although all four authors have law degrees, this book should not be construed to constitute legal advice. Readers with specific legal questions should consult with a legal professional in their jurisdiction. Second, this book is intended to be a primer, which means that we provide an overview of select topics that are relevant to forensic mental health professionals. Many of the topics we cover can be (and have been) the focus of an entire book. To that end, we provide readers with many citations to other useful sources.

We appreciate the outstanding support we received from Oxford University Press, particularly Emily Benitez, Lacey Harvey, and Sarah Harrington, who have made this book much stronger. We also thank David Koller, Esq., and Jordan Santo, Esq., for their helpful feedback on select portions of this book. Finally, we thank the many clinicians, researchers, consultants, legal professionals, and students who continue to shape the psychology-law field.

Dave DeMatteo
Daniel A. Krauss
Sarah Fishel
Kellie Wiltsie

Chapter 1
United States Legal System
Structure and Function

We begin from the premise that mental health professionals who work within, or adjacent to, the legal system should have a sufficient understanding of the laws relevant to their work. Indeed, Section 2.04 of the American Psychological Association's *Specialty Guidelines for Forensic Psychology* highlights the necessity for forensic psychologists to have "a fundamental and reasonable level of knowledge and understanding of the legal and professional standards, laws, rules, and precedents that govern their participation in legal proceedings and that guide the impact of their services on service recipients" (American Psychological Association, 2013, p. 9). Similarly, the ethical guidelines applicable to forensic psychiatrists (*Ethics Guidelines for the Practice of Forensic Psychiatry*) highlight the need for forensic psychiatrists to understand the relevant legal rules and procedures (American Academy of Psychiatry and the Law, 2005).

Recognizing the need for forensic mental health professionals to have a sufficient understanding of the legal system, prominent scholars have expressed concern regarding forensic mental health professionals' lack of legal knowledge. Nearly 40 years ago, Grisso (1986, 2003) identified five concerns (known colloquially as the five "I's") related to forensic mental health assessments: ignorance of the law, irrelevance of the expert's opinion, intrusion into matters of law, insufficiency of evidence supporting an expert's opinion, and incredibility (i.e., lack of credibility) of information provided by experts. It is not surprising that ignorance of the law is the first of the five concerns identified by Grisso (1986, 2003).

As "guests" in the legal system, forensic mental health professionals, regardless of whether they are clinicians, researchers, or consultants, should have (at least) a working knowledge of the structure and function of the legal system. Possessing an understanding of the legal system can increase competence in performing forensic mental health assessments, conducting forensically relevant research, providing consultation to the legal system, and communicating results to legal decision-makers. As such, this chapter provides an overview of the United States legal system, which serves as foundational material for the remainder of this book.

Forensic Mental Health Practice and the Law. David DeMatteo, Daniel A. Krauss, Sarah Fishel, and Kellie Wiltsie, Oxford University Press. © Oxford University Press (2025). DOI: 10.1093/9780197686591.003.0001

Classifications of Law

There are two primary classifications of law in the United States legal system: criminal law and civil law.[1] Criminal law addresses harms against society, while civil law, which is often broadly defined as all non–criminal law matters, deals largely with private disputes in which individual rights or interests have been violated by an individual, organization, or other entity. The United States developed this dual system of laws that permits parallel causes of action in both systems because each system of law has unique remedies, which means that an aggrieved individual can potentially bring legal actions in both systems (criminal and civil) based on the same alleged misdeed. Regarding the latter point, most criminal offenses have a civil analog. For example, the crime of murder has a civil analog of wrongful death, and the crime of kidnapping has a civil analog of false imprisonment. If someone is physically harmed, for example, the alleged perpetrator can be criminally prosecuted for assault in criminal court and sued for battery in civil court. We provide more detail on the differences between criminal law and civil law in the sections that follow.

Proof: Standards and Burdens

To prevail in a court case (criminal or civil), the party alleging the misdeed—either the prosecution in a criminal case or the plaintiff in a civil case—bears the burden of proving its case to a specified level of proof. There are three primary standards of proof in the United States legal system, with each standard being used in specific criminal or civil contexts (see Allen & Stein, 2013; Kaplow, 2012).[2] The lowest standard of proof is preponderance of the evidence, which is defined as more likely than not. This standard of proof can be conceptualized as slightly tipping the scale in the burden-holder's favor. Although many scholars and commentators believe that it is not possible to quantify the two higher standards of proof (discussed below), preponderance of the evidence is often conceptualized as 51%.[3] The preponderance standard is used in most civil contexts, and it is the easiest standard to meet in terms of the strength of evidence needed to satisfy it.

The mid-level standard of proof is clear and convincing evidence, which is used in some civil and criminal contexts. This standard requires the party bearing the burden to prove that a particular fact is substantially more likely than not to be true. Some commentators have noted that most jury instructions on clear and convincing evidence do not define the required degree of belief and instead simply highlight the amount and quality of evidence that is necessary to satisfy the burden (see McCauliff, 1982).

The most stringent standard of proof in the United State legal system is beyond a reasonable doubt, which is the standard used for convictions in criminal cases. The Supreme Court of the United States has never explicitly defined "beyond a reasonable doubt" and has concluded that the standard "defies easy explication" (*Victor v. Nebraska*, 1994, p. 5). In *Victor v. Nebraska* (1994), which is a Supreme Court case that devoted considerable space in the opinion to discussing the reasonable doubt standard, the Court held that the United States Constitution neither requires nor prohibits trial courts from defining reasonable doubt. The only requirement, per the Supreme Court in *Victor*, is that trial courts instruct the jury on the necessity for the prosecution to prove the defendant's guilt beyond a reasonable doubt. What is clear, however, is that beyond a reasonable doubt does not require absolute certainty (Kaplow, 2012).

Criminal Law

A crime is viewed as an offense against society. Although criminal behavior is typically associated with a specific victim, a criminal offense is also conceptualized as inflicting harm on society because the alleged wrongdoer has violated a social norm expressed in the form of a law. As such, a criminal case is brought by the government (state or federal) against the alleged perpetrator of the criminal offense. For state crimes, the criminal case is the State versus the alleged perpetrator (e.g., *California v. Jones*), while the federal government is responsible for prosecuting federal crimes (e.g., *United States v. Jones*). The prosecutor represents the government (and society) and is responsible for proving the criminal charges against the defendant; there are no private prosecutions for criminal offenses in the United States. During a trial, the prosecutor must prove each element of the charged offense(s) beyond a reasonable doubt, and the verdict is reached by the judge or jury; defendants have a constitutional right to choose a jury trial, but they can also choose to have their case heard solely by a judge, which is referred to as a bench trial.

The goals of the criminal justice system are invariably described as incapacitation (to physically prevent the convicted individual from engaging in further criminal behavior), retribution (i.e., "just desserts" for the convicted individual), specific deterrence (to prevent the convicted individual from committing future criminal acts), general deterrence (to set an example that deters other would-be perpetrators from engaging in criminal behavior), and rehabilitation (to provide opportunities for the individual to reform their behavior) (see Slobogin et al., 2020). To accomplish these goals, various punishments may be imposed when someone is convicted of a criminal offense, including monetary fines, community supervision (e.g., probation, parole), intermediate sanctions (e.g., house arrest, boot camp), incarceration, and death.

There are several pleas available to defendants in the United States legal system. The basic pleas, which are a decision that must be made by the defendant (not defense counsel) before a trial begins, are not guilty, guilty, and no contest (with variations on some of these pleas described below). A plea of not guilty indicates that the defendant does not believe the prosecution can satisfy its burden of proving the case. The defendant may be proclaiming factual innocence by denying any wrongdoing, or the defendant may simply believe that the prosecution cannot satisfy its burden of proving the charges against the defendant beyond a reasonable doubt.

A plea of guilty indicates that the defendant wishes to avoid trial and accept the punishment imposed by the court. Pleading guilty results in the waiver of certain rights, including the right to a trial (and therefore the right to force the prosecution to prove the defendant's guilt beyond a reasonable doubt), the right to file further motions in trial court (e.g., a motion alleging evidence was obtained in violation of the defendant's constitutional rights), the right to testify at trial and/or confront witnesses that would testify against the defendant, and the right to an appeal (based on most legal grounds). Most cases in the criminal justice system are resolved through a plea deal in which the defendant pleads guilty in exchange for a disposition that is more lenient than what could have been imposed if the defendant were to be convicted at trial. In recent years, approximately 98% of federal criminal cases were resolved via plea bargains (Hitt, 2022). Although exact numbers in state courts are harder to find, it is estimated that 90–95% of state criminal cases are resolved via plea bargains (Devers, 2011); some jurisdictions have not held a trial in several years because all of their cases were resolved via pleas (American Bar Association Criminal Justice Section, 2023).

A specific type of guilty plea is the *Alford* plea, which is when a defendant pleads guilty but maintains factual innocence (*North Carolina v. Alford*, 1970; see Redlich & Özdoğru, 2009). In *North Carolina v. Alford* (1970), the Supreme Court of the United States held that it is constitutionally permissible for a judge to accept a guilty plea from a defendant who is also maintaining their innocence. Some scholars have raised concerns about *Alford* pleas because they permit courts to punish defendants who have not been found guilty or admitted to the criminal offense (see Conklin, 2020, for a discussion of arguments for and against *Alford* pleas). Nevertheless, *Alford* pleas are available in almost every jurisdiction.

There is a variation of a plea deal called an open plea. Typically, when a defendant pleads guilty as part of a plea deal, the defendant is aware of the punishment being recommended by the prosecutor, and that punishment is usually less severe than what could have been imposed if the defendant had been convicted at trial. The deal needs to be approved by the court, but the court often gives leeway to the prosecution and defense to agree on a disposition. However, in an open plea, the defendant pleads guilty without any promise from the prosecution regarding the recommended punishment, and the court is responsible for ruling on the verdict and fashioning the disposition.

A plea of no contest is similar to a guilty plea, although the defendant is not admitting guilt. Like a guilty plea, a defendant pleading no contest will be convicted without a trial, and certain procedural rights are forfeited. A key difference between a guilty plea and a no contest plea is the effect the plea has in another legal case stemming from the same alleged misdeed. Specifically, if a defendant pleads guilty in a criminal case, the guilty plea can be used against the defendant in a subsequent civil case based on the same misdeed; the defendant's admission of guilt associated with a guilty plea can be "transferred" to the civil court and used as evidence against the defendant in the civil proceedings. However, a plea of no contest does not involve an express admission of guilt, so the plea cannot be used against the defendant in a subsequent civil case.

There are variations on the basic pleas available to defendants. For example, in jurisdictions that offer the insanity defense, a defendant can plead not guilty by reason of insanity (or however the specific plea is worded in that jurisdiction) (Melton et al., 2018; Slobogin et al., 2020). By using this plea, the defendant is acknowledging that they committed the criminal offense, but asserting that they should not be held criminally responsible, typically due to the presence of mental health symptoms that interfered with their ability to understand right from wrong or their ability to conform their behavior to the requirements of the law (see Packer, 2009).[4]

Another plea (and/or verdict) in some jurisdictions is guilty but mentally ill (GBMI), which provides a vehicle for the court to find a defendant guilty of a crime while also acknowledging that the defendant was experiencing mental illness at the time of the offense (see Slobogin et al., 2020). It is important to note that a defendant who pleads GBMI or is found GBMI is considered fully culpable for the offense and can receive any sentence, including a death sentence, that is available for the offense in that jurisdiction (Emanuel, 1989). Further, GBMI does not guarantee that the convicted defendant will receive any mental health treatment as part of the disposition (Morse & Hoffman, 2008), although all inmates are constitutionally entitled to basic medical and mental health treatment.[5]

The manner in which criminal cases are adjudicated confers some advantages on the prosecution and some advantages on the defense. A key advantage for the prosecution is the availability of resources. A criminal case is brought by the state or federal government against an individual, so the prosecution has access to government resources (e.g., money, crime labs, experts, investigators). Some criminal defenses are mounted by a government agency, such as a public defender's office, which affords similar advantages, but public defenders are only available to indigent defendants. Criminal defendants represented by private counsel may have fewer resources available to them due to financial limitations and other barriers.

The prosecution has other advantages. For example, when grand juries are used to screen criminal indictments, there are less restrictive rules, which means that the defendant has no right to counsel, prosecutors can typically rely on hearsay evidence, and there is no duty on the prosecution to provide exculpatory evidence (prior to the grand jury hearing). A final advantage for the prosecution is primacy because the prosecution has the first opportunity to tell the court its theory of the case, thereby priming the jury to receive the evidence in a way that is favorable to the prosecution.

Despite these prosecutorial advantages, the balance of the criminal justice system is arguably tipped slightly in favor of the defendant, most likely based on the underlying premise that it is better to protect innocence than punish guilt.[6] A key defense advantage is the *Brady* Doctrine. This is a pretrial discovery rule established by the Supreme Court of the United States which holds that the prosecution must turn over exculpatory evidence (related to guilt or punishment) to the defense prior to trial (*Brady v. Maryland*, 1963; see Serota, 2011). Failure of the prosecution to turn over exculpatory evidence can result in the dismissal of charges or a mistrial,[7] along with potential sanctions on the prosecutor (Harris, 2006). By contrast, the defense has no obligation to turn over inculpatory evidence to the prosecution.

Another advantage for the defense is that it has more peremptory challenges of jurors than the prosecution, which provides the defense with more opportunities to remove potential jurors without providing a reason or explanation for the removal (Leak, 2021). Use of peremptory challenges arguably provides the defense with an opportunity to choose a defense-friendly jury (Flanagan, 2015). Some researchers and commentators have expressed concern that the use of peremptory challenges (by the defense or prosecution) is racially discriminatory (e.g., DeCamp & DeCamp, 2022).

The burden and standard of proof in criminal cases confer another significant benefit on the defense. As noted, the prosecution must prove every element of the charged offense(s) beyond a reasonable doubt, which is a high and exacting standard, and the prosecution's failure to carry the burden results (or should result) in the defendant's acquittal. The defense has no burden to prove that the defendant is not guilty; rather, the entire burden of proof rests with the prosecution. Defendants are also protected by the Double Jeopardy Clause of the Fifth Amendment to the United States Constitution, which prevents the government from re-prosecuting a defendant for an offense for which the defendant has been found not guilty.[8]

Civil Law

Civil cases arise between two parties, and each party—plaintiff and defendant—is responsible for mounting their legal position. Civil cases can include personal injury suits, contract disputes, malpractice actions, and actions based on alleged discriminatory behavior (e.g., employment discrimination cases based on membership in a protected class). A common civil action is a tort, which is a civil wrong other than breach of contract for which the law provides a remedy. Although parties in a civil case are typically individuals, companies, or corporations, the State can be party to certain civil proceedings that have forensic relevance (e.g., civil commitment, parental rights cases based on alleged abuse/neglect).

The remedies available in civil cases are legal and equitable. Legal remedies are monetarily based, including both compensatory damages (to make the injured party whole) and punitive damages (to punish the wrongdoer). Equitable remedies typically require specific performance by a party to the action. For example, the court may issue an injunction (which prevents a party from engaging in certain actions), a cease-and-desist order (which requires a party to discontinue certain actions), or an order compelling contract performance (which requires a party to adhere to a previously executed contract). Consistent with these remedies, the goals of the civil legal system are restoration (i.e., make the aggrieved party whole) and sometimes punishment (i.e., sanction the wrongdoer). The dispositions in civil court—liable or not liable—are determined by a jury or judge, depending on the legal context and jurisdiction. The standard of proof in civil cases is typically preponderance of the evidence, which is the lowest evidentiary burden in the United States legal system, although certain legal issues with forensic relevance, such as civil commitment, require clear and convincing evidence (see *Addington v. Texas,* 1979). Further, because of the nature of the sanctions in the civil system, which are considered less punitive than criminal punishments, the civil system does not provide the same constitutional protections that are afforded in the criminal system.

Sources of Law

Laws come from several sources, so understanding the "law" can be a surprisingly convoluted process (see DeMatteo et al., 2013). **Constitutions** are the foundation of the United States legal system, and they provide specific rights and protections. Individuals are protected by both the United States Constitution and their state constitution. Importantly, the United States Constitution should be seen as providing the minimum foundational rights and protections, and state constitutions may provide citizens of their state with more protection than the United States Constitution (but not less protection). Individuals are protected by constitutions, while the government (e.g., legislatures, courts, executive agencies, law enforcement) is bound by them.

Statutes are laws enacted by legislatures, either Congress at the federal level or state legislatures. A related concept is an ordinance, which is enacted by a local legislature (typically city or county). Statutes are often called "law on the books" or "black letter law," and they are typically written using general language so they have broad applicability in a wide range of legal contexts. Statutes may be revised by the legislature to address concerns relating to content (e.g., delete outdated provisions that no longer apply) or scope (e.g., ensuring the statute is not too narrow or too broad). Further, as part of the checks and balances in our legal system, legislatures may revise statutes—either voluntarily or at the risk of having the statute declared unconstitutional—in response to court decisions about how the statute is to be interpreted or whether the statute is even constitutional.

After a statute is enacted, courts are responsible for interpreting and applying statutory law in the context of specific disputes, which means that courts are an important source of laws. In the process of applying the statute in the contexts of specific cases, courts determine, *inter alia*, whether, where, how, and when the statute applies; whether there are exceptions to its application; and how statutory language should be interpreted. A collection of judicial decisions amasses as courts apply and interpret statutes in cases, and those court decisions are collectively referred to as **case law** (or common law).

Administrative law is the branch of law that governs the creation, operation, and regulation of administrative (executive branch) agencies. At the federal level, Congress delegates rule-making power to administrative agencies to define and clarify the intent of Congress and to effectuate the intent of federal legislation. For example, if Congress passes a law to reduce air and water pollution from factories, the Environmental Protection Agency may be tasked with operationalizing the law through a series of administrative regulations that carry the force of law.

Because laws are created by multiple entities (e.g., legislatures, courts, administrative agencies) and at multiple levels (e.g., federal, state, local), it is not uncommon for laws to be inconsistent and conflicting. Although federal laws and state laws often address different content areas, there is often some overlap in the areas that are covered by federal and state laws. For example, use of recreational cannabis is legal in some states, but individuals in those states can be prosecuted under federal law, which currently does not permit recreational cannabis use. Conflicts of laws is a complex topic (and some law schools devote an entire course to this topic). A good starting point in sorting through conflicts is the Tenth Amendment to the United States Constitution, which outlines that the powers not delegated to the United States by the Constitution, nor prohibited by it to the states, are reserved to the states. Although an oversimplification, when there are conflicts between federal law and state law, federal law typically trumps state law. This is captured by the Supremacy Clause (Article VI, Paragraph 2) of the United States Constitution, which establishes that the United States Constitution and federal laws generally take precedence over state laws (and even state constitutions).

There is an important distinction between primary sources and secondary sources. Constitutions, statutes, and case law are **primary sources of law** because they provide enforceable laws; violation of constitutional, statutory, or case law can lead to consequences in the criminal and civil legal systems. There are also various **secondary sources of law**. Although somewhat circular, secondary sources of law can be anything that describes or summarizes law that is not primary source. Secondary sources of law are not enforceable (unless they are adopted into law, in which case they become part of a primary source of law). Common examples of secondary sources of law include legal dictionaries (e.g., Black's Law Dictionary), legal encyclopedias (e.g., American Jurisprudence, Corpus Juris Secundum), legal summaries (e.g., hornbooks, nutshells), law journals, books, and American Law Institute (ALI) publications.

Two secondary sources of law—law journals and ALI publications—deserve special comment. Most law schools and some independent entities publish law journals or law reviews. The articles in these journals provide more context to the law, and they offer opportunities for legal scholars to provide opinions, identify areas of clarification, or discuss shortcomings with laws, procedures, or systems. For those familiar with social science journals, it is important to note that most law reviews are run by law students and the articles are not peer-reviewed in the same manner as social science publications. Although law review articles are fact-checked and often heavily cited, they often offer more of a subjective commentary on legal issues as opposed to an objective presentation of data or facts, particularly when the law review article is classified as a "note," which is typically a law review article written by a law student.

The ALI, which is an independent organization composed of legal scholars with expertise in a range of legal topics, publishes various documents that are often highly influential. ALI organizes and summarizes common law, and it publishes restatements, model penal codes, and principles. ALI restatements synthesize cases and statutory law on topics ranging from tax law to family law, the model penal codes offer suggestions (that may be codified by legislatures) for statutes and regulations, and the principles outline best practices for procedural matters. ALI restatements straddle the distinction between primary and secondary sources of law. They are considered secondary sources of law because they synthesize the law in a given area without carrying any force of law, but it is not unusual for judges to rely on restatements as persuasive authority in deciding a novel legal issue. Further, legislatures sometimes adopt the work produced by ALI, particularly model codes, which then gives the model code the force of law.

Structure of the United States Court System

Courts in the United States are divided into tiers that form a pyramidal/vertical structure, and the most basic division is between state courts and federal courts. State courts hear state matters—that is, crimes violating the state criminal code, civil disputes between residents or entities of the same state, and other matters governed by state law. Federal courts hear federal matters—that is, crimes violating federal law, disputes arising between residents or entities of different states, cases in which the amount in controversy reaches a certain threshold, and other issues that are expressly reserved for federal courts. In both the state and federal court systems, all courts are either trial courts or appellate courts (described more fully below).

State Courts

Most states have three levels of courts—trial courts, intermediate appellate courts, and the high court—although some smaller states only have trial courts and a high court. Different states use different names for each level of court, which can be a source of confusion. In Pennsylvania, for example, the three levels of courts are the court of common pleas, superior court, and supreme court, whereas the three levels of courts in New Jersey are the superior court, superior court appellate division, and supreme court. In New York, trial courts are called supreme courts (which is a major source of confusion when mental health professionals are not familiar with New York's unusual convention), the intermediate courts are called appellate courts, and the state high court is the court of appeals.

Trial courts are the lowest level of courts in each state,[9] and their tasks are to determine facts and settle disputes. Some states separate trial courts into courts of limited jurisdiction and courts of general jurisdiction. Trial courts of limited jurisdiction typically hear relatively minor matters, such as parking tickets, accrued fines, and minor offenses (e.g., vandalism), while trial courts of general jurisdiction hear the majority of criminal and civil cases. Trial court judges (and judges at higher levels) are either elected or appointed, depending on the court and jurisdiction.

The next step up from trial courts is the intermediate appellate courts. These courts have appellate jurisdiction (not original jurisdiction), which means they only hear cases that have been appealed from the trial court. Not all cases are eligible for an appeal, and simply being unhappy with a trial court's decision does not provide a sufficient legal basis for an appeal. An exception is death penalty cases, which are automatically appealed in almost every death penalty state. In other contexts, a party must have sufficient grounds to be eligible for an appeal. Grounds for appeal vary by case and jurisdiction, but they often involve procedural error, such as judicial rulings regarding objections, decisions regarding the admissibility of evidence, and a party's failure to properly or promptly turn over evidence via discovery. Further, being eligible for an appeal does not guarantee that the appellate court will grant the appeal. Unlike trial courts, which determine facts and settle disputes, appellate courts rarely reexamine the facts of a case and instead treat the facts as established by the trial court as dispositive; rather, appellate courts examine if the trial court correctly applied the governing law in reaching its verdict and disposition. As such, appellate courts typically resolve issues of law, not issues of fact. In some legal contexts, appellate courts grant de novo review, in which the appellate court will make a factual determination without reference to the trial court's decision.

Each state also has a high court, which is typically called the state supreme court. As an appellate court, a state high court only hears cases for which it has granted an appeal. In most states, the state high court is a discretionary court that is not required to hear any cases on appeal (with the possible exception of death penalty cases that are automatically appealed). Typically, for state matters, once the state high court rules on an issue, the court's decision is final. However, as discussed below, it is possible that some cases resolved or rejected for appeal by the state high court can be reheard in the federal court system.

Federal Courts

Federal courts are courts of limited jurisdiction, which means they can only hear cases authorized by the United States Constitution or federal statutes. Federal judges are nominated by the president and must be confirmed by the Senate.[10] Federal courts have the same three levels of courts as state courts (trial, intermediate appellate, and high court), but the federal system uses consistent names for the courts across jurisdictions. Trial courts in the federal system are called district courts. As a trial court, district courts determine facts and settle disputes. There are 94 district courts spread out geographically across the continental United States and outlying states and territories. There is at least one district court in each state and Washington, DC, and four United States territories have district courts (Puerto Rico, Virgin Islands, Guam, and Northern Mariana Islands). There are also some federal district courts that have nationwide jurisdiction, such as the United States Tax Court, United States Court of Federal Claims (for suits against the federal government), and the United States Court of International Trade.

As in the state court system, cases can move up the federal court system through the appeals process. The intermediate federal appellate courts are the United States Circuit Courts of Appeal. Any case with a final decision from a district court may be appealed to a circuit court.[11] These appellate courts review the procedures and decisions of the district courts to see if the proceedings were fair and the proper law was applied correctly. There are 13 circuit courts of appeal in the federal court system, including 11 regional courts, the 12th Circuit Court for Washington, DC, and the Federal Circuit Court (which has nationwide jurisdiction and hears special cases, including those involving patents and international trade).

Each circuit court has jurisdiction over a specified number of district courts. For example, the United States Court of Appeals for the Third Circuit has appellate jurisdiction over the district courts in Delaware, New Jersey, Pennsylvania, and the Virgin Islands, and the United States Court of Appeals for the First Circuit has appellate jurisdiction over the district courts in Maine, Massachusetts, New Hampshire, Puerto Rico, and Rhode Island. Appeals in each circuit court are heard by a three-judge panel, although on rare occasions all of the circuit court judges may hear a case (known as an *en banc* hearing), typically on a rehearing after the case has already been heard by the three-judge panel. The size of circuit courts varies considerably. For example, the United States Court of Appeals for the First Circuit currently has six judges, while the United States Court of Appeals for the Ninth Circuit currently has 29 judges.

The highest court in the federal system is the Supreme Court of the United States. The Supreme Court, which was established by Article III, Section 1 of the United States Constitution, has original jurisdiction over cases involving disputes between states, actions involving various public officials, disputes between the United States and a state, and proceedings by a state against the citizens (or aliens) of another state. The Supreme Court has appellate jurisdiction over cases decided by federal appellate courts and state court decisions based on the United States Constitution or federal law.

The Supreme Court is currently composed of eight Associate Justices and one Chief Justice, although there is no constitutional basis for setting the number of Supreme Court Justices at nine. Article III of the United States Constitution authorizes Congress to establish the number of Supreme Court Justices, and the size of the Supreme Court has changed several times. In fact, the size of the Supreme Court changed seven times in its first 80 years of existence, from as few as five Justices to as many as 10 Justices (McKeever, 2020). The Judiciary Act of

1869 set the number of Justices at nine, and the Supreme Court has remained at this size since then. As with the other federal courts, Supreme Court Justices are nominated by the United States President and confirmed by the Senate, and they serve for life unless they retire or are impeached. There are also no constitutional requirements for Justices regarding age, experience, or citizenship.

When functioning as an appellate court (as opposed to a court of original jurisdiction), the Supreme Court only hears cases for which it has granted an appeal. If a writ of certiorari is issued, the Supreme Court has granted an appeal and will hear the case; the writ is a request for the lower court to send the case to the Supreme Court for review. At least four of the nine Justices must agree to hear a case—known as the Rule of Four—for a writ of certiorari to be issued, and the Supreme Court typically hears less than 1% of the cases that are presented to it on appeal. As the highest court in the United States, all decisions by the Supreme Court are final.[12]

State and Federal Courts

Typically, a case in the state court system or federal court system is heard in the lowest court in the jurisdiction, which is called the court of first instance. However, through appeals, cases can move up the hierarchy to be reviewed by higher courts with greater authority. It is also possible in some contexts for a case to "jump" from state court to federal court; the reverse situation—going from federal court to state court—is not permissible in the United States legal system. A common way of jumping from state court to federal court is through a writ of habeas corpus. Technically, a writ of habeas corpus is an appeal for a federal court to hear a case based on a challenge to the legitimacy of the defendant's detainment. However, in practice, a habeas corpus petition is an assertion that an inmate's federal constitutional rights (e.g., Fourth Amendment right against unreasonable search and seizure, Sixth Amendment right to effective assistance of counsel, Fourteenth Amendment right to due process of law) were violated on the way to detainment. Additionally, some cases can jump from a state high court to the Supreme Court of the United States if the United States Constitution or federal law is implicated.

Precedent: Binding Authority Versus Persuasive Authority

Precedent plays an important role in United States courts. Courts typically follow the principle of *stare decisis*, which "requires" courts to follow earlier judicial decisions when similar legal issues arise again. *Stare decisis* can be applied horizontally or vertically. When applied horizontally, there is an expectation that courts will follow their own precedent when again faced with the same (or highly similar) issue. When applied vertically, there is an expectation that lower courts will reach the same decision as a higher court in their jurisdiction when faced with the same (or highly similar) issue. For example, all lower courts in Pennsylvania are bound by the decisions of the Pennsylvania Supreme Court, and all federal courts are bound by the decisions of the Supreme Court of the United States. Among other benefits, following precedent lends some predictability to the law.

A key distinction when it comes to precedent is between binding authority and persuasive authority. As noted above, if an earlier court decision came from a higher court in the same jurisdiction, then a lower court in that jurisdiction is expected to follow the precedent established by the higher court. The higher court's decision is referred to as binding authority because the lower court is bound by the higher court's decision.[13] However, court decisions from a lower court in the same jurisdiction or from a court in a different jurisdiction do not carry the same weight. A state court in California, for example, is not bound by the precedent established by a state court in Nebraska. But considering how other courts have resolved a legal issue can be informative, particularly when a court is faced with a novel legal question, so it is referred to as persuasive authority.

There is, however, no requirement per se that courts follow precedent, even if it is binding authority. A key aspect of good lawyering is convincing judges to deviate from precedent based on new facts, changed societal standards, or some other distinction. A judge will not be punished for failing to follow precedent, but the judge's decision could be reversed on appeal, or perhaps the judge may not be reappointed or reelected if they make decisions against established precedent. Departing from precedent results in new law. A familiar example is the Supreme Court's decision in *Brown v. Board of Education* (1954) (holding that racial segregation in public schools is unconstitutional), which overruled the Supreme Court's earlier decision in *Plessy v. Ferguson* (1896) (upholding racial discrimination in public schools as long as the facilities were "separate but equal").

A final point regarding precedent relates to the interplay between state courts and federal courts. All decisions by the Supreme Court of the United States are binding on all federal courts, but not all Supreme Court decisions are binding on state courts. The determining factor is whether the legal issue addressed by the Supreme Court has implications for state courts. For example, if the Supreme Court holds that a particular activity violates the United States Constitution, all states are bound by the Court's decision because the legal issue is relevant for the states. However, if the Supreme Court issues a ruling about how the Federal Rules of Evidence should be interpreted, that decision is not relevant to state courts because the Federal Rules of Evidence only apply in federal courts. In that circumstance, states are free to adopt or reject the Court's position.

Jurisdiction

A final topic is jurisdiction, which is the authority of a court to hear a case. As with several other topics covered in this chapter, jurisdiction is a complicated and nuanced topic with important implications. Some law schools devote an entire course to this topic, so we will necessarily provide a simplified discussion. For a court to hear a case, the court must have both subject matter jurisdiction and personal jurisdiction. Subject matter jurisdiction is the power of a court to hear the type of legal claim being asserted. For example, cases involving the United States Constitution, federal statutes, and federal treaties are heard in federal courts, as are lawsuits filed against the federal government. State courts do not have subject matter jurisdiction to hear these types of cases. Most criminal matters and civil lawsuits are heard in state courts, which have primary subject matter jurisdiction to hear those types of legal claims. Disputes about subject matter jurisdiction are not uncommon, and those disputes need to be addressed before the case proceeds.

Although seemingly straightforward, the concept of subject matter jurisdiction can be somewhat complex. In criminal matters, for example, a court's jurisdiction is affected by the nature of the victim and the location of the alleged crime. For example, murder is typically a state crime that is heard in state courts, but murder is a federal offense if the victim was a federal employee (e.g., DEA agent, U.S. mail carrier). Drug possession is typically a state crime that is heard in state courts (although it depends on the amount of the drug and several other factors), but it is a federal offense if the drug possession occurred on federal property (e.g., national park). Stealing a car is typically a state crime, but it is a federal crime if the stolen car is driven across state lines.

Whereas subject matter jurisdiction relates to the type of claim being asserted, personal jurisdiction is the power of a court over the parties. Even if a court has proper subject matter jurisdiction, the court cannot adjudicate the case unless it also has jurisdiction over the parties. A state court in Texas, for example, would not have jurisdiction over a person from another state unless personal jurisdiction is established. There are two types of personal jurisdiction: *in personam* and *in rem*. For *in personam* jurisdiction, the potential party must have "minimum contact" in a particular state for the state (and therefore courts) to have jurisdiction over the person. State rules differ, but minimum contact might be established by proving that the party lives in the state, works in the state, has a post office box in the state, or engaged in the alleged conduct in the state. A court has *in rem* jurisdiction over a person if the person owns property in the state, even if they do not reside in the state. A third way in which a court can have personal jurisdiction over a person is if they consent to give the court jurisdiction.[14] Many contracts specify which court has jurisdiction to hear contract-related disputes, which gives the court personal jurisdiction over the parties to the contract.[15]

Conducting Legal Research

Conducting methodologically sound legal research does not require a law degree or formal legal training, but it requires a basic understanding of the law and legal systems. The information discussed in this chapter up to this point provides the necessary foundation for conducting legal research. For example, issues relating to jurisdiction may greatly change the legal framework applicable to the forensic issue in dispute. If a practitioner has a question about expert testimony, admissibility standards vary both between the federal and state levels and also among the states. Furthermore, some definitions of psycholegal concepts may vary between the criminal and civil court systems, even within the same jurisdiction. A mental health professional may also need to know about the authority granted by different types of law. Finally, because influential court decisions may be overturned by a subsequent case or a revised statute, forensic mental health professionals must have a basic understanding of what constitutes "good law."

This section reviews best practices for conducting legal research. After offering suggestions for identifying the scope of the research and the proper methodology for answering the question, we provide a basic framework for understanding case law and common sources of legal scholarship. We conclude with some tips for conducting efficient legal research.

Identifying and Tailoring the Scope

An important step in legal research is tailoring the scope of the question. Different legal systems often have different standards, laws, or approaches to a certain legal concept. Thus, when asking a question, it is imperative to have a solid understanding of the proper type of law and relevant jurisdiction. The scope of legal research (and therefore the relevant legal question) may be so large as to require a review of the relevant statutes and case law in all 50 states, or it may be as narrow as examining one court opinion. Regardless, if the scope is either ill-defined or undefined, the legal basis of the research may be mischaracterized or not applicable to the question. There are two major legal considerations when defining the scope of a research question—the classification of the law or legal issue and the jurisdiction of interest.

Classifications of Law

As a reminder, the United States legal system has two broad classifications of law: criminal and civil. The stakes are different between the two systems. Criminal laws are enforced and prosecuted by the government, and individuals accused of violating the criminal code have more robust due process because of the severity of punishments that may be imposed. Alternatively, the civil system arbitrates disputes between or among individual entities, so the processes and safeguards that protect individual rights are not as robust because the consequences are less intrusive.

In conducting initial research, the terminology differences between the civil and criminal systems are particularly relevant. For example, a criminal case is brought by a prosecutor on behalf of the government, and a civil case is brought by a plaintiff on behalf of themselves or an entity. Whereas someone is found guilty in a criminal case, they are found liable in a civil case. What may seem like small semantic differences are important distinctions that should be considered when conducting legal research.

Though utilizing accurate terminology in conducting legal research is important, so, too, are the larger structural differences between the criminal and civil systems. As a reminder, in the civil court system, the plaintiff is required to convince the jury of their position by a preponderance of the evidence, while the standard of proof in criminal court is at the more stringent level of beyond a reasonable doubt. If a mental health professional is studying how mock jurors would decide a case, they would need to be aware of these differences and provide the correct standard of proof to preserve both the construct and ecological validity of their study.

Jurisdiction

Recall that the structure of the legal system and the principle of *stare decisis* generally require lower courts to follow the precedent established by a higher court in the same jurisdiction (or a court with greater authority). Thus, when conducting legal research, it is important to remember that a decision from a federal appellate court is binding on the district courts within the appellate court's jurisdiction, but a decision from a court outside of the relevant jurisdiction would only be persuasive authority. Also, equivalent mid-level courts in the federal system, or equivalent state courts in the state system, may make legal decisions that differ from one another. For example, the United States Court of Appeals for the First Circuit may make a decision that is different from the United States Court of Appeals for the Third Circuit, even when both courts are addressing the same legal question. In the federal system, this disjunction among appellate courts is referred to as a "circuit split," and it is ripe ground for legal research and commentary. Until (and unless) a higher court addresses the legal issue and makes an official ruling, the contradictory laws stand. In this example, a ruling from the Supreme Court of the United States[16] would resolve the circuit split and provide binding authority for all federal courts.

In summary, jurisdiction is a primary consideration when identifying relevant law. An example is the legal definition of insanity, which is something forensic mental health professionals must be aware of when conducting mental state evaluations. In the federal system, the legal definition of insanity applies when "the defendant, as a result of a severe mental disease or defect, was unable to appreciate the nature and quality or the wrongfulness of his acts" (18 U.S.C. § 17). The definition of insanity in Kansas, however, does not offer a morality prong and instead defines insanity as existing only when "the defendant, as a result of mental disease or defect, lacked the culpable mental state required as an element of the crime charged" (Kan. Stat. Ann § 21-5209).[17] Though different from the federal standard, the Supreme Court of the United States affirmed Kansas's freedom to define insanity in a way that differs from the federal definition (see *Kahler v. Kansas*, 2020). Whether conducting research for scholarly or clinical purposes, it is essential to be familiar with the different laws that are applicable in different jurisdictions.

Sources of Information

When the scope of the question is identified, the next step in conducting legal research is identifying the appropriate source of information. As previously noted, information about the law can come from primary sources, such as enforceable laws, or secondary sources, such as legal commentary, law dictionaries, or ALI restatements. Each of these sources can be identified and researched through formal means, such as legal databases, or informal means, such as general Internet searches. Primary sources of law, such as constitutions and statutes, are generally available on the Internet and in legal databases, and some court opinions are available free of charge on the Internet. However, some court opinions that are available on the Internet are "unpublished" and are prohibited in certain jurisdictions from being cited or used. Other court decisions are only available from a legal database. Regarding secondary sources, some are available free of charge on the Internet, while others require a subscription fee or can only be accessed via a legal database (which requires membership and/or a fee).

Legal Databases

As noted, most sources of law are available through general Internet sources. However, when conducting extensive legal research or looking through case law more systematically, legal databases provide the most efficient means of conducting legal research. Some of these databases are available online for free; a few of the more commonly used free legal databases are Justia, Oyez, FindLaw, and the Legal Information Institute (available through Cornell University Law School). Savvy researchers can also use more traditional approaches, such as Google Scholar, to find some legal opinions and journals.

The two most comprehensive legal databases for conducting legal research (of both primary and secondary sources) are Westlaw and LexisNexis. Both are closed-universe search tools specifically for legal information (i.e., case law, briefs, statutes, law review articles, and other legal documents). Although legal professionals tend to prefer one database over the other, often based on their level of comfort and familiarity with the database, Westlaw and LexisNexis have similar structures, tools, and functionality, with some small differences. These databases were designed to facilitate legal research, so they provide efficient modes of legal research wherein the user can search for specific issues, case law, statutes, or other sources of law. These databases also permit users to follow a specific case and its progeny. They allow for the use of terms and operators most researchers are familiar with from other search tools (e.g., OR, *, NOT). Helpful guides for conducting research with connectors, and the use of these connectors specifically on Westlaw and LexisNexis, can be found through a quick Internet search.

It is important to note that these legal databases can be quite expensive (depending on the specific services one chooses). Many universities have open access subscriptions, while smaller organizations or entities that do not require regular or widely cast legal research, including some small law firms, have pay-per-use subscriptions in which charges are based on the number of searches or the number of resources "clicked on." Thus, understanding the fundamentals of research, combined with an understanding of the law and how to identify "good" or "bad" law, is essential to the economic use of these powerful legal resources (both in terms of time and money).

Understanding the Law

Once a source of information is identified, the next step in conducting legal research is ensuring that you have a sufficient understanding of the law. This includes knowing how to cite the law, understanding the weight assigned to the source of law, and determining whether the law is "good." Being able to quickly assess a source of law for these purposes is critical in terms of understanding the law and its impact.

Anatomy of a Citation

Most of those reading this chapter will be familiar with the citation format promulgated by the American Psychological Association (APA). The most recent iteration of the APA manual, the *Publication Manual of the American Psychological Association* (7th ed.) (APA, 2020; APA7), defers the citation format of legal materials to that of the legal profession as outlined in *The Bluebook: A Uniform System of Citation* (21st ed.) (Columbia Law Review, Harvard Law Review, University of Pennsylvania Law Review, & Yale Law Journal, 2020) (colloquially known as the Bluebook). Bluebook citation format diverges from APA7 in a few important ways, so we provide a review of the general rules for citing key legal sources (Note: references to Rules in the following discussion refer to rules in the Bluebook).

Abbreviations

The Bluebook includes multiple tables for abbreviating geography, organizations, legal actors, months, commonly used words, and other legal terminology. Some of these are commonsense abbreviations, though others may differ from what someone without legal training would expect. When in doubt, it is best to look up the abbreviation to confirm the true meaning of the word.

Symbols

There are a few commonly used symbols in Bluebook citation (see Rule 3.3). The two most popular are those assigned to "section" (§) and "paragraph" (¶).

Pin Cites

One of the most useful differences with Bluebook citations (versus APA7) is the use of pin cites. Regardless of whether the statement is a direct quote or a paraphrased assertion, the author is required to identify the page(s) from which the statement is derived via a pin cite. By contrast, APA7 typically requires a page number only when material is being quoted.

Short Form Citations

Full citations can be lengthy and sometimes clumsy, so the Bluebook offers rules that truncate previously cited materials or that minimize the use of repetitive citations. The concept of a short form citation should be familiar to those who understand the style and formatting rules of APA7, which also provides for in-text short form citations in some contexts. *Supra* and *infra* can be used to indicate that a full citation or discussion can be found in either a future (supra) or previous (infra) footnote.[18] *Hereinafter* signals to the reader that a shorter title will be utilized moving forward. *Id.* can be used to indicate that the source of the information in the current sentence follows from the source of information in the preceding citation (see Rule 4).

Statutes

Rule 12 governs the citation of statutes. A statute is cited using the name of the act (if relevant), its title, the name of the source, the section, and the year: Act (if applicable), Title Number, Source § Number (year published). An example used earlier in this chapter to clarify the impact of jurisdiction on definitions of psycholegal constructs highlighted the federal insanity defense. This definition can be found in Title 18 of the United States Code, Section 17, which was last amended in 1986. Thus, the proper citation is: 18 U.S.C. § 17 (1986). The definition of insanity used by the State of Kansas would be cited differently. It has no title number, but can be found in the Kansas Statutes, Annotated, Chapter 21, Article 5209, and was effective 2011. Thus, its citation is Kan. Stat. Ann. § 21-5209 (2011).

Case Law

The citations for case law are outlined in Rule 10 and follow the structure of the individual or entity bringing the action, the recipient of the action, the source volume, source name, page on which the opinion begins, pin cite, and year the case is decided. The template, therefore, is *Action Bringer v. Recipient*, Volume # Source Page #, Pin cite (year). The volume information is particularly relevant for case law because cases can make their way up and down the various courts based on the issue raised. Though a case name may seem ubiquitous, citing the opinion based solely on the case name without the contextual information of the volume could result in gross inaccuracies. Using *Kahler v. Kansas* as an example, the full citation for the Court's decision on the constitutionality of Kansas's definition of insanity is *Kahler v. Kansas*, 140 S. Ct. 1021 (2020). However, if someone were simply to look for the case name and cite whatever information came up first, they may come across the following citation: Kahler v. Kansas, 139 S. Ct. 1318 (2019). This latter citation is not the full opinion, but rather the Supreme Court's decision to hear the case in full. The entirety of the opinion is "Motion of petitioner for leave to proceed *in forma pauperis* granted. Petition for writ of certiorari to the Supreme Court of Kansas granted." Therefore, use of this second citation when referencing the full opinion would be inaccurate and may raise questions as to the accuracy of the material in which the improper case citation is found. Returning now to the discussion of case law citations, if the source of the information comes from a portion of the opinion that is not the majority opinion, the author and weight (discussed further in the next section) should be indicated in parentheses following the citation. Therefore, a citation to the dissenting opinion in *Kahler* may be *Kahler v. Kansas*, 140 S. Ct. 1021, 1038–1050 (2020) (Breyer, J., dissenting).

Periodicals

APA7 preserves the use of its own citation format for journals relating to the law. As such, we will only briefly mention the Bluebook's Rule 16 (covering periodicals) so that researchers will be able to quickly "translate" the relevant information necessary to cite a periodical regardless of the system of citation. Rule 16 requires the full name of the author(s), the title of the article, volume number, periodical name, first page of the article, pin citation, and the year published. A template for the Bluebook citation of a periodical would be: Author First, Last, *Title of Article*, Vol # Journal[19] First Page #, pin cite (year).

To provide an example, if one were to search for a psychologal perspective of the decision in *Kahler*, they may come across an article published in 2022 by the authors of this book. The article, titled "The United States Supreme Court's Enduring Misunderstanding of Insanity," is in Volume 52 of the *New Mexico Law Review*, beginning on page 34. *Kahler v. Kansas* is discussed in depth on pages 59–62 of that law review article. Applying the Bluebook citation format, the proper legal citation for the article would be:

> David DeMatteo, Daniel A. Krauss, Sarah Fishel, & Kellie Wiltsie, *The United States Supreme Court's Enduring Misunderstanding of Insanity*, 52 N.M. L. REV. 34, 59–62 (2022).

To compare, the APA7 citation of the same article would be:

> DeMatteo, D., Krauss, D. A., Fishel, S., & Wiltsie, K. (2022). The United States Supreme Court's enduring misunderstanding of insanity. *New Mexico Law Review, 52*(1), 34–69.

There are other rules and nuances when citing statutes, case law, periodicals, and other legal materials in their proper form. A full review of these conventions is outside the scope of this chapter, and those who wish to learn more should refer to the Bluebook (which can be purchased from a number of book vendors). We hope this brief overview provides some basic information that will allow those from a social science background to be more informed and adept consumers of legal materials and citation.

Weight of the Opinion

When conducting legal research, it is important to know how to properly "weigh" the materials reviewed. Materials derived from a legislative branch are binding to those within the authority of that branch. In other words, you must follow the letter of the law as written by your legislature. Scholarly work such as books, journal articles, reference guides, or other secondary sources are opinion pieces. Though they may be persuasive to lawmakers or legal decision-makers, they do not hold any weight or require adherence. When it comes to legal opinions written by judges, however, there are several factors that contribute to how much weight an opinion is given.

The weight of the opinion refers to how much deference others must give to the court's decision. The principle of legal precedence or *stare decisis* ("let the decision stand") formalizes this custom. In effect, it means that courts look to each other's decisions when making their own ruling on a legal issue. As previously discussed, *stare decisis* can be applied horizontally, wherein courts follow their own precedent, or vertically, wherein lower courts follow the precedent of higher courts.

There are three important caveats to note with legal precedence. The first caveat returns us to the topic of jurisdiction. As noted, though courts often consider the opinions of courts outside of the deciding court's jurisdiction (e.g., a court in a different state, a court in a different federal circuit, a federal opinion for a current state case), the extra-jurisdictional decision is considered persuasive rather than binding. This custom preserves the autonomy of jurisdictions while also acknowledging the importance of some level of uniformity of law across the United States. However, when a decision is from a higher court within the same jurisdiction as the current case, or when it comes from the Supreme Court of the United States, the higher court's decision must be followed by the lower court (i.e., constitutes binding authority).

The second caveat, though perhaps obvious, is that *stare decisis* is a principle, not a steadfast rule. As society and opinions change, so, too, can the way courts approach the law. We used the example of *Brown v. Board of Education* (1954) earlier in this chapter to highlight how the Supreme Court can overrule itself. There are examples of the Supreme Court overturning a precedent set by itself in various areas of mental health law. For example, in *Atkins v. Virginia* (2002), the Court determined that executions of defendants with intellectually disability are "cruel and unusual punishments" prohibited by the Eighth Amendment to the

United States Constitution. *Atkins* overturned the Court's earlier ruling in *Penry v. Lynaugh* (1989), which held that defendants who are intellectually disabled are not categorically excluded from the death penalty (although intellectual disability could be a mitigating factor that calls for a lesser sentence).

The third caveat requires a closer look at the opinion itself. A legal opinion represents the views of the court from which it is published. When more than half of the judges come to an agreement, one of the judges (or their clerk) will author a document that discusses the history of the case, reviews the issue, presents the decision, and outlines the reasoning. Although one judge is the lead author, the others who agree with the decision will sign on. This is called the majority opinion because it represents the beliefs of the majority of the court. Occasionally, the court will publish an opinion that is not signed but still represents the consensus of the group. This is called a per curium opinion and is treated the same as a majority opinion.

As is expected with any decision-making body, judges do not always agree. When a judge declines to sign the majority opinion, they often write a dissenting opinion (or dissent). This document is attached to the opinion as published, but it does not have any binding authority because it was not signed by a majority of the court. Even when judges agree on the ultimate conclusion, there may be disagreement or differences in the reasoning that led to the conclusion. When a judge who signed the majority opinion wants to elaborate on these points, they can offer a concurring opinion. As with a dissent, a concurrence does not have binding authority.[20]

In some cases, the court cannot come to a consensus. For this reason, most courts are composed of an odd number of judges so there are no ties. However, circumstances may lead to a situation in which an even number of judges are deciding a case or a majority consensus cannot be reached; this results in a plurality opinion (granted to the argument with the greatest number, though not a majority, of votes). Though there is some disagreement as to what portion of a plurality opinion is binding, the Marks Rule, established in *Marks v. United States* (1977), grants precedence only to the holding(s) on which the greatest number of judges agree "on the narrowest grounds" (p. 193). Putting this rule into effect is perhaps easier said than done. If one wishes to understand the weight that should be accorded to a plurality opinion, it is best to seek consultation and familiarize oneself with their jurisdiction's approach to binding precedent. When citing a portion of the overall opinion that does not come from the majority and, therefore, is not binding, the citation will note this deviation in parentheses (see *Kahler* example above). This provides an easy visual cue to those reading the research that identifies the weight of the underlying authority from which the assertion is derived.

Identifying "Good Law"

After identifying the relevant topic and jurisdiction, conducting a search of the case law, and finding a case or statute that is on point, the last step is determining whether the law is "good." In this context, "good" and "bad" laws are not a moral description, but rather a way to identify whether the law, legal principle, or issue that has been decided still stands. Case law is considered "good" if the specific legal issue in question has not been overruled by the same court or a court with greater authority. However, if the ruling in question has been overturned, it is considered "bad" law. Notice that even though the law in general is referred to as "good" or "bad," this does not necessarily invalidate the case in its entirety. When a decision is overruled, it can be overruled in whole or in part. If a case is overruled in whole, the higher court disagreed with the entire decision of the lower court and none of the lower court's opinion stands. If it is overruled in part, then only a specific issue, and not the entire decision, has been called into question. Therefore, when researching case law, if the reader were to come across a case that has been overruled, additional research may be warranted before disregarding the precedential value of the case because it is possible that the specific legal ruling is still applicable.

Determining whether a rule or ruling is good law can sometimes be done through a quick Internet search. However, this is where the major legal databases are particularly useful, as both Westlaw and LexisNexis have tools for efficiently accomplishing this goal. Westlaw offers "KeyCite," a tool that flags legal materials that have negative subsequent history. An issue is flagged yellow if it has had some negative treatment but has not been overruled or reversed, red if at least one point of law or issue has been invalidated, blue if it is in the process of being appealed, and an orange caution symbol is present if the decision relies on other cases that are no longer good law (Thompson Reuters, n.d.).

LexisNexis offers a similar service through its "Shepard's Signals." The signals similarly assign a color based on the subsequent history of the decision. Red indicates a warning that the case is likely no longer good law, orange law is "questioned," yellow is associated with a "caution," dark blue is a neutral mention, green is a positive mention, and light blue is associated with no specific information (LexisNexis, 2020). In addition, cases can be "Shepardized," which produces further graphics, including "Ravel View," an analysis of the case's history since the decision was published.

Regardless of whether the research is conducted on Westlaw or LexisNexis, these tools (and others) help to streamline the analytical review of a case or statute and offer suggested materials for related content. Each legal database also publishes guides, videos, and other materials to provide helpful suggestions for maximizing the research conducted on their platform. With some basic knowledge of how these databases work, non–legally trained professionals can develop efficient and useful legal researching skills.

Reading and Interpreting the Law

We have outlined several steps when conducting research and understanding the law, including identifying the scope of the question, the relevant jurisdiction, and the system of law in which the question lies; thinking through the necessary source material and where to obtain the information; and finding a potentially applicable resource that has binding precedent and that is still good law. The final step is having (at least) a basic understanding of the content of the material itself, which requires the ability to read and interpret the law. We will assume that the average reader of this book is adept at reading, interpreting, and synthesizing the secondary materials (i.e., books, journal articles, legal guides) they may find during the course of their research. This section focuses instead on providing additional advice specifically for reading and interpreting legislative materials and case law.

Navigating a Statutory Code

Most statutory codes are written like books, with overarching titles, parts, chapters, and sections. At each junction, the law within is more narrowly defined. Therefore, there are two methods to research a specific topic or definition outlined in the statute. Both will ultimately achieve the goal, but the first uses a more targeted method, whereas the second uses a funnel approach that provides more context to the statute. The first method is to search for the relevant law by name or topic. For example, when searching for the federal statutory framework for insanity, an Internet search would lead to 18 U.S.C. § 17, which provides the definition of the affirmative defense of insanity and the required burden of proof. This targeted approach quickly identifies the information sought, but it does not provide much context to that information.

If, instead, someone is interested in the context in which the definition of insanity is set, they could look to the larger statute. This constitutes the second ("funnel") approach. A statutory code is constructed like a book with a table of contents describing the titles, parts, chapters, and sections. Most statutes begin each level with an introduction that provides definitions for later concepts and terms. Therefore, when searching for the legal definition of insanity, a researcher using the funnel approach could look generally to the first chapter of the United

States Code to find definitions and rules of construction (i.e., guidance on how to read and interpret the language of the statutes therein) for the code itself. Therefore, Title 1 (General Provisions), Chapter 1 (Rules of Construction) of the United States Code would provide the greatest context for the Code's later provisions.

Using the above example, someone interested in the definition of insanity would next turn to Title 18 (Crimes and Criminal Procedure). Again, each level of classification is outlined in the table of contents and can be easily identified by the name used to describe the content therein. Part 1 of Title 18 provides a definition of each crime that can be federally charged in the United States. Title 18 (Crimes and Criminal Procedure), Part 1 (Crimes), Chapter 1 outlines the general provisions, or introductory concepts, applied throughout the Title. A glance at the table of contents shows that Section 17 provides a definition of the insanity defense.

The benefit of using this funnel approach is the context provided to the statute. Topics are often grouped together. Therefore, research into one area will provide information that a targeted approach would possibly miss. Turning again to federal insanity, once someone understands the statutory definition of insanity, they might want to understand the process by which a defendant is evaluated for insanity. Without any prior knowledge of the statute or workings of the criminal code, the researcher could still be successful in their efforts by using the funnel approach.

Because insanity is a question that focuses on the individual who was charged, the answer would be found in Title 18, Part III (Prisons and Prisoners). If someone mistakenly initially thought the topic was procedural in nature and looked to Part II (Criminal Procedure), they would only lose a few moments of their time perusing the table of contents before moving on. Within Part III, Chapter 313 is titled "Offenders with Mental Disease or Defect," and a review of the descriptions accompanying the sections within show several helpful sources, such as § 4242, titled "Determination of the existence of insanity at the time of the offense"; § 4243, "Hospitalization of a person found not guilty only by reason of insanity"; and § 4247, "General provisions for chapter." These sections are where the desired information is found.

Sifting Through an Opinion

A basic understanding of the structure of a judicial opinion can expedite legal research. As jurisdictional issues, citations, and the weight of the authority have already been discussed in this chapter, further consideration of these components is not reevaluated below. A brief caution will suffice. For the purpose of identifying binding authority on a legal issue, the majority opinion in a relevant jurisdiction is what matters. Furthermore, citations provide helpful context and, as in other types of research, looking to the citations in the relevant identified case and legal decisions in which that case is cited is a useful method that can further guide the legal research.

A judicial opinion will almost always follow a formal structural format. It will begin with the case name, docket number, and the dates when the case was argued and decided. When viewing the opinion online, some databases will provide additional information, such as the attorneys who argued the case and a review of the prior history if the case is being heard on appeal. Cases from appellate courts, and particularly cases from the Supreme Court of the United States, will begin with a syllabus. The case syllabus is not written by a judicial authority. It is more akin to an abstract provided at the beginning of a paper, which summarizes the content to follow. The case syllabus is a useful summary of the facts, holding, and reasoning, but it does not hold any weight and is often written by the legal database in which the opinion is found.

The majority opinion will follow, with identification of the decision author. The majority opinion ends with the signatures of the judges who are in agreement. If there is disagreement among the judges, the majority opinion may be followed by a concurring and/or dissenting opinion. A well-written opinion will begin with a short introduction to the case that outlines the facts, the relevant legal issue, the arguments, and the holding (i.e., decision). This serves as a roadmap paragraph, and each of the subsections follows in order. Thus, the introduction paragraph will be followed by a review of the facts of the case and the procedural history of how the case came before the current court. Next, the opinion will discuss the legal issue or issues raised by the petitioner(s) and their arguments supporting their position. The court will then review the relevant legal framework, statutes, cases, and other authority before applying them to the facts of the case. After the proper groundwork is laid, the court will put forth its holding, grounded in the authority previously discussed, followed by a short conclusion paragraph. This general format is repeated for each issue presented to the court by the petitioner(s).

If the case is heard on appeal, the opinion will end with an order from the court that the decision of the lower court be affirmed (i.e., deemed correct and will stand), reversed (i.e., deemed incorrect and overturned), or reversed and remanded (i.e., the conclusion is determined to be incorrect, but more information is needed to decide the ultimate outcome of the case). When the case is remanded, it is returned to the lower court to gather the necessary information and come to a new conclusion based on the guidance provided by the higher court.

Case Briefs

Judicial opinions can be lengthy, with word counts sometimes in the thousands (American Bar Association, 2022). They can also be dense, convoluted, and full of legal jargon. When reading a case that has come to a court on appeal, multiple issues can be raised and therefore only a fraction of the case may be relevant to those not interested in the procedure or other issues presented. One method for circumventing these loquacious documents is to find a "case brief."

A case brief is a legal "cheat sheet" that provides important information about a case in a succinct format. Briefing cases is a method taught in law schools to help law students search through case law and quickly identify the relevant and important aspects of the case, preserving only those components necessary for a broad understanding of the relevant issue or rule. Though case briefs may follow one of several formats, they generally include the name of the case and a brief discussion of the facts, relevant legal issue, holding, and legal reasoning. Some may also include the rule derived from the opinion, or the legal consequence of the ruling.

Case briefs for seminal cases and, therefore, most of the relevant psycholegal cases, are available on the Internet. However, not all case briefs are high quality and, as with other secondary sources of information, the accuracy of the brief is correlated with the quality of the source from which it is disseminated. Furthermore, just as one would not expect to gain a nuanced understanding of an article from the abstract, it is best to read the complete opinion to fully appreciate a case. As such, case briefs can be a useful tool, but they must be utilized with caution.

Conclusion

As forensic mental health professionals, we provide our services to or within the legal system, so there is a responsibility to be familiar with the "rules of the game." It is certainly not necessary to receive formal legal training to enhance one's familiarity with the legal system, and there are several resources (besides this book) that can improve someone's understanding of the legal system. A related "obligation" is the ability to be able to conduct basic legal research and, importantly, understand how to read, understand, and interpret the law. Being familiar with the legal system, both in terms of its structure and process, will increase our confidence, allow us to function more effectively in our forensic roles, and ultimately improve the quality and utility of our work.

Chapter 2
Forensic Mental Health Professionals and the Law

Mental health professionals have been providing a range of services to the legal system for many years, but there has often been an uneasy relationship between the two professions (e.g., Bersoff & Glass, 1995; Monahan & Walker, 2022). When describing the relationship between courts and social scientists, a prominent legal scholar once stated that "if that relationship were to be examined by a Freudian, the analyst would no doubt conclude that it is a highly neurotic, conflict-ridden ambivalent affair (I stress affair because it is certainly no marriage)" (Bersoff, 1986, p. 155). Part of the conflict between the mental health professions and the law stems from the inherent differences between the two disciplines. As recently stated by DeMatteo and Scherr (2023), "Psychologists and lawyers come from different cultures, with different interests, different approaches to solving problems, different research methodologies, different attitudes toward confrontation and argument, and different ways of arriving at the 'truth'" (p. ix).

Despite the differences between the mental health professions and the legal profession, the two disciplines have managed to form a working and oftentimes productive relationship. Currently, mental health professionals who work within the legal system provide many different services to a variety of legal actors and entities, including courts, attorneys, law enforcement agencies, legislators, policymakers, forensic hospitals, and correctional facilities (see Bartol & Bartol, 2018; Huss, 2014; Melton et al., 2018). Given the nature of their work, which functions at the intersection of mental health and the law, the psychologists, psychiatrists, and social workers who provide these services are referred to as forensic mental health professionals (DeMatteo et al., 2020; Heilbrun & Brooks, 2010).

The relationship between mental health and the law can be traced back many centuries, but a brief history will suffice (see Grisso & Brodsky, 2018). Ancient Greek, Roman, and Hebrew civilizations more than 2,000 years ago considered an alleged wrongdoer's mental health when assessing legal responsibility. But the modern history between mental health professionals and the law was shaped by several key events in the 19th and 20th centuries. For example, the

Forensic Mental Health Practice and the Law. David DeMatteo, Daniel A. Krauss, Sarah Fishel, and Kellie Wiltsie, Oxford University Press. © Oxford University Press (2025). DOI: 10.1093/9780197686591.003.0002

first psychology-law research laboratory was established by Wilhelm Wundt at the University of Leipzig in the 1870s, Harvard psychologist Hugo Munsterberg published his influential book *On the Witness Stand* in 1908, and William Healy founded the Chicago Juvenile Psychopathic Institute around the same time (see DeMatteo & Scherr, 2023).

Later in the 20th century, the Supreme Court of the United States relied on social science research, often conveyed to the Court via *amicus curiae* briefs, in several landmark legal decisions, including the seminal school desegregation case of *Brown v. Board of Education* (1954). After the United States Court of Appeals for the District of Columbia Circuit decided *Jenkins v. United States* in 1962, which held that properly trained and qualified psychologists could offer expert testimony on mental health disorders, the field of forensic psychology experienced considerable growth as forensic psychologists began routinely conducting forensic mental health assessments on a variety of legal issues in criminal and civil cases (Melton et al., 2018; Otto & Heilbrun, 2002). Prior to *Jenkins*, expert testimony regarding mental health disorders was the almost exclusive domain of psychiatrists.

The forensic mental health field has grown considerably in more recent decades. There are several national and international professional organizations devoted to psychology/psychiatry and law (e.g., American Academy of Psychiatry and the Law; American Psychology-Law Society; Australian and New Zealand Association of Psychiatry, Psychology, and Law; European Association of Psychology and Law; International Academy of Law and Mental Health; International Association of Applied Psychology; International Association for Correctional and Forensic Psychology; and International Association of Forensic Mental Health Services). There are also hundreds of books, book chapters, and articles devoted to forensic mental health, and many journals have been developed that publish empirical, theoretical, and practice articles relevant to law and mental health (e.g., *Behavioral Sciences and the Law*; *Criminal Justice and Behavior*; *International Journal of Forensic Mental Health*; *Journal of the American Academy of Psychiatry and the Law*; *Law and Human Behavior*; *Psychology, Crime and Law*; and *Psychology, Public Policy, and Law*).

Another indicator of the growth of the psychology-law field is the continued development of interdisciplinary training programs. Currently, there are nearly 40 doctoral programs and several joint-degree programs that provide some form of specialized training in forensic psychology (Haigh, 2023). There are also several predoctoral internships, postdoctoral training programs, and continuing education programs that provide opportunities for work with forensic populations and specialty training in forensic psychology/psychiatry (Burl et al., 2012; DeMatteo et al., 2009, 2016).

Roles of Forensic Mental Health Professionals

The growth of forensic psychology/psychiatry, along with growing recognition that mental health professionals can provide useful information in various legal contexts, led to an expansion of the services that mental health professionals provide to the legal system. However, before exploring the various roles that can be assumed by forensic mental health professionals and the services they provide, it is important to define what is meant by forensic mental health generally. The way in which the profession of forensic mental health is defined is pivotal in understanding what activities are properly considered "forensic." As described below, forensic psychology and forensic psychiatry have slightly different definitions that reflect the nature of the training and expertise of those two professions.

Forensic Psychology and Forensic Psychiatry

At base, forensic psychology can be conceptualized as the application of the science and practice of psychology to questions and issues relating to the law and the legal system. That conceptualization is quite broad, and it leaves a great deal of room (and debate) regarding the professional activities that should be considered as falling within the scope of forensic psychology. Defining which activities are forensic is important because mental health professionals who provide forensic services have some different ethical obligations than mental health professionals who limit their activities to traditional therapy (discussed more thoroughly in Chapter 8).

Rather than adopting a narrow and restrictive definition of forensic psychology that only includes providing clinical psychological expertise to justice-involved individuals, we endorse a broad and inclusive definition that is consistent with the definitions adopted by leading forensic psychology authorities in the United States. For example, the American Board of Forensic Psychology (ABFP) (n.d.), which is a specialty board of the American Board of Professional Psychology (ABPP) and the premier board certification entity for forensic psychologists in the United States, defines forensic psychology as the "application of scientific, technical, or specialized knowledge of psychology to inform matters of law within the judicial system, legislative bodies, and administrative agencies." ABFP (n.d.) further states that forensic psychology "includes, but is not limited to, conducting psychological evaluations, treatment, or research in anticipation of future legal, contractual, or administrative proceedings; offering expert psychological opinions in the form of testimony or amicus briefs; and, trial consultation."

Similarly, the *Specialty Guidelines for Forensic Psychology*, which were adopted as official policy of the American Psychological Association in 2011, define forensic psychology as the "professional practice by any psychologist working within any subdiscipline of psychology (e.g., clinical, developmental, social, cognitive) when applying the scientific, technical, or specialized knowledge of psychology to the law to assist in addressing legal, contractual, and administrative matters" (American Psychological Association, 2013, p. 7). The *Specialty Guidelines for Forensic Psychology* further state:

> These Guidelines apply in all matters in which psychologists provide expertise to judicial, administrative, and educational systems including, but not limited to, examining or treating persons in anticipation of or subsequent to legal, contractual, or administrative proceedings; offering expert opinion about psychological issues in the form of amicus briefs or testimony to judicial, legislative, or administrative bodies; acting in an adjudicative capacity; serving as a trial consultant or otherwise offering expertise to attorneys, the courts, or others; conducting research in connection with, or in the anticipation of, litigation; or involvement in educational activities of a forensic nature. (American Psychological Association, 2013, p. 7)

Finally, the *Specialty Guidelines for Forensic Psychology* clarify that "[p]sychological practice is not considered forensic solely because the conduct takes place in, or the product is presented in, a tribunal or other judicial, legislative, or administrative forum" (American Psychological Association, 2013, p. 7); the psychological services must be intended to assist in addressing legal, contractual, and administrative matters. The broad definitions of forensic psychology adopted by ABFP and in the *Specialty Guidelines for Forensic Psychology* encompass the primary roles of forensic psychologists—clinical, research, and consultation—that are discussed throughout this book.

The definition of forensic psychiatry is focused primarily on the provision of clinical services in legal contexts. The *Ethics Guidelines for the Practice of Forensic Psychiatry*, which were promulgated by the American Academy of Psychiatry and the Law in 2005, define forensic psychiatry as a subspecialty of psychiatry involving the application of scientific and clinical expertise in civil, criminal, correctional, or legislative matters, and in specialized consultation in areas such as employment and risk assessment. Given the nature of the education and training received by psychiatrists (which is not focused on conducting research), forensic psychiatrists conduct forensic mental health assessments and consult with various legal entities, but they are less involved in conducting research.

It is important to note that although we are primarily focusing on the clinical, research, and consulting activities of forensic mental health professionals, a range of other activities is considered forensic. For example, the *Specialty Guidelines for Forensic Psychology* state:

> These Guidelines apply in all matters in which psychologists provide expertise to judicial, administrative, and educational systems including, but not limited to, examining or treating persons in anticipation of or subsequent to legal, contractual, or administrative proceedings; offering expert opinion about psychological issues in the form of amicus briefs or testimony to judicial, legislative, or administrative bodies; acting in an adjudicative capacity; serving as a trial consultant or otherwise offering expertise to attorneys, the courts, or others; conducting research in connection with, or in the anticipation of, litigation; or involvement in educational activities of a forensic nature. (American Psychological Association, 2013, p. 7)

Some of these forensic activities will be referenced in the sections that follow in this chapter and later in this book. Now we turn to discussions of the three major roles—clinicians, researchers, and consultants—of forensic mental health professionals.

Forensic Clinicians

There are a variety of clinical-forensic activities for mental health professionals with clinical expertise. Due to the specific expertise required for clinical-forensic work, these activities are performed by psychologists trained in clinical psychology (or a closely related field, such as counseling psychology), psychiatrists, and sometimes licensed clinical social workers. Broadly speaking, clinical-forensic activities fall into the categories of assessment and intervention/therapy.

Forensic Mental Health Assessments

Clinically trained mental health professionals may conduct forensic mental health assessments (FMHAs) of justice-involved individuals in a variety of legal contexts (Heilbrun et al., 2014, 2023; Melton et al., 2018). The legal contexts in which FMHAs may be used are quite broad, encompassing criminal, civil (including family law), administrative, and juvenile contexts (see DeMatteo & Scherr, 2023, Drogin et al., 2011, and Jackson & Roesch, 2016, for chapters on FMHAs in a variety of contexts). In this capacity, forensic mental health professionals are retained by attorneys or appointed by courts to conduct an evaluation of a justice-involved person to assist the legal decision-makers to make better-informed decisions. FMHAs may assist attorneys in better representing their clients by addressing whether the attorney's client can, for example, satisfactorily participate in the legal proceedings (competence to stand trial) or testify with sufficient capacity (testamentary capacity), or the FMHA may address the viability of a plaintiff's claim (e.g., workers' compensation) or a defendant's mental health defense (e.g., insanity). FMHAs can assist courts (judges and juries) to make better-informed decisions about the guilt and disposition of an individual in a criminal context, the merit of a plaintiff's claim in civil court, the appropriate child custody schedule in family court, or the appropriate disposition of an adolescent in juvenile court. FMHAs may even assist a state ethics board in determining whether another mental health professional engaged in unethical conduct.

Evaluations conducted in a forensic context differ in important respects from evaluations conducted in traditional clinical contexts. Several authors have described these differences (e.g., DeMatteo et al., 2011, 2020; Greenberg & Shuman, 1997, 2007; Heilbrun, 2001; Heilbrun et al., 2014; Melton et al., 2018). However, given the foundational importance of the distinction, which further clarifies the role and scope of forensic psychology/psychiatry, we will highlight the primary differences between evaluations conducted in a traditional clinical setting and evaluations conducted in a forensic context.

Purpose

Perhaps the most important distinction between FMHAs and traditional clinical assessments is the respective purpose of the evaluations. The purpose of a traditional clinical assessment is typically to provide a psychiatric diagnosis and/or assessment of an individual's presenting problems or symptoms, and these evaluations are often used to develop an appropriately tailored treatment plan. The individual's well-being is the paramount consideration, and the clinical assessment is used to enhance the provider's quality of care.

By contrast, the purpose of FMHAs is to assist a legal decision-maker. FMHAs address legal questions, not clinical questions. The individual's mental health functioning and treatment needs may be (and often are) addressed in FMHAs, but only if those things are relevant to the legal question. Further, although traditional clinical assessments are designed to yield results that will presumably benefit the individual who was examined (e.g., diagnoses, case conceptualizations, treatment plans), the results of FMHAs may lead to results that do not necessarily appear to be in the best interests of the individual who was examined (e.g., longer term of incarceration, rejection of a mental health defense), although the legal outcome may be in the best interests of the legal system and society.

Client

The client in a traditional clinical context is the person being evaluated or treated, whereas the client in a forensic assessment context is the person or entity that requested the evaluation (e.g., attorney, court, employer, insurance company). The identity of the client in an evaluation context is important because the ethics that govern mental health professionals impose certain obligations on the mental health professional vis-à-vis the client. For example, in a traditional clinical context, the mental health professional owes a duty of confidentiality to their client, but that duty is defined differently (and more restrictively) in a forensic context because the client is the retaining attorney or court (or other legal entity), not the person being evaluated.

Relationship

A therapeutic relationship between a mental health professional and their client is often characterized by empathy, support, emotional safety, and overarching concern for the client's well-being. Mental health professionals use techniques such as active listening to develop a rapport with their clients, which can help the client feel more comfortable in the therapeutic environment and potentially lead to better clinical outcomes. In forensic assessment contexts, mental health professionals may seek to establish a rapport to the extent that a good rapport will facilitate obtaining information from the person being evaluated, but mental health professionals may simultaneously strive to remain somewhat detached from the examinee. In a forensic context, the focus is obtaining complete and accurate information relevant to the legal question being addressed.

Voluntariness and Autonomy

Most therapeutic relationships are initiated by the client who voluntarily seeks an evaluation or treatment to address distressing mental health symptoms or behaviors (e.g., depression, anxiety, eating disorders, substance use). Some people may feel (or be) pressured into therapy by a significant other, friend, or employer, or be court-ordered to attend in some circumstances, but the decision to enter therapy is typically made voluntarily, which means that the client can discontinue therapy at any time, for any reason, and typically without any negative consequences (except perhaps the failure to address the problems that led the client to enter treatment). Depending on the type of therapy, the therapeutic relationship may be collaborative and provide the client with a greater role in determining the nature and direction of the therapy (e.g., types of interventions, treatment targets, length of treatment).

However, in forensic assessment contexts, the evaluation may not be voluntary because the individual being examined may have been ordered by a court, employer, or insurer to undergo an evaluation. Even if the FMHA is technically voluntary, the individual may be undergoing the evaluation at the strong request of their attorney in preparation for a criminal or civil case. In some forensic contexts, there is no option for the individual to decline participation (e.g., a defendant being evaluated by the prosecution's expert in an insanity case), and the individual may be forced to undergo an evaluation that could ultimately yield information that is unfavorable to their legal case.

Confidentiality

Confidentiality is a bedrock ethical obligation in a clinical relationship. With few exceptions (e.g., mandated reporting obligations relating to child or elder abuse or the dangerous propensities of a client), clients can be confident that a mental health professional will not disclose information obtained during therapy. Individuals undergoing FMHAs must understand that the results of the evaluation will not remain confidential; the results will be shared with the retaining party and, under certain circumstances, with the opposing party and court. FMHA reports may also become part of the public record in certain contexts.

Consent

Clients in a traditional clinical context provide consent to be evaluated or treated. Client consent is either provided implicitly (based on the client's initiation of therapy) or explicitly (via a consent form). By providing consent, the client is agreeing to the therapeutic procedures, limits on confidentiality, and other important aspects of the therapeutic relationship. As noted, in some situations, an individual may be court-ordered to receive therapy, or someone may be involuntarily hospitalized, but the typical clinical scenario is one in which the individual consents to the treatment.

However, obtaining consent from the person being evaluated is not always required in a forensic context. If the FMHA is being conducted at the request of the individual's attorney, the person being evaluated has the right to decline participation, which means the forensic mental health professional should obtain consent before conducting the evaluation. If, however, the FMHA is court ordered, the individual is required to participate in the evaluation and their consent is not necessary; they may choose to provide limited or no information, but that may have detrimental legal consequences. When consent is not required, the forensic mental health professional should nevertheless provide the individual being evaluated with information regarding key aspects of the FMHA (often termed "notification of purpose"), including who requested the evaluation, the purpose of the evaluation, how the results of the evaluation will be used, the limits on confidentiality, and who will see the report.

Response Style

Clients in a traditional therapeutic context are typically not motivated to provide inaccurate or distorted information to their therapist. Therapy clients often recognize that the therapist needs accurate information to provide high-quality, individually tailored care. As such, there is often an assumption that information provided by a client is honest and reliable (to the extent the client is capable of providing such information).

However, the nature and potential consequences of legal involvement can provide motivation for some justice-involved individuals to provide inaccurate or distorted information during FMHAs (see Rogers & Bender, 2018; Rogers et al., 2023). In a criminal context, the defendant may exaggerate or fabricate symptoms of serious mental illness in an effort to avoid trial or to receive a more lenient disposition. Litigants in civil cases may fabricate or exaggerate mental health symptoms to obtain disability benefits or a financial settlement in a personal injury case. By contrast, a litigant in a child custody context may minimize or deny psychological problems in an effort to appear well-adjusted, psychologically healthy, and capable of parenting a child, or someone may deny having mental health symptoms to avoid being involuntarily hospitalized in a psychiatric facility. Given the motivation for justice-involved individuals to potentially provide distorted information, forensic mental health professionals should not assume that the individual being evaluated is providing fully truthful information.

Data Collection and Sources of Information

In a clinical context, the primary source of information for the therapist is the client, and it is typically not necessary for the therapist to obtain information from other sources. In some clinical contexts, someone other than the client may provide information (e.g., parents providing information to the child's therapist; spouse providing information to assist the therapist in treating their significant other), but the norm is that the client is the sole source of information. However, in FMHA contexts, it is consistent with best practices for the forensic mental health professional to consider multiple sources of information (besides the person being evaluated), including records (e.g., mental health, medical, criminal, school, employment) and collateral interviews (Heilbrun, 2001). These sources of information can supplement and corroborate information provided by the person being evaluated.

Pace and Setting

Traditional therapy often takes place in private, comfortable settings that facilitate the development of the relationship between the therapist and client. Treatment length may be determined in advance or open-ended (depending on presenting symptoms and treatment goals),[1] and the professional and client can often proceed at a pace that is comfortable for both parties. By contrast, FMHAs in criminal contexts may be conducted in correctional facilities or forensic psychiatric hospitals that offer limited privacy and sometimes poor testing conditions. Moreover, rather than proceeding at a comfortable pace, FMHAs in both criminal and civil contexts are subject to deadlines imposed by the legal process, which could lead to time pressure to conduct the evaluation and produce the report.

Report

In traditional clinical contexts, there is no written report per se; there may be session notes, but a formal report is not typically needed, and there is no expectation that anyone other than the therapist will see the session notes. Even in therapeutic or evaluation contexts in which a formal report is needed, such as a neuropsychological evaluation to determine if an individual should be permitted to retain their driver's license, or when a student is evaluated for an Individualized Education Plan, the report is often relatively brief. In a forensic context, the resulting reports are often lengthy, detailed, and comprehensive (depending on the referral question), and the reports may be reviewed by the retaining attorney, opposing attorney, and judge (or administrative body) (DeMier & Krauss, 2023). Further, although clinical reports focus exclusively on the client's mental health functioning (and perhaps a treatment or remediation plan), forensic reports focus on how the individual's mental health functioning is related to the legal question being addressed.[2]

Testimony

In a traditional clinical context, it is unlikely that the therapist will be asked to testify regarding the client in a deposition, hearing, or trial. Although some mental health professionals may be called as a fact witness in court proceedings to discuss, for example, the client's psychiatric diagnosis and course of treatment, it is often contraindicated for the therapist to serve as an expert witness (i.e., one who addresses the legal question being decided by the court); serving two roles vis-à-vis the same client, such as being a therapist and expert witness, can lead to an unacceptable conflict of interest that is inconsistent with best practices and governing ethics (American Psychological Association, 2013, 2017). However, forensic mental health professionals should assume that testimony based on their evaluation will be needed (although forensic mental health professionals offer testimony in only 15–20% of their cases; see DeMatteo et al., 2020).

Now that we have discussed the primary differences between FMHAs and traditional clinical practice, we will focus on various types of FMHAs. To facilitate this description, we will group FMHAs into the broad categories of criminal, civil, family law, juvenile, and administrative, although we recognize that there may be overlap among these broad legal categories. Rather than providing an exhaustive discussion of the types of FMHAs that may be conducted in each of these contexts, we will highlight some of the more common evaluations that are conducted.

Criminal Contexts

Forensic mental health professionals perform a variety of FMHAs in criminal contexts. The most common type of FMHA conducted in the United States is **competence to stand trial** (Melton et al., 2018). In the landmark case *Dusky v. United States* (1960), the Supreme Court of the United States held that the United States Constitution requires that defendants in criminal cases be competent before they can stand trial for their crime. The *Dusky* requires that the defendant have a sufficient factual and rational understanding of their legal situation and be able to meaningfully assist their attorney in mounting a defense (see *Drope v. Missouri*, 1975; Zapf & Roesch, 2009). Relatedly, the Supreme Court has held that defendants in criminal cases must be **competent to enter a guilty plea** (*Boykin v. Alabama*, 1969; see Redlich, 2016) and **competent to waive their right to counsel** (*Johnson v. Zerbst*, 1938), and the Supreme Court held that satisfying the *Dusky* standard would establish competence to stand trial, waive counsel, and plead guilty (*Godinez v. Moran*, 1993). However, the Court has also held that if a defendant wants to waive counsel and also act as their own attorney (referred to as acting pro se), a standard slightly higher than *Dusky* must be satisfied to determine if the person has sufficient **competence for self-representation** (*Indiana v. Edwards*, 2008). Specifically, in *Edwards*, the Supreme Court held that a criminal defendant who is competent to stand trial can nevertheless be found incompetent for self-representation if the court believes the defendant's mental illness and/or impairment would interfere with their ability to manage trial proceedings by themselves.

An individual suspected of having committed a criminal offense cannot be subjected to a custodial interrogation unless they waive their *Miranda* rights (*Miranda v. Arizona*, 1966). A typical *Miranda* warning, which highlights rights that stem mostly from the Fifth and Sixth Amendments to the United States Constitution, notifies custodial suspects that they have the right to remain silent, anything they say can and will be used against them in a court of law, and they have the right to have an attorney present during the interrogation. Forensic mental health professionals may be asked to assess whether a suspect was **competent to waive their *Miranda* rights**, particularly if the resulting interrogation led to a confession. The focus of these evaluations is whether the suspect understood the rights as presented by the police and whether the suspect knowingly, intelligently, and voluntarily waived those rights before being interrogated (see Goldstein & Goldstein, 2010; Kelley et al., 2018).

Evaluations of a criminal defendant's **mental state at the time of the offense** focus on the defendant's thinking, feeling, and behavior at the time of the alleged offense. The most common mental state evaluation is **insanity**, which is a (rarely raised) criminal defense in which the defendant argues that they should not be held legally responsible for a crime because of mental illness (Packer, 2009; Packer & Kois, 2023). There are several legal definitions of insanity used in various jurisdictions (see DeMatteo et al., 2022), but they typically require that the defendant's mental health symptoms at the time of the offense resulted in the defendant's inability to recognize their criminal actions as wrong or to control such actions. A related mental state evaluation is **diminished capacity**. To be precise, the "defense" of diminished capacity is not actually a defense, at least in the way in which insanity is conceptualized as a defense. Rather, diminished capacity is a defense strategy that seeks to challenge the prosecution's ability to prove the *mens rea* (i.e., intent) element of the criminal offense (DeMatteo et al., 2022; see Slobogin et al., 2020).

Forensic mental health professionals also conduct evaluations to help state and federal courts determine appropriate sentences for defendants who have been convicted of a crime. In most states, an individual's mental health functioning and any risk the individual may pose to the public are relevant factors when courts are determining an appropriate disposition. These **sentencing evaluations** focus on factors that courts can consider when determining what type of sentence to impose and whether to impose a harsher or more lenient sentence.

In the sentencing phase of a capital case, forensic mental health professionals may be asked to assist the jury in determining whether the defendant should be sentenced to either death or life in prison. These **capital mitigation evaluations** may be used by the defense to argue that death is not an appropriate punishment for a particular defendant due to the presence of mitigating factors that would make a death sentence too harsh (Cunningham, 2010, 2016; see Fairfax-Columbo et al., 2023). Because mitigating factors are interpreted broadly by both legislatures and courts, these evaluations can address any relevant factor that could be seen as calling for a more lenient sentence for a given defendant (DeMatteo et al., 2011).

Defendants who have been convicted of a capital offense and sentenced to death can only be executed if they are **competent to be executed**. In *Ford v. Wainwright* (1986), the Supreme Court of the United States held that the Eighth Amendment's prohibition against cruel and unusual punishment prohibited executing those who are incompetent. Although this holding was in line with common law that existed in almost every state, it was the first time the Supreme Court held that the prohibition was constitutionally based. Unfortunately, the Supreme Court did not define a legal standard for determining incompetence and instead charged each state with developing appropriate procedural protections. However, Justice Powell's concurring opinion in *Ford* stated that the Eighth Amendment should prohibit "execution of those who are unaware of the punishment they are about to suffer and why they are to suffer it" (*Ford*, 1986, p. 422). Most courts and forensic mental health professionals adopted Justice Powell's standard (Otto, 2009). More than 20 years after *Ford*, the Supreme Court in *Panetti v. Quarterman* (2007) held that competence for execution requires both factual awareness and a rational understanding of the reasoning behind the execution. Brodsky et al. (2001) described evaluations of an inmate's competence to be executed as "low demand, high impact evaluations" (p. 21), and several prominent scholars have identified guiding frameworks and professional standards for these evaluations (e.g., Zapf, 2009, 2016; Zapf et al., 2003).

In many jurisdictions, inmates serving a prison sentence can be released from incarceration on parole before the end of their sentence (although not in the federal correctional system if they were sentenced after 1987).[3] When determining the appropriateness of releasing an inmate on parole, a state parole board may request an evaluation of the inmate to assist the board in making its decision. These **conditional release evaluations** often focus on the likelihood that the inmate will commit another crime if released.

Civil Contexts

In civil law contexts, forensic mental health professionals may evaluate individuals who are involved or may become involved in litigation or some other civil proceeding. As with FMHAs conducted in criminal contexts, these evaluations can be requested by attorneys and courts, but they may also be requested by employers and insurance companies.

We previously noted that individuals in the criminal justice system must be competent at various points and for various reasons. Similarly, individuals need to be competent to perform certain activities and make certain decisions that fall within the civil law system. There are various **civil competencies**, including the need to be competent to enter into a contract, execute a will, or make certain medical or treatment decisions (see Kim, 2010). Forensic mental health professionals are often asked to evaluate these types of civil competencies.

In some employment contexts, employees who believe they are not able to perform the essential functions of their jobs due to mental health symptoms may seek disability benefits. Forensic mental health professionals who conduct **disability evaluations** assist insurance companies in determining whether claimants should receive the disability benefits they are seeking. These evaluations focus on assessing the scope and extent of the claimant's mental health impairment (Piechowski, 2011, 2023). Another evaluation stemming from an employment context focuses on the effects of **alleged workplace discrimination and harassment** (Goodman-Delahunty & Foote, 2011). In these contexts, forensic mental health professionals may be asked to assess the nature and scope of the plaintiff's mental health symptoms and the degree to which the defendant's alleged behavior led to (or exacerbated) the plaintiff's mental health functioning.

Individuals who believe they have suffered psychological harm (broadly defined to include emotional and cognitive harm) due to the actions of another can potentially sue the person or organization that allegedly inflicted or caused the harm. For example, an individual injured in a car accident may sustain physical injuries (e.g., broken bones), psychological injuries (e.g., posttraumatic stress disorder), and/or cognitive injuries (e.g., traumatic brain injury). Forensic mental health professionals who conduct **psychological damages** evaluations are asked to assess the scope of emotional, psychological, and cognitive harm sustained by the injured party, which will assist the court in determining liability and appropriate damages (Kane & Dvoskin, 2011).

Individuals who are mentally ill and present an imminent risk of serious harm to themselves or others, or who are unable to properly care for themselves without assistance in the community, can be committed to a secure psychiatric facility against their will. Forensic mental health professionals may be asked to assist a legal decision-maker to determine if **civil commitment** (involuntary psychiatric hospitalization) is appropriate. Among other things, these evaluations may address whether someone is being inappropriately hospitalized, which is a significant loss of liberty that raises constitutional implications, and if some other type of less restrictive alternative is available to protect the needs of the individual and society (Pinals & Mossman, 2011).

Forensic mental health professionals who conduct **guardianship/ conservator evaluations** assess whether the individual has mental health impairments that result in the person lacking the capacity to meet the essential requirements for personal health care, safety, therapeutic needs, financial needs, or habitation (living situation) without the assistance of a guardian (Drogin & Barrett, 2010). They can evaluate whether an individual lacks ability in all these areas, a plenary guardianship, or if the individual's deficits are more circumspect to one or more of these areas, a limited guardianship.

Roughly half of U.S. states have sexually violent predator laws that provide for the postrelease involuntary civil commitment of offenders who have committed identified threshold sexual offenses and are nearing the end of their term of incarceration (DeMatteo et al., 2015). Despite several challenges to the constitutionality of these laws, the Supreme Court of the United States has upheld them (*Kansas v. Hendricks*, 1997; *United States v. Comstock*, 2010; see Witt & DeMatteo, 2019). When conducting **sexually violent predator evaluations**, forensic mental health professionals are typically asked to offer an opinion about whether the individual is mentally ill (as defined in the governing statute) and likely to engage in future predatory acts of sexual violence (Witt & Conroy, 2009).

Individuals applying for certain professional positions or who hold certain positions may be asked or required to undergo a **fitness evaluation** (or fitness for duty evaluation) to determine if they can perform the essential functions of the position. These types of evaluations may be conducted in law enforcement contexts, for example, to assess the suitability of the individual to perform the functions of the job (Corey & Zelig, 2020).

If a consumer of mental health services believes that the mental health professional has provided substandard professional care, the consumer can sue the mental health professional for malpractice. If the lawsuit is successful, the mental health professional may be required to pay monetary damages to the consumer. In these **malpractice evaluations**, a forensic mental health professional may be asked to offer an opinion about whether the mental health professional's conduct fell below a minimally acceptable threshold of professional behavior.

Family Law Contexts

Family law is part of the civil law system, and forensic mental health professionals are asked to conduct a variety of FMHAs in the family law context (see Brank, 2019). Forensic mental health professionals are often asked to conduct **child custody evaluations** to assist courts in determining the "best interests of the child" when divorcing partners are not able to amicably reach a child custody arrangement (Fuhrmann & Zibbell, 2012; Gould & Mulchay, 2023). In cases of suspected **child abuse or neglect**, forensic mental health professionals may be asked to help determine the validity of the allegations and the scope or effects of the alleged abuse. Forensic mental health professionals who conduct **parental fitness evaluations** assess the capacity of a parent to provide the necessary emotional, cognitive, and financial support for children (Budd et al., 2011).

Juvenile Contexts

There are a variety of FMHAs that may be conducted in the juvenile legal system (see Heilbrun et al., 2016, 2017; King et al., 2023). As with adults, justice-involved juveniles must be **competent to be adjudicated** (Kruh & Grisso, 2009),[4] and many states use the same competence standard for adults and adolescents (Riggs Romaine et al., 2010). Another common evaluation (in many jurisdictions) focuses on whether an adolescent who has been charged in criminal court due to the seriousness of the alleged offense should have their case transferred to the juvenile court (often called family court) system. In **juvenile waiver evaluations**, forensic mental health professionals assess the adolescent's maturity, treatment needs, and risk to public safety to help courts determine the appropriate venue in which to hear the case (see Heilbrun et al., 2017). A closely related topic is evaluations of juveniles for **sentencing in criminal court**, which is attracting increasing attention from researchers, scholars, and lawmakers (Kavanaugh & Grisso, 2021).

Administrative Contexts

If a mental health professional is alleged to have engaged in substandard professional care in the provision of services, the consumer of those services can bring a civil suit for malpractice (as discussed above) and/or an ethics complaint. Unlike a civil suit filed in court, an ethics complaint is filed with the state board of psychology that oversees the mental health professional. Whereas successful civil suits can result in the awarding of monetary damages to the victim, a successful ethics complaint can result in the imposition of fines, mandated training or education, and restrictions on the ability of the mental health professional to practice (e.g., suspended license, requirement to practice under supervision, loss of license).

Forensic Therapy/Intervention

Besides conducting a range of FMHAs for individuals involved in the legal system, the practice of clinical-forensic psychology or psychiatry may also include providing mental health treatment to justice-involved individuals. It is important to note that simply providing therapeutic services to a justice-involved individual does not automatically render the activity "forensic" per se, even if the treatment takes place in a correctional facility or forensic psychiatric hospital. Instead, mental health treatment is only properly considered forensic if it is provided to a criminal offender or civil litigant in a legal context in which a legal decision-maker needs to make a decision about the offender or litigant (see American Psychological Association, 2013).[5]

Forensic mental health professionals often provide therapeutic services that are tailored to the context of a specific legal proceeding. For example, a forensic mental health professional employed in a secure forensic psychiatric hospital may provide restorative therapy to individuals who have been determined by a court to be incompetent to stand trial, or they may provide therapy to reduce the risk of violence posed by an offender who has been found not guilty by reason of insanity. Some forensic mental health professionals work with individuals convicted of sex offenses in an effort to reduce the risk posed by the individual, or they work with adolescents detained in a juvenile detention center to reduce the likelihood that they will engage in antisocial behavior once they are released. Again, the therapy must be provided in a context in which the mental health professional "reasonably expects to, agrees to, or is legally mandated to provide expertise on an explicitly psycholegal issue" (American Psychological Association, 2013, p. 7).

Forensic Researchers

The broad definition of forensic mental health practice endorsed in this book and by several leading organizations is not limited to clinical practice (assessment and intervention) with justice-involved individuals. For some clinically trained forensic mental health professionals, research is a core part of their professional activities, and the work of non–clinically trained forensic mental health professionals may consist primarily or solely of conducting research and disseminating findings that can be useful to legal decision-makers. The discussion of research in forensic contexts is less relevant for forensic psychiatrists because their training/education typically does not prepare them to conduct research (although some forensic psychiatrists have made exceptionally meaningful contributions to the research literature). Forensic research, which we broadly define as research that can be used to inform a legal decision, is a core part of forensic mental health practice (see DeMatteo & Scherr, 2023, for chapters on major and emerging topics in forensic psychology).

There are various specialty areas within the psychology field that can contribute forensic research (see DeMatteo et al., 2020, for a review). Clinical psychologists with expertise in assessment, intervention, and psychometrics may focus on developing valid and reliable screening measures to assess mental health functioning, examine the incremental predictive validity of violence risk assessment instruments, or examine the effects of interventions in reducing recidivism among justice-involved individuals. Social psychologists, who have expertise in understanding the impact of social influences on individual behavior, might study jury decision-making, jury selection, gang violence, and racial discrimination in various contexts. Cognitive psychologists might study eyewitness identification (Cutler & Kovera, 2010), false confessions, investigative interviewing, deception detection, and memory accuracy because of their expertise in human thinking, reasoning, sensation and perception, and memory. Developmental psychologists might study the development of antisocial behavior, the reliability of courtroom testimony provided by children, decision-making among children and adolescents, risk and protective factors for juvenile delinquency, and the effects of divorce on children. Two caveats are in order.

First, this list of research topics is far from exhaustive. Second, the lines among different types of psychological expertise are inherently blurry, so it is not uncommon for psychologists trained in one specialty field to conduct research that spans several specialty areas.

Forensic research can either be used in the context of a specific criminal, civil, or administrative case, or it can be used more broadly in some other aspect of the justice system (see DeMatteo et al., 2020). When research is used in a specific case, a forensic mental health professional may be asked to testify as a teaching expert (sometimes referred to as a pure expert). In that capacity, the mental health professional educates the court about a topic area that is relevant to the matter before the court. For example, a mental health professional may testify about the relationship between gang involvement and violent behavior in a case involving a defendant who is alleged to have been part of a gang, or a mental health professional may testify about the unreliability of eyewitness evidence in a case with eyewitness testimony. In these situations, the mental health professional has not conducted an FMHA (and they may not even be trained to do so); rather, they are offering their expertise to the court about a particular topic area that is relevant to the court's decision.

Forensic research may also be used more broadly outside of the context of a specific case. For example, a mental health professional may provide their expertise in an *amicus curiae* brief, which is a "friend of the court brief" submitted by a nonparty to the case that may assist the court in reaching a decision. These briefs often include summaries of relevant social science research, and forensic mental health professionals may play important roles in conducting the underlying research and/or accurately summarizing and contextualizing the research in the *amicus curiae* brief. The American Psychological Association has submitted more than 250 *amicus curiae* briefs over the past 60 years, including more than 50 *amicus curiae* briefs filed in the Supreme Court of the United States (Bersoff, 2013). As another example, a forensic mental health professional may testify before a legislative or administrative body when their expertise is relevant to a matter before those bodies (Bornstein & Meissner, 2023). For example, if a state legislature is considering adopting legislation that widens the jurisdiction of criminal courts over juvenile offenders, a mental health professional may offer testimony before the legislature that summarizes the relevant research.

Forensic Consultants

There are also many opportunities for forensic mental health professionals to serve as consultants in some part of the legal system. The consultation provided by these professionals can be circumscribed to a particular case or broadly applicable in a larger context (see Drogin & Barrett, 2013; Drogin

& Hagan, 2023). For example, in a specific court case, forensic mental health professionals can act as jury consultants (see Lieberman & Olson, 2009). In that capacity, they are assisting the retaining attorney to (among other things) eliminate potential jurors during the *voir dire* process who are predicted to render a verdict that would be unfavorable to the attorney's client. In other cases, forensic mental health professionals may be retained by attorneys to assist in critiquing an expert psychological report submitted by the opposing party's expert. The forensic mental health professional might, among other things, highlight strengths and weaknesses in the expert's report and assist the retaining attorney in developing cross-examination questions for the opposing expert.

Mental health professionals may also act as consultants in larger contexts. For example, in a correctional context, a mental health expert may be asked to recommend an efficient, valid, and reliable screening procedure to classify inmates based on their risk of harm to self or others, or they may be asked to consult on the pros and cons of segregating inmates by offense type, gang affiliation, or some other factor. Mental health professionals may be asked to advise the correctional facility on the use of solitary confinement, train correctional staff on crisis intervention and de-escalation strategies, or develop/implement a therapeutic intervention for the inmates. These are just a few examples of the ways in which forensic mental health professionals can consult with correctional facilities.

Mental health professionals are increasingly being asked to consult with law enforcement and other government entities. Some of these services provided to law enforcement may be evaluative (e.g., fitness for duty evaluation), while other consultation may focus more broadly on developing tools to select the strong candidates for police training. Forensic mental health professionals may assist police departments in developing mental health assessment and treatment protocols for officers involved in shootings. Given some recent high-profile negative police–citizen interactions, mental health professionals have taken a larger role in training police officers and other first responders (e.g., emergency dispatch, emergency medical technicians) to interact more effectively with individuals who are mentally ill, drug-involved, or military veterans (e.g., crisis intervention training). Mental health professionals may also be asked to consult with a variety of other entities, including schools (e.g., to develop effective active-shooter safety protocols), courts (e.g., develop/evaluate problem-solving courts), government agencies (e.g., improving the mental health services provided to justice-involved individuals in the community; advise on organizational policies for agencies that address child abuse and neglect), and legislative bodies (e.g., advise on how laws or policies can be developed or modified based on social science research) (see Bornstein & Meissner, 2023).

Conclusion

Over the past few decades, forensic mental health professionals have become an integrated and integral part of the justice system in the United States. Whether they are functioning as clinicians, researchers, or consultants—or some of the other roles identified in the literature—forensic mental health professionals are increasingly providing their services in a range of legal contexts. This suggests that the value of forensic mental health science and practice is being recognized in various legal domains. As emphasized in Chapter 1, the forensic mental health professionals who provide these services must be sufficiently knowledgeable about the legal system, and that foundational legal knowledge will enhance their ability to provide high-quality and useful services.

Chapter 3
Discovery

Discovery is the pretrial process by which parties to litigation obtain information from each other. The primary mechanisms of discovery are document production, interrogatories, and depositions. Forensic mental health professionals may become involved in the discovery process through their role as an expert witness or consultant. The forensic mental health professional's response to discovery is dependent both on the professional's role in the case and the applicable law in the relevant jurisdiction. This chapter will discuss the primary federal rule governing discovery (Federal Rules of Civil Procedure 26); procedures and best practices regarding document production, subpoenas, interrogatories, and depositions; and common mistakes forensic mental health professionals make during discovery.

Relevant Federal Law

The Federal Rules of Civil Procedure (FRCP) govern civil proceedings in the United States federal district courts. Their purpose is "to secure the just, speedy, and inexpensive determination of every action and proceeding," and they generally provide rules for how parties in litigation must behave (Federal Rules of Civil Procedure 1). Prior to 1938, federal courts had separate rules for civil cases for "suits in equity" and "suits in law." The primary distinction between suits in equity and suits in law is that suits in law were eligible for a trial by jury, while suits in equity were not. An example of a suit in equity would be to quiet title to a parcel of land, while a breach of contract claim would be a suit in law (*Schoenthal v. Irving Trust Co.*, 1932). In 1938, the Federal Rules of Civil Procedure combined suits in equity and suits in law. The Federal Rules of Criminal Procedure were established shortly after in 1944. Although discovery occurs in both civil and criminal cases, this chapter will focus on discovery processes that occur in civil litigation.

The primary rule that governs discovery in federal courts is FRCP 26, which outlines required disclosures, discovery scope and limits, requesting protective orders, timing and sequence of discovery, supplementing disclosures and responses, party conferencing and discovery plans, and discovery requests, responses, and objections. Discovery is meant to ensure that cases are decided

Forensic Mental Health Practice and the Law. David DeMatteo, Daniel A. Krauss, Sarah Fishel, and Kellie Wiltsie, Oxford University Press. © Oxford University Press (2025). DOI: 10.1093/9780197686591.003.0003

on the merits, so the scope of discovery is typically broad and extensive (with several enumerated limitations and exceptions). FRCP 26(b)(1) states: "Parties may obtain discovery regarding any nonprivileged matter that is relevant to any party's claim or defense and proportional to the needs of the case.... Information within this scope of discovery need not be admissible in evidence to be discoverable." Although the scope is broad, documents obtained during discovery may not ultimately end up being admitted at trial because they must also pass several hurdles included in the Federal Rules of Evidence. As such, discovery casts a wider net than admissibility.

There are, however, limits to the scope of discovery, such as privileged information and information irrelevant to the party's claims. As used in the legal context, the term *privileged* does not mean that the forensic mental health professional simply does not wish to disclose information; rather, it means that there is a basis in law that allows or requires the forensic mental health professional to avoid disclosing information (Bronstein, 2012). Examples of privileged relationships that give rise to privileged information that is outside the scope of discovery include attorney–client privilege and doctor–patient privilege. Whether information is deemed relevant to the party's claims depends largely on the type of lawsuit, the type of information being requested, and the requesting party's reason for the request. Jurisdictions vary on the question of whether an attorney receiving a request for discovery who deems the information to be irrelevant can unilaterally redact the irrelevant information prior to sending documents to the opposing party. For example, in *IDC Fin. Pub., Inc. v. BondDesk Grp., LLC* (2017), the United States District Court for the Eastern District of Wisconsin ordered defendants to produce the unredacted versions of over 600 documents because of the court's concern about abuse in the discovery process.

FRCP 26(a)(2)(A) requires a party "to disclose the identity of any witness it may use at trial to present evidence under Federal Rule of Evidence 702, 703, or 705." This includes expert witnesses that plan to testify at trial. Conversely, the identity of a forensic mental health professional who is retained as a consultant and does not plan to testify generally does not need to be disclosed. FRCP 26(b)(4)(D) states: "Ordinarily, a party may not, by interrogatories or deposition, discover facts known or opinions held by an expert that has been retained or specially employed by another party in anticipation of litigation or to prepare for trial and who is not expected to be called as a witness at trial."

There are two exceptions to the general prohibition on discovering nontestifying expert witnesses. The first occurs if the expert witness has conducted a physical or mental examination of a relevant party under FRCP 35(b). This also includes situations in which notes from a nontestifying expert or conclusions of a nontestifying expert are included in the report or testimony of the testifying expert witness. In this case, the notes of the nontestifying expert may become subject to discovery (Walker & Shapiro, 2020). Second, the identity of a nontestifying expert witness needs to be disclosed "on showing exceptional circumstances under which it is impracticable for the party to obtain facts or opinions on the same subject by other means" (FRCP 26(b)(4)(D)(ii)). This exception to the general rule is designed to prevent one party from taking advantage of another party's investigative work and to protect the work of a consulting expert. For example, exceptional circumstances may be present where one party's experts cannot duplicate a test or an observation by a consulting expert. In *Sanborn v. Kaiser* (1968), which centered on a defective pipe, the United States District Court for the Eastern District of Kentucky found that exceptional circumstances were present because only the plaintiff's expert was present to collect evidence when the pipe was removed and the pipe was destroyed prior to litigation. In this situation, it was impossible for the defendant to collect the same evidence surrounding the removal and present condition of the defective pipe. The court held that this constituted exceptional circumstances under FRCP 26(b)(4)(D)(ii) and permitted discovery of the nontestifying expert witness.

If a forensic mental health professional "is one retained or specially employed to provide expert testimony in the case or one whose duties as the party's employee regularly involve giving expert testimony," then FRCP 26(a)(2)(B) requires the disclosure of an expert witness's identity to be accompanied by a written report that is prepared and signed by the witness. The report must contain the following:

> i) a complete statement of all opinions the witness will express and the basis and reasons for them; ii) the facts or data considered by the witness in forming them; iii) any exhibits that will be used to summarize or support them; iv) the witness's qualifications, including a list of all publications authored in the previous 10 years; v) a list of all other cases in which, during the previous 4 years, the witness testified as an expert at trial or by deposition; and vi) a statement of the compensation to be paid for the study and testimony in the case. (FRCP 26(a)(2)(B))

Although FRCP 26(a)(2)(B) technically requires all of those things to be included in the expert's report, experts will often supplement their report with their curriculum vitae (CV) (which includes their qualifications and publications), a list of cases in which the expert offered testimony in the prior 4 years, and a statement regarding compensation in the case. Of note, FRCP 26(a)(2)(B)(ii) in practice requires every document the expert created, relied upon, reviewed, or possessed in the course of work on the case to be disclosed. If a testifying expert witness does not fall under FRCP 26(a)(2)(B), then the retaining attorney is required to disclose "the subject matter on which the witness is expected to present evidence under Federal Rule of Evidence 702, 703, or 705, and a summary of the facts and opinions to which the witness is expected to testify" (FRCP 26(a)(2)(C)). The expert is not required to prepare a report under FRCP 26(a)(2)(C) but may be asked to prepare one to assist the retaining attorney in summarizing the expert's testimony for the court.

To facilitate compliance with the discovery rules governing a testifying expert witness who must submit a report, forensic mental health professionals should diligently update their resumes and CVs to reflect all publications authored within the past 10 years. Additionally, it is good practice to maintain documentation of all cases in which the professional provided testimony (deposition, hearing, or trial). When setting fees for evaluations or expert testimony, forensic mental health professionals should be aware that their compensation will be disclosed to the opposing parties (at least in federal civil cases) and may be brought up on cross-examination.

Generally, both draft reports and communications between attorneys and expert witnesses required to provide a report under FRCP 26(a)(2)(B) are not discoverable. Specifically, FRCP 26(b)(3)(A) states: "Ordinarily, a party may not discover documents and tangible things that are prepared in anticipation of litigation or for trial by or for another party or its representative" unless they are otherwise discoverable under the general scope of Rule 26 discussed above, or "the party shows that it has a substantial need for the materials to prepare its case and cannot, without undue hardship, obtain their substantial equivalent by other means" (FRCP 26(b)(3)(A)(ii)). Because draft reports are prepared by an expert in anticipation of litigation for a party, they fall squarely under this prohibition. Even if a court orders discovery of an expert witness's draft reports under subsection (b)(3)(A)(ii), "it must protect against disclosure of the mental impressions, conclusions, opinions, or legal theories of a party's attorney or other representative concerning the litigation" (FRCP 26(b)(3)(B)). Communications between attorneys and expert witnesses are covered under these same provisions because they often were either conducted in anticipation of litigation or involve the mental impressions, conclusions, opinions, or legal theories of a party's attorney concerning the litigation.

Subpoenas

There are multiple ways that an attorney may request information from a forensic mental health professional retained by opposing counsel in a case, including an informal request, subpoena, or court order. These requests increase in severity for failure to respond or comply. The first type of request occurs when an attorney for a party in the litigation contacts the expert and asks for information; this request should be made through the retaining attorney. The second type of request is a subpoena, which will be discussed in depth later in this chapter. The third type of request is a court order, which is an official document from a court. Court orders are signed by a judge, magistrate, or commissioner (rather than a lawyer). It is important for a forensic mental health professional to distinguish among the types of requests because while informal requests by attorneys do not require a response (although a response may often be provided), both subpoenas and court orders require a response and often outline how the professional should appropriately respond. Further, failure to comply with a court order can constitute contempt of court and carry a range of punishments, including monetary fines and jail time.

There are two primary types of subpoenas. A subpoena, which is Latin for "under penalty," is a writ commanding a person to appear subject to penalty for failing to comply. A standard subpoena requires the designated person to testify on a certain date and time. Conversely, a subpoena duces tecum, which is Latin for "you shall bring it with you," is an instrument compelling testimony and the production of specific documents or other items. A subpoena duces tecum requires the individual to deliver the stated items to a designated place at a specific date and time. Subpoenas are typically issued by attorneys during the pretrial discovery process but can also be issued by the court after a judicial hearing. In the federal system, anyone over the age of 18 can serve a subpoena as long as they are not involved in the legal proceedings in question (FRCP 45(b)(1)). Subpoenas are typically served by a neutral party, although some jurisdictions only allow service by the U.S. Post Office. In some jurisdictions, when a forensic mental health professional is being called as a fact witness (e.g., to provide factual information as opposed to an expert opinion), the only compensation provided to the witness is the statutory witness fee in that jurisdiction. For example, in Missouri, witnesses are compensated $25 per day plus mileage (Revised Statutes of Missouri Section 491.280(1)), whereas witnesses are compensated $5 per day plus mileage in Pennsylvania (Pennsylvania Consolidated Statutes 42 § 5903(b)). As such, forensic mental health professionals may wish to add language to their fee agreement indicating how much they will charge for testimony provided in response to a subpoena and who is responsible for paying the fee.

Receiving a subpoena can be an anxiety-provoking experience, particularly the first time. Fortunately, the practice literature includes some effective guidance in responding to subpoenas. Before discussing appropriate responses to subpoenas, it is important to note that there is a critical distinction between *responding* to a subpoena and *complying* with a subpoena. Although all subpoenas deserve a response, it may not be advisable—that is, it may be unethical (and perhaps illegal, depending on the context)—to comply with the subpoena. The *Specialty Guidelines for Forensic Psychology*[1] state that forensic mental health professionals should "recognize the importance of complying with properly noticed and served subpoenas or court orders directing release of information . . . unless there is a legally valid reason to offer an objection" (American Psychological Association, 2013, p. 14). However, as noted, it may be unethical to comply with a subpoena without taking appropriate steps to protect against the consequences of disclosure. For example, a subpoena, by itself, does not provide a sufficient basis to break confidentiality (American Psychological Association Committee on Legal Issues, 2016). In states where the APA's *Ethical Principles of Psychologists and Code of Conduct*[2] has been adopted by the state psychology licensing board and/or otherwise incorporated into state law, the ethics code becomes enforceable by law against forensic mental health professionals. If a forensic mental health professional is in doubt about how to respond to a subpoena, the *Specialty Guidelines for Forensic Psychology* (see Guideline 8.01) recommend that they seek assistance from the retaining party, retain/seek legal advice from their own attorney, or formally notify the issuer of the subpoena of the uncertainty and conflicting ethical/legal obligations (American Psychological Association, 2013).

There are several informative resources that offer guidance for forensic mental health professionals who receive subpoenas, including two articles by the American Psychological Association's Committee on Legal Issues (2006, 2016). As shown in Figure 3.1, a threshold first step is determining whether the subpoena is valid (i.e., carries the force of law). For a subpoena to be valid, the issuer (typically an attorney but sometimes a court) must have appropriate jurisdiction, service must be proper, and the request must provide sufficient time for the recipient to comply. FRCP 45 governs the required content, proper service, duties in responding to a subpoena, and subpoena enforcement, and a subpoena can be formally challenged if there are deviations from the governing rules regarding service, content, and other matters. A forensic mental health professional is advised to consult with an attorney if there are questions about the validity of the subpoena. Although an invalid subpoena may not require a response, a valid subpoena requires a formal response, which could be compliance with the subpoena or opposition to the subpoena's demands (in whole or in part) (American Psychological Association Committee on Legal Issues, 2016; American Psychological Association Practice Organization, 2012). Prior to proceeding with the next steps in planning a response or challenge to a subpoena, the forensic mental health professional should temporarily cease all routine or otherwise planned document destruction, including electronic systems that automatically delete email correspondence or draft/backup documents after a certain period of time has passed. The goal is to preserve as much information

The following steps may be taken, as appropriate:

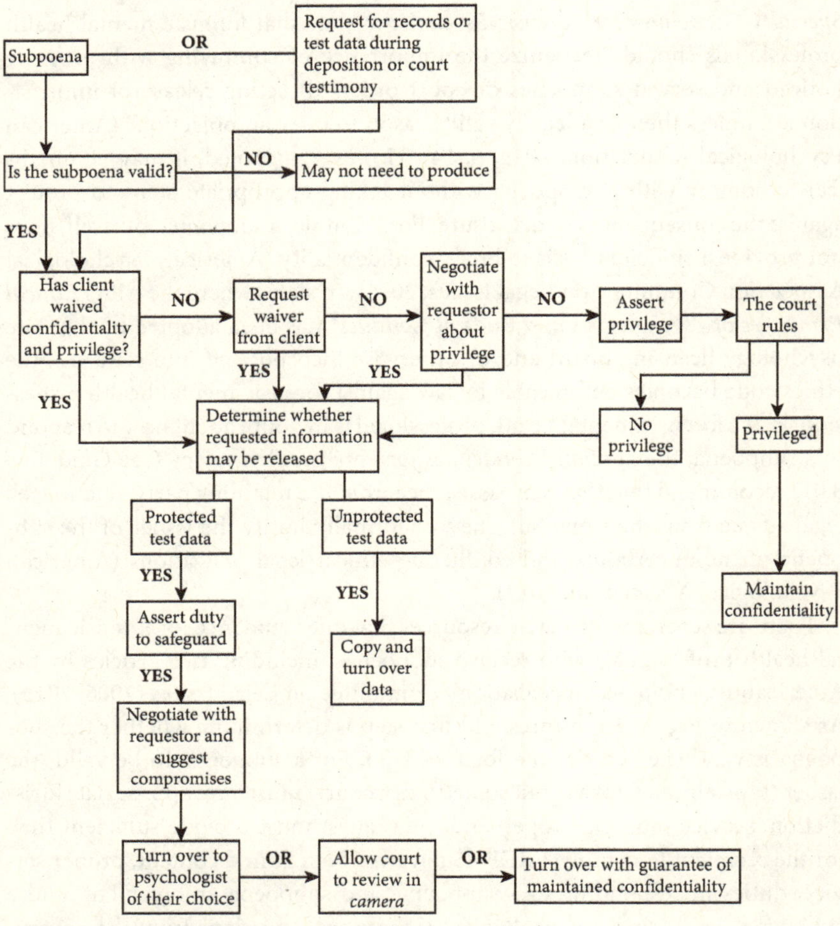

Figure 3.1 Disclosure Issues Flow Chart

Note: This flow chart was created by the American Psychological Association in 2016 to assist private practitioners in coping with subpoenas or compelled testimony. From "Strategies for Private Practitioners Coping with Subpoenas or Compelled Testimony for Client/Patient Records or Test Data or Test Materials," by the American Psychological Association Committee on Legal Issues, 2016, *Professional Psychology: Research and Practice*, *47*(1), p. 11. Copyright © 2016 by American Psychological Association. Reprinted with permission.

as possible at the time the subpoena was received in case the challenge to the subpoena's validity is unsuccessful.

The next step is for the forensic mental health professional to contact the client impacted by the subpoena (see Figure 3.1). If a forensic mental health professional is retained by an attorney to conduct an evaluation of another individual, the client in this situation is the retaining attorney, not the person who is being evaluated. Therefore, the retaining attorney can consent to the release of information and production of records to enable an expert to comply with the subpoena. However, the client is not able to designate the scope of what is released under the subpoena, and this consent does not extend to the disclosure of proprietary test manuals and test protocols that may have been used in evaluation or treatment (American Psychological Association Committee on Legal Issues, 2016).

If the client is unwilling to consent to the release of information to enable compliance with the subpoena, the forensic mental health professional should next contact the counsel or attorney for the requesting party; note that this may be done through the forensic mental health professional's attorney. The forensic mental health professional should present both the legal and ethical arguments against disclosure and assert privilege on the client's behalf if applicable. The forensic mental health professional can attempt to negotiate with the requesting attorney to determine if there is a way to achieve the requestor's objective without releasing confidential or proprietary information. If negotiation is not possible with the requesting party, the forensic mental health professional should contact the court governing the subpoena and ask the court to rule on whether disclosure is required.

There are two types of motions that can be filed on behalf of the individual impacted by the disclosure by the party's attorney. Of note, courts are generally more receptive to these types of motions if they are made by the individual impacted by the disclosure via their attorney, rather than the forensic mental health professional on their behalf (American Psychological Association Committee on Legal Issues, 2016). The first is a motion to quash, where the party is filing a formal application requesting the court to vacate the subpoena or declare it invalid in whole or in part. The second type of motion is for a protective order asking the court to protect against the consequences of disclosing information. The goal of protective orders is to prevent or limit the number of individuals to whom the sensitive/protected information may be disclosed and to provide parameters for the maintenance and possible destruction of the confidential material (American Psychological Association Committee on Legal Issues, 2016). There have been multiple instructive cases on the disclosure of testing information during the course of litigation. For example, in the landmark case of *Carpenter v. Superior Court* (2006), the First District Court of Appeals of California held that copyright law did not prevent disclosure of written psychological test questions and answers to the opposing party. The court reasoned that if the psychological tests were disclosed subject to a protective order, this eliminates any copyright law concerns (*Carpenter v. Superior Court*, 2006). Protective orders will be discussed more in depth below. As a general rule, forensic mental health professionals who perform psychological testing for treatment purposes may receive a subpoena to disclose test information. In this situation, the client would be the individual being assessed, and to disclose test data, the psychologist would need a release authorization form from the patient or a valid court order. The forensic mental health professional should also consult the relevant laws in their jurisdiction around how to respond to these requests. For example, Iowa law states "the test material shall not be disclosed in any administrative, judicial, or legislative proceeding," while (conversely) New Mexico law states "if test materials are sought by the subpoena or discovery request, the psychologist shall seek a protective order from a court of competent jurisdiction in order to maintain test security. Thereafter, the psychologist shall comply with the court order" (IA Code, 2014; NM Admin. Code, 2018).

A separate but related issue that is subject to the use of protective orders relates to a forensic mental health professional's testing materials (see Frederick et al., 2024, for an informative discussion). The Ethical Principles of Psychologists and Code of Conduct (EPPCC) distinguishes between test materials, which are defined as "manuals, instruments, protocols, and test questions or stimuli" (APA, 2017, p. 13), and test data, which are defined as "raw and scaled scores, client/patient responses to test questions or stimuli, and psychologists' notes and recording concerning client/patient statements and behavior during an examination" (APA, 2017, p. 12). Generally, test materials are provided with greater protection by APA than test data. Section 9.11 of the EPPCC states that "psychologists make reasonable efforts to maintain the integrity and security of test materials and other assessment techniques consistent with law and contractual obligations, and in a manner that permits adherence to this Ethics Code" (APA, 2017, p. 13). Conversely, Section 9.04 states: "Psychologists may refrain from releasing test data to protect a client/patient or others from substantial harm or misuse or misrepresentation of the data or the test, recognizing that in many instances release of confidential information under these circumstances is regulated by law" (APA, 2017, pp. 12–13).

If a psychologist is subpoenaed to disclose test materials, the psychologist (through the retaining attorney) should resist the initial request, cite the relevant sections of the EPPCC and *Specialty Guidelines for Forensic Psychology*, and propose an alternative course of action that satisfies the request and the psychologist's legal and ethical obligations to the extent possible (Otto et al., 2014; see Frederick et al., 2024). Specifically, Guideline 10.02 of the *Specialty Guidelines for Forensic Psychology* states that "given the stakes involved in forensic contexts, forensic practitioners strive to ensure the integrity and security of test materials and results" (American Psychological Association, 2013, p. 15). Examples of alternative solutions that are available with protective orders are discussed below. When the requesting attorney has requested a court order mandating disclosure of testing materials, jurisdictions have varied in their response. In *Gavin v. Hilton Worldwide, Inc.* (2013), the United States District Court for the Northern District of California advised the requesting party to subpoena the tests from the test publisher rather than from the opposing party. Other courts have declined to order the disclosure of the testing materials to the requesting attorneys, but have allowed disclosure of testing materials to any qualified psychologists serving as experts in the case (*Collins v. TIAA-CREF*, 2008; *Walton v. North Carolina Dept. of Agriculture*, 2011). Conversely, other courts have ordered the disclosure of testing materials to the requesting attorney with protections in place offered by the test publishers via protective order (e.g., *Carpenter v. Superior Court*, 2006; *Taylor v. Erna*, 2009). These protections included:

> a) restricting access to the materials and any testimony regarding the materials to the most limited audience possible, preferably only to counsel and experts engaged by the parties who are professionals qualified to use and interpret the tests; b) restricting use of the test materials only to that required for the resolution of the pending proceeding; c) requiring the prompt return of the materials produced and the destruction of any copies made at the conclusion of the proceeding; and d) sealing the record to the extent any portion of such materials are disclosed in pleadings, test, exhibits, or other documents which would otherwise be available for public inspection. (Vanderpool, 2014, p. 43)

If a psychologist's efforts are unsuccessful in challenging the subpoena, the EPPCC states: "If psychologists' ethical responsibilities conflict with law, regulations, or other governing legal authority, psychologists make known their commitment to the Ethics Code and take steps to resolve the conflict. If the conflict is unresolvable via such means, psychologists may adhere to the requirements of the law, regulations, or other governing legal authority" (American Psychological Association, 2017, p. 4). Some other common examples of reasons for protective orders include requests to prevent the wide dissemination of confidential information and requests to limit the categories of information that need to be released to comply and requesting an *in camera* hearing.

In addition to the grounds mentioned above, forensic mental health professionals can also challenge subpoenas if the psychologist does not have custody or control of the records, if the information is not relevant to the requesting party's claim, on behalf of the interests of third parties not involved in the litigation but impacted by the disclosure, if the disclosure conflicts with applicable laws, regulations, or ethical standards and guidelines, or if the disclosure presents an undue burden (American Psychological Association Committee on Legal Issues, 2016). Forensic mental health professionals can also be proactive in planning a response to anticipated subpoenas by training a Subpoena Response Designee.

This individual controls document retention and compliance with subpoenas. They should also be familiar with the forensic mental health professional's document retention plan and practice procedures as applicable.

In summary, forensic mental health professionals should remember that only a valid subpoena requires a response, and it does not necessarily require compliance. There are various strategies for challenging subpoenas or otherwise limiting the disclosure of information to protect the interest of others, including the protection of copyrighted testing materials. To the extent possible, forensic mental health professionals should create a plan for handling subpoenas when choosing to work on cases pending litigation.

Interrogatories

Interrogatories are written questions drafted by the opposing party's attorney that are answered under oath prior to trial (Otto et al., 2014). Although interrogatories are most commonly exchanged between attorneys, they can also be used to gather information about experts and what testimony can be expected at trial. Interrogatories may address the expert's credentials and background, data that were considered or generated, and opinions and work completed on the case at hand (Otto et al., 2014). To ease the burden on expert witnesses, testifying experts are often permitted to submit their written report as required by FRCP 26 in lieu of answering interrogatories. Interrogatories are often of limited utility when it comes to expert witnesses because attorney-drafted responses may be incomplete or unclear. However, although interrogatories are technically directed to the parties involved in the litigation, forensic mental health professionals who are serving as an expert witness may be called on to provide the necessary information or draft the interrogatory response. For example, interrogatories may require a party to provide information regarding the subject matter on which the expert is expected to testify, the conclusions and opinions of the expert as well as the underlying bases for these opinions, and the qualifications of the expert (Lubet & Boals, 2020). As an alternative to interrogatories, many attorneys attempt to gain early access to an expert witness's expected testimony through depositions.

Depositions

A deposition is a sworn statement given before trial to give parties access to a witness's testimony. Depositions involving expert witnesses are typically arranged by the party's attorneys via agreement. Attorneys, witnesses, clients, opposing experts, and someone authorized to administer oaths may all be present at a deposition, but there is no judge. Depositions typically take place in the office of an attorney, the court reporter, or the expert witness's office (Lubet & Boals, 2020). Failure to appear in response to a formal deposition request by an attorney can result in monetary sanctions against the attorney who retained the expert, exclusion of the expert's testimony in the party's case, and holding the expert witness in contempt of court. The goals of depositions are for attorneys to find out an expert's opinions, the bases for these opinions, and the expert's methods for reaching these opinions (Otto et al., 2014). Attorneys are also often evaluating the expert witness's testimony performance, testing which theories may be most successful at trial, assessing whether the expert has a bias in favor of either the plaintiff or defense, or seeking to facilitate settlement by weakening the opposing party's case or scope of their expert's testimony (Walker & Shapiro, 2020). Expert witnesses may be advised by attorneys to provide short but honest answers to avoid future impeachment. Impeachment of an expert can arise when an expert's trial testimony meaningfully differs from deposition testimony. Additionally, depositions can establish the scope of trial testimony. To avoid having the scope of their testimony limited, forensic mental health professionals should avoid categorical statements and provide qualified answers to questions, even if they initially appear to be straightforward. If requested to participate in a deposition, the forensic mental health professional should not bring anything to the deposition unless documents are specifically requested. If an expert witness brings notes or draft reports to aid them in their deposition, these notes and draft reports become discoverable notwithstanding the provisions discussed above.

In some cases, depositions are taken so that the transcript of the deposition can be offered in lieu of the witness's appearance at trial. These depositions are known as *de bene esse* depositions (Greiffenstein & Kaufman, 2012). FRCP 32(a)(4) states that a deposition may be used if a witness is unavailable for a variety of reasons, including death, infirmity, distance from the proceedings, inability to procure the witness's appearance by subpoena, or other exceptional circumstances. For most cases, however, depositions are taken with the expectation that the witness will testify at trial.

Under FRCP 30(d)(1), a deposition is limited to 1 day consisting of 7 hours of testimony. However, under Rule 26(b)(2), "By order, the court may alter the limits in these rules on the number of depositions and interrogatories or on the length of depositions under Rule 30." The court may similarly alter the rules surrounding depositions "if needed to fairly examine the deponent or if the deponent, another person, or any other circumstance impedes or delays the examination" (FRCP 30(d)(1)). During the deposition, the expert answers questions presented by the attorney requesting the deposition, then answers questions by the attorney retaining them, followed by questions from any other attorney that is party to the litigation (Otto et al., 2014).

At the conclusion of a deposition, the expert witness will be asked whether they would like to "read or waive signature." FRCP 30(e) states that "on request by the deponent or a party before the deposition is completed, the deponent must be allowed 30 days after being notified by the officer that the transcript or recording is available" to review the transcript or recording and "if there are changes in form or substance, to sign a statement listing the changes and the reasons for making them." If the deponent or a party does not request a transcript review, the transcript becomes the official record at the conclusion of the deposition.

There are multiple advantages to being an expert witness involved in the discovery process. Expert witnesses are designated experts for a reason: They often have the most knowledge about the subject matter they are testifying about and have many years of education and training to rely on when testifying. By having a plan for responding to attorney requests and subpoenas, forensic mental health professionals can set themselves up for success in dealing with court procedures (Bronstein, 2012). Additionally, forensic mental health professionals will often know going into testimony where the "grey" areas of their specialty field are and thus are in the best position to avoid these pitfalls simply by possessing that knowledge and brushing up on how to explain the field's current understanding of a complex topic accurately (Lubet & Boals, 2020). An expert witness should also not be afraid to acknowledge if there are things they do not know, for example, if the topic is an ongoing area of research or exploration in the field of forensic mental health assessment.

However, it is also important for forensic mental health professionals to be aware of where attorneys may have the most advantage in discovery proceedings. Attorneys typically know the procedures better than the expert witness. Attorneys are also aware of common weaknesses that apply to expert witnesses as a category (e.g., experts may be biased) and can attempt to expose these weaknesses during cross-examination. Lastly, attorneys have the benefit of "requiring" consistency across an expert's participation in interrogatories, depositions, and in-court testimony. If an expert is not careful in reviewing their prior testimony and responses under oath, it is very easy to be impeached with prior inconsistent statements, which can discredit an expert's testimony in totality for the fact finder (Lubet & Boals, 2020; Malone & Zwier, 2014).

There are common pitfalls that forensic mental health professionals fall into when testifying in court or in depositions. Expert witnesses should avoid making overly broad assertions. For example, an expert should not state that they can testify with "100% certainty" in their conclusions. Forensic mental health professionals should also avoid arguing or engaging in rapid-fire question-and-answer while under cross-examination. This can both increase the probability that an expert will make a mistake in their testimony (which may facilitate impeachment). Similarly, forensic mental health professionals should tailor their demeanor to be professional, direct, and knowledgeable without appearing arrogant, argumentative, or biased. Expert witnesses should refrain from "thinking out loud" or musing about topics not directly related to the case at hand. By straying off topic, the expert risks confusing the fact finder about the relevant issues or losing their attention in the technical details. Forensic mental health professionals should openly acknowledge the limits of their expertise and stay within these boundaries during both direct and cross-examination testimony. If an expert goes beyond the bounds of their expertise, they risk being both incorrect and losing credibility with the fact finder about the scope of their expertise. Similarly, experts should also openly admit and acknowledge any mistakes made, preferably on direct examination, when possible. By proactively addressing the weaknesses of their testimony, the expert limits the opposing attorney's scope on cross-examination and bolsters their credibility with the fact finder.

Conclusion

Discovery is an opportunity for forensic mental health professionals to prepare themselves for potential impending litigation. Regardless of whether involvement in litigation is a regular practice or rare occasion, forensic mental health professionals should be familiar with the discovery rules in their jurisdiction to avoid running afoul of both the law and ethical standards. If faced with a subpoena, forensic mental health professionals should remember that a valid subpoena requires a response, but not every subpoena requires compliance. When in doubt, the professional should consult the relevant ethics codes and consult with fellow professionals and/or an attorney.

There is significant guidance both in this chapter and in the relevant professional codes surrounding disclosure of psychological testing materials, and forensic mental health professionals are ethically required to protect against the consequences of disclosure of these materials. If called to testify in a deposition, forensic mental health professionals should exercise caution when deciding what materials to bring to aid them in their testimony (as these become discoverable). Forensic mental health professionals can avoid many of the pitfalls surrounding discovery by being proactive. Expert witnesses should discuss with the retaining attorney what will be expected during the discovery portion of the proceedings, tailor their fee agreement and create a subpoena plan to account for time constraints during the discovery process, and prepare for questions that may arise during interrogatories and depositions.

Chapter 4
Legal Bases for Expert Testimony

The prospect of providing testimony at a deposition, hearing, or trial can elicit a variety of responses from mental health professionals, both substantively and emotionally. It is our hope that fostering a deeper understanding of the legal workings at play during a trial will serve the dual purposes of providing mental health professionals with the necessary information to fulfill their duties on the stand and assuage some of the anxiety that comes from not being fully familiar with the legal procedures.

Mental health professionals do not need to have an understanding of court rules and procedures that is commensurate with the understanding possessed by legal professionals. Ultimately, it is the job of the lawyers to ask the necessary questions and the judge to make the appropriate determinations regarding what information is allowed in the courtroom. However, effective experts will seek to educate themselves on these legal procedures to foster awareness of how the law impacts their work product and how they convey the concepts from their work to others through testimony.

To accomplish this goal, this chapter provides forensic mental health professionals with an understanding of the legal bases for expert testimony. We include a discussion of the relevant Federal Rules of Evidence, clarification regarding the inclusion of hearsay in expert reports and testimony, and a review of the legal standards governing expert reliance on inadmissible evidence in reports and testimony.

Although some researchers in the field may be tempted to skim these pages, or skip the chapter entirely, we believe the information in this chapter is beneficial to any mental health professional engaged in forensic work. Clinicians may be most likely to provide expert testimony, but researchers may also be asked to testify (e.g., presenting the state of the science in a particular topic area to the court). Similarly, consultants may be asked to guide attorneys or other professionals through the many overlapping and sometimes seemingly contradictory legal requirements and limitations on expert testimony. Given the variety of roles mental health professionals may play in the courtroom (and behind the scenes), the chapter begins with a brief history to provide context to the landscape of expert testimony regarding mental health.

Forensic Mental Health Practice and the Law. David DeMatteo, Daniel A. Krauss, Sarah Fishel, and Kellie Wiltsie, Oxford University Press. © Oxford University Press (2025). DOI: 10.1093/9780197686591.003.0004

History

The Etiology of the Expert Witness

Xi Yuan Lu (translated as either *Collected Cases of Injustice Rectified* or *The Washing Away of Wrongs*), which is widely considered the first book on forensic science, was published in the 13th century. The author, Song Ci, used medical practices to explain, among other things, how to determine the cause of death of an individual and, specifically, how to determine whether a death was accidental or the product of homicide.

Xi Yuan Lu described the utility of science in court proceedings using an example from 1235 AD. According to the text, a peasant from a village in China was murdered, and it was quickly determined that the murder weapon was a hand sickle, a common tool possessed by most peasants in the area. To identify the attacker, the magistrate called all the suspects to the town square and had them lay their sickles in the sun. As the crowd watched, a group of flies were attracted to a single sickle, suggesting the presence of trace amounts of blood and tissue. The owner of the sickle confessed to the murder and was prosecuted. This story was used in the text to convey the utility of insect behaviors as an aid to investigations and mortality analyses (see Sung [1981] for the useful translation by McKnight).

Turning specifically to expert witnesses in the systems that influenced the current United States legal landscape, it is interesting to note that juries in medieval England were selected based on their relevant knowledge, thus circumventing the need for outside expertise (Milroy, 2017). This practice continued from the medieval court systems into the more modern common law system and was only abolished in England in 1971 (Milroy, 2017). When experts did not have a place on the jury, they were called in as "neutral" consultants to the court (Golan, 2008). In this role, they did not directly offer opinions regarding the legal case but instead provided information to the court as needed throughout the trial process.

As the landscape and structure of judicial proceedings changed, so, too, did the need for scientific advisors to the court. The Industrial Revolution brought about a surge of advancements in science, technology, and skilled knowledge. However, the modern-day scientific method lagged behind these advancements, as did professional standards for practice. Against this backdrop, court cases began to require knowledge of scientific processes that judges did not possess. At the same time, "experts" with varied and often questionable qualifications were brought before the court in droves, offering opposing testimony that further muddied, rather than clarified, the facts in question (Golan, 2008).

English courts eventually adopted "the expert" as a distinct entity in the late 1700s. During that time, the court system was evolving into something closer to what we recognize in England and the United States today, with an adversarial system in which each party called witnesses (Milroy, 2017). The rules regarding testimony were crystallizing, and the distinction between lay and expert witnesses was formalized in *Folkes v. Chadd* in 1782. In his opinion, Lord Mansfield recognized scientifically derived, opinion-based expert testimony as distinct from the fact-based testimony (to which witnesses were limited at the time). As a result, Lord Mansfield permitted the expert testimony, citing the specific expertise that could be provided by an expert regardless of whether they had firsthand knowledge of the facts of the case.

The legal doctrine outlined in *Folkes* set the foundation not only for expert testimony but also for the rules of evidence that continue to provide the basis for expert testimony in modern legal systems. The black letter and case law that developed in the centuries that followed further delineated the role of the expert witness and of science in the courtroom. At the same time, the burgeoning science of human behavior led to a parallel and highly contested discussion regarding the role and professional qualifications required of experts offering mental health testimony.

Mental Health Testimony in the United States

The history of mental health testimony in the United States court system is characterized by a pattern of leaps forward, skepticism, backpedaling, and then measured progress. Some accounts indicate that mental health professionals began lending their expertise to courts in the United States as early as 1846 (Ewing, 2003). The practice of psychologists serving as expert witnesses was first propagated by Hugo Münsterberg in 1908 in *On the Witness Stand* (Erickson & Ewing, 2012; Ewing, 2003). *On the Witness Stand* vehemently argued for the nascent field of forensic psychology and its place in the courtroom. In the book, Münsterberg praised the psychological profession and chastised the legal profession. He expressed "astonish[ment] that the work of justice is ever carried out in the courts without ever consulting the psychologist" (p. 194) and claimed that against the utility of psychology "[t]he lawyer alone is obdurate" (Münsterberg, 1908, p. 10).

Speaking directly of the court's general view of the psychologist as an expert witness, Münsterberg (1908) lamented that "while the alienist is always a welcome guest in the courtroom, the psychologist is still a stranger there" (p. 46).[1] This commentary brought forth not only the ire of legal professionals but also the sardonic amusement of professions that have traditionally been accepted as experts in the courtroom (and those specifically mentioned in *On the Witness Stand*), such as medical doctors, psychiatrists, and professionals from "hard" sciences (e.g., chemistry, engineering) (Bartol & Bartol, 2013; Erickson & Ewing, 2012).

The most scathing commentary came from John Henry Wigmore, a leading evidentiary expert at the time. Wigmore (1909) published a satirical article structured as a mock trial for libel. Rife with allusion and allegory, the "suit" listed Münsterberg as the defendant in which the "plaintiff" (whose name is a mixture of those belonging to foundational legal scholars) sought to "vindicate the honor and the intelligence of the profession to which they belonged" (Wigmore, 1909, p. 404). The commentary pokes fun at Münsterberg's work, cites 127 articles and treatises to support its claims, and ultimately finds for the plaintiff, calling Münsterberg both obstinate and incompetent in the process.

At this time, psychologists were occasionally admitted as expert witnesses when discussing experimental research, but they were generally barred from opining on issues related to mental health (Bartol & Bartol, 2013). This practice was cemented in *West Virgina v. Driver* (1921), which is the first published United States case with a psychologist. One issue in *Driver* was the credibility of a 12-year-old female victim of attempted rape. During the trial, Dr. Florence Mateer, the chief psychologist for the Bureau of Juvenile Research in Ohio, was admitted as an expert due to her "extensive training and study in the examination of delinquents" (p. 191). As an expert, she was allowed to provide general testimony regarding the definition of the word "moron," but she was prohibited from providing more specific testimony regarding the victim.

Importantly, a closer reading of the case suggests that Dr. Mateer's testimony regarding the victim was ruled inadmissible because of the method by which her opinion was reached (and *not* her training or credentials). The court classified the opinion regarding the victim's mental health (i.e., the "class of moron" to which she was prescribed) as "character evidence" because it was related to the question of whether she was likely to lie about the attempted rape. The court ruled that once the jury heard the expert testimony, the jury was suited to come to a conclusion regarding the veracity of her claims. Specifically, the court opinion states the testimony "was an attempt in a measure to substitute the opinion of the experts for that of the jury, and to tell them that they should disregard her evidence" (*West Virginia v. Driver*, 1921, p. 192). Thus, the issue was not necessarily whether the psychologist could properly render an opinion on the victim, but whether the opinion (a) was best characterized as character evidence and inadmissible, and/or (b) embraced an "ultimate issue" best left to the jury.

As a result of this legal precedent, psychologists remained "strangers" to mental health testimony in the court for the next two decades. However, incremental progress was made in the 1940 case of *Michigan v. Hawthorne*. Hawthorne was convicted of manslaughter after unsuccessfully raising the insanity defense, and he appealed his case to the Supreme Court of Michigan. Among other things, he argued that the trial court had improperly refused to qualify a professor of psychology as an expert witness for the defense. In the opinion, Judge McAllister affirmed the conviction. Dressed in ever so complicated legal trappings, however, was a small win for forensic psychologists. McAllister's opinion ruled that the trial court was not in error when it excluded the professor's testimony.[2] In describing his reasoning, McAllister summarized that the professor:

> [H]ad never treated insanity nor was he licensed to practice medicine in any form. His qualifications, as submitted to the court, were that he had received degrees of bachelor of arts, master of arts, bachelor of divinity, doctor of philosophy, and doctor of psychology; that he had studied at eight different colleges and had taught at four; that he gave courses in general psychology, and had written books and articles on the subject; and that he had given "mental tests." Insanity, however, is held to be a disease [. . .] and, therefore, comes within the realm of medical science, which comprises the study and treatment of disease. Only physicians can qualify to answer hypothetical questions as experts in such science. (*Hawthorne*, p. 20)

However, in a majority concurrence, Judge Butzel argued the opposite. Describing the qualifications of the proposed expert, he asserted:

> I do not think we further the cause of justice by insisting that only a medical man may completely advise on the subject of mental condition. The proposed witness was a graduate of Tilton School in New Hampshire, Wesleyan University, Yale University, and Harvard Foundation, and held the degrees of Bachelor of Arts, Master of Arts, Bachelor of Divinity, and Doctor of Philosophy in Psychology. As a graduate student he had attended the University of California, Columbia University, Boston University, Harvard University Medical School, and the Boston Psychopathic Hospital. He was a full professor of Central College, Fayette, Missouri; Baker University; University of Kansas, and Michigan State Normal College; he had been connected with the latter institution for 11 years up to the time of the trial. He had given courses in normal and abnormal psychology, experimental psychology, educational psychology, mental tests and measurements, psychology and criminology, problems in marriage and family, and problems of child-welfare. One of his texts has been through five editions since the first publication in 1927. He has written articles on the subject of human behavior that have appeared in publications throughout the United States. He specialized in the particular field of psychology devoted to motivation and motives of human conduct. He had no medical degree and, of

> course, could not practice medicine, though he knew about the anatomy of the brain, having studied physiological psychology and neurology. He had given insanity and diseases of the brain special study. I do not think it can be said that his ability to detect insanity is inferior to that of a medical man whose experience along such lines is not so intensive. (*Hawthorne*, pp. 22–23)

Butzel went on to contend "no case has been called to my attention where a general medical training has been held to be the sine qua non of the competency of a trained specialist to advise on the matter of insanity" (*Hawthorne*, p. 23), and therefore:

> There is no magic in particular titles or degrees and, in our age of intense scientific specialization, we might deny ourselves the use of the best knowledge available by a rule that would immutably fix the educational qualifications to a particular degree. (*Hawthorne*, p. 25)

Though the concurrence is not legally binding, it is the first time a published legal argument was made for allowing individuals outside of the medical profession to provide expert testimony regarding mental health.[3]

The 1950s and 1960s also saw the emergence of clinical and counseling psychology (Erickson & Ewing, 2012; Otto & Heilbrun, 2002). These specialty areas followed the training of psychiatry more closely than experimental psychology. Clinical and counseling psychologists obtained specific training in mental health conditions using a disease-based or medical model of psychiatric conditions, and they were taught how to use objective measures and assessments in diagnosing conditions. These training programs also provided a framework for treatment that existed outside of the medical model; shifting the focus from the psychopharmacological treatments provided by psychiatrists, clinical and counseling psychologists used psychotherapy to treat those under their care.

Thus, the arguments in *Hawthorne*, though not legally binding, became essential to these professionals—psychologists could now assess, diagnose, and treat in ways that psychiatrists could not. If there was no longer "magic" in the medical doctorate, and the qualification of an expert on mental health was instead knowledge of mental conditions, then what, other than precedent, was barring clinical and/or counseling psychologists from providing this expert testimony?

The next leap forward came in the civil arena. In 1954, the United States Court of Appeals for the Fourth Circuit heard *Hidden v. Mutual Life Insurance Company*. In *Hidden*, two physicians and a psychiatrist were called to testify regarding the impact of a car accident on the insured driver. These doctors were all admitted as experts and their testimony was heard. However, a fourth expert was called—a doctoral-level clinical psychologist. The insured driver was referred to the psychologist for testing by one of the testifying psychiatrists. After examining the driver, the psychologist opined that the driver was disabled at the time of examination (1952) and at the time the original claim was filed (1949).

The trial court excluded the testimony of the psychologist on the grounds that he was "not qualified as an expert" and it rejected his attempts to further explain his opinion (*Hidden*, p. 820). The appellate court reversed the trial court's decision on the admissibility of the psychologist's testimony, opining that "[t]he uncontradicted evidence received at the trial tended to show that the expert was qualified in his field by academic training and by experience" (*Hidden*, p. 821). The court stated that the objective tests used by the psychologist and integrated into the opinion of the referring/testifying psychiatrist buttressed the qualification of the psychologist. For the first time in modern American jurisprudence, a clinical psychologist was regarded as a qualified expert and allowed to testify regarding an individual's mental health.

That same year, the Council and Business Meeting of Members of the American Psychoanalytic Association, the Council of the American Psychiatric Association, and the Board of Trustees of the American Medical Association, published the *Joint Resolution on the Relationship of Psychotherapy to Medicine* (1954). In the resolution, the organizations argued that psychotherapy is a form of medical treatment and thus subsumed by the medical profession. Thus, although other professions such as psychology (and counselors, teachers, nurses, etc.) use "psychological understanding" to achieve the goals of their profession(s), they are *not* "practicing psychotherapy" (p. 814). Therefore, while these other professionals may work in "contributing roles in medically supervised settings," when the issue at hand is diagnosis and treatment of mental illness, "their professional contributions must be coordinated under medical responsibility" (p. 815). In other words, though psychologists can participate in the mental health sphere, the ultimate arbiters and, therefore, experts on the topic are medical doctors.

The question of whether clinical psychologists were qualified as expert witnesses and able to provide opinion testimony regarding mental disorders in a criminal context reached a critical point in 1962 with *Jenkins v. United States*. Jenkins was charged with housebreaking with intent to commit an assault, assault with intent to rape, and assault with a dangerous weapon, to which he pled not guilty by reason of insanity. Jenkins subsequently underwent psychological and psychiatric evaluations for competency to stand trial and to assess his mental state at the time of the alleged offense. Though multiple psychiatrists and psychologists were initially allowed to provide testimony, the trial court instructed the jury to disregard the opinion testimony of the psychologists relating to whether Jenkins had a mental disease when he committed the crimes. Specifically, the court instructed:

> A psychologist is not competent to give a medical opinion as to a mental disease or defect. Therefore, you will not consider any evidence to the effect that the defendant was suffering from a mental disease or defect on June 10, 1959 according to the testimony given by the psychologists. (*Jenkins*, p. 643)

The court in *Jenkins* also instructed the jury to disregard some aspects of the testimony of the psychiatrists when based on the reports of the psychologists, stating only "there isn't any testimony here that is based on any proper evidence that he was suffering from a mental disease. I am not going to allow it on the basis of a report of a psychologist" (*Jenkins*, p. 640). Jenkins was ultimately found guilty and appealed the case, partially arguing that the trial court's exclusion of the expert witness testimony was improper.

Jenkins was highly controversial. The American Psychiatric Association filed an *amicus curiae* brief arguing against overturning current precedent,[4] and the American Psychological Association filed its first *amicus curiae* brief arguing for reversal (*Jenkins v. United States*, 1962; see APA *Amicus Curiae Brief Program*). In forming its opinion, the United States Court of Appeals for the District of Columbia Circuit relied heavily on the legal basis for the role of the expert witness at the time, which required no specific degree, but instead special knowledge and skill that allows them to render an opinion to "aid the trier [of fact] in the search for truth" (*Jenkins*, p. 644).

The appellate court reviewed the training and education requirements specifically for psychologists with a doctorate in clinical psychology. Finding first that "[t]he determination of a psychologist's competence to render an expert opinion based on his findings as to the presence or absence of mental disease defect must depend on the nature and extent of his knowledge" rather than the title of "psychologist," the court asserted "[w]hen completion of such training is followed by actual experience in the treatment and diagnosis of disease in association with psychiatrists or neurologists, the opinion of the psychologist may properly be received in evidence" (*Jenkins*, p. 645). Furthermore, it offered guidance that clinical psychologists who are certified by the American Board of Examiners in Professional Psychology should, as a result of the qualifications necessary for board certification, generally be admitted as expert witnesses.[5]

The majority opinion in *Jenkins*, though the last case cited in this brief review, was not the end of the debate on whether psychologists should be admitted as expert witnesses for the purpose of providing mental health testimony.[6] Regardless, it set new precedent and provides the legal foundation for psychologists as expert witnesses. The field has since grown in its understanding of psycholegal issues, and in 2001 the American Psychological Association recognized the specialty of forensic psychology (Otto & Heilbrun, 2002).

Almost 100 years after Münsterberg's vehement argument for the role of psychology in the courtroom, Justice Breyer of the Supreme Court of the United States observed that scientific issues permeate the law (Breyer, 2000). Speaking specifically about mental health testimony, he emphasized the import and severity of the consequences associated with this testimony when highlighting expert predictions of a defendant's future dangerousness, which can be persuasive on juries in the sentencing phase of death penalty cases (Breyer, 2000). Münsterberg would likely be happy to hear that questions such as these are currently accepted as falling squarely under the purview of clinical psychology, forensic psychology, and other mental health professions.

The Legal Foundation of Expert Testimony

Understanding the *Jenkins* decision can be helpful for contextualizing the historical controversy surrounding the question of which professionals are allowed to offer mental health expert testimony. However, any professional who aims to offer their expertise to the court must also understand the legal foundation for the testimony. There are specific rules and case law to guide expert testimony, including rules regarding (a) how expert testimony differs from lay testimony, (b) how to determine whether an individual is qualified to provide expert testimony, (c) the scope of the testimony, (d) the methodology used by the expert to come to a conclusion, and (e) how those conclusions are communicated in court. The rules that provide the legal basis for expert testimony generally, and their application to mental health testimony specifically, are reviewed in detail below.

As a reminder, from a legal perspective, an expert witness is there to provide information to the trier of fact (judge or jury) to help the court make a decision. The information used by the expert, any written product produced by the expert, and any testimony given during a deposition, hearing, or trial, is considered evidence. Thus, the legal definition of evidence covers a wide range of material, including physical (e.g., murder weapon), written, or spoken (also called testimonial evidence). Additionally, the evidence used in a case may be described as *horizontal*, in that multiple forms of evidence are used, or *vertical*, in that one form of evidence relies on another. Expert testimony often falls into this vertical structure because it is a type of testimonial evidence that relies upon other types of evidence, such as interviews, testing administration, and existing records.

The Rules of Evidence

Not all evidence is treated equally in court. In fact, most evidence gathered in a case is not allowed to be introduced to a jury or other legal fact finder. The reasons and associated guidelines are codified in each jurisdiction's rules of evidence. The Federal Rules of Evidence (FRE) serve as a general guideline that will be discussed throughout this chapter and book. However, there are two caveats to the following discussion. First, the FRE are not applicable in state courts, but nearly every state has adopted the FRE in whole, in part, or with only minor modifications (Dreyer et al., 2011; see Table 4.1 for states that have modeled their rules after the FRE). Before offering their expertise, forensic mental health professionals should familiarize themselves with the rules specific to the court in which they are providing testimony. Second, the FRE apply to all hearings and proceedings, but FRE 1101 carves out exceptions—that is, the FRE do not apply to admissibility or grand jury proceedings. Of particular importance for mental health professionals, the federal exception states that the FRE do not apply in sentencing hearings (FRE 1101(d)(3)).[7] Though the judge will make the determination of which evidence is admissible, forensic mental health professionals should be familiar with the rules and the legal foundation they set for expert testimony.

Table 4.1 State Codes Modeled After the Federal Rules of Evidence

State	Relation to FRE	Citation
Alabama	Modeled	Ala. R. Evid. 102
Alaska	Modeled	Alaska R. Evid. (Commentary)
Arizona	Modeled	Ariz. R. Evid. Prefatory Comment
Arkansas	Modeled	State v. Terrazas, 944 P.2d 1194 (1997)
California	Modeled	State of California Evidence Code with Comments (1965)
Colorado	Modeled	Colo. R. Evid. (see generally)
Connecticut	No	Conn R. Evid. 1–2(a) (Commentary)
Delaware	Modeled	Del R. Evid. (Commentary)
District of Columbia	Common law	D.C. Super. Ct. Crim. R. 26
Florida	Modeled	H.B. 7015, 2013 Reg. Sess. (Fla. 2013)
Georgia	Modeled	H.B. 24, 2011 Reg. Sess. (Ga. 2013)
Hawaii	Modeled	Barkai, John. (2018). *Hawaii Rules of Evidence Handbook.*

Continued

Table 4.1 *Continued*

State	Relation to FRE	Citation
Idaho	Modeled	Amendments Recommended by the Idaho Evidence Rules Advisory Committee (2018, January 15)
Illinois	Modeled	Illinois Rules of Evidence Committee Commentary (2011, January 1)
Indiana	Modeled	Drew, E. R., & Wanker, A. A. (2014). Recent developments in Indiana evidence law. *Indiana Law Review*, *47*, 1065–1092. *Griffith v. State*, 31 N.E.3d 965 (Ind. 2015).
Iowa	Modeled	*In the matter of adopting amendments to the Iowa Rules of Evidence in* Chapter 5 *of the Iowa Court Rules* (Iowa Sept. 14, 2022)
Kansas	Uniform Rules	*State v. Price*, No. 86,243 (Kan. 2003)
Kentucky	Modeled	In Re: Order Amending Kentucky Rules of Evidence (Ky. 2007)
Louisiana	Modeled	Force, R. & Ciolino, D. S. (2022). *Handbook on Louisiana Evidence Law.*
Maine	Modeled	Me. R. Evid. 101
Maryland	Modeled	McLain, L. (1994). Maryland's adoption of a code of evidence. *ScholarWorks.*
Massachusetts	Unofficially modeled	Supreme Judicial Court Advisory Committee on Massachusetts Evidence Law (2024 ed.). *Massachusetts Guide to Evidence.*
Michigan	Modeled	A.O. No. 2021-8. Establishment of the Michigan Rules of Evidence Review Committee (2021, Dec. 22)
Minnesota	Modeled	Thompson, P. N. (1976). Presumptions and the new rules of evidence in Minnesota. *William Mitchell Law Review*, *2*(1), 167–186.
Mississippi	Modeled	Miss. R. Evid. (Commentary)
Missouri	Common Law	Mo. Sup. Ct. Op. R 15.01
Montana	Modeled	Clarke, D. P. (1978). Montana Rules of Evidence: A general survey. *Montana Law Review*, *39*(1), 79–140.
Nebraska	Modeled	Naylor, Jr., K. E. (1978). Section 609 of the Nebraska Evidence Rules: A need for clarification. *Nebraska Law Review*, *57*(1), 26–43.

State	Relation to FRE	Citation
Nevada	Modeled	*Mitchell v. Eighth Judicial Dist. Court*, 131 Nev. 163 (2015)
New Hampshire	Modeled	N.H. R. Evid. (Preamble)
New Jersey	Modeled	2017–2019 Report of the Supreme Court Committee on the Rules of Evidence (2019, Jan. 15)
New Mexico	Modeled	*State v. Martinez*, 145 N.M. 220 (2008)
New York	Common law	Guide to NY Evid. *Rule 1.01 Purpose and Construction*. (accessed Aug. 20, 2024).
North Carolina	Modeled	*State v. Bogle*, 324 N.C. 190 (N.C. 1989)
North Dakota	Modeled	N.D. R. Evid.
Ohio	Modeled	Weinstein, J. B. (1977). The Ohio and Federal Rules of Evidence. *Capital University Law Review*, *6*(4), 517–532.
Oklahoma	Modeled	*Christian v. Gray*, 65 P.3d 591 (Okla. 2003)
Oregon	Modeled	*State v. O'Key*, 321 Or. 285 (Or. 1995)
Pennsylvania	Modeled	225 Pa. Code Sec. 101 (Preface to Comments)
Rhode Island	Modeled	*State v. Mallett*, 600 A.2d 273 (1991)
South Carolina	Modeled	Hon. G. Ross Anderson, Jr. (1996). Unmined Gold in 803(18) *South Carolina Lawyer* 32.
South Dakota	Modeled	*State v. Swallow*, 405 N.W.2d 29 (S.D. 1987)
Tennessee	Modeled	Banks, Jr., R. (1990). Some comparisons between the new Tennessee Rules of Evidence and the Federal Rules of Evidence Part III. *Memphis State University Law Review*, *21*(1), 1–58.
Texas	Modeled	*Cole v. State*, 839 S.W.2d 798 (Tex. Crim. App. 1992)
Utah	Modeled	Utah R. Evid. (Preliminary Note)
Vermont	Modeled	Martindale-Hubbell Law Digest: Vermont (2008)
Virginia	Modeled	Virginia Inns of Court (2011). *Rules of Evidence*.
Washington	Modeled	*Condon Bros. v. Simpson Timber Co.*, 92 Wn. App. 275 (Wash. Ct. App. 1998)
West Virginia	Modeled	*State v. Sutphin*, 195 W. Va. 551 (W. Va. 1995)
Wisconsin	Modeled	*State v. Heft*, 185 Wis. 2d 288 (1994)
Wyoming	Modeled	*In the matter of the adoption of Wy. R. Evid.* (Wyo. 1977)

Relevancy and Admissibility

Turning now to the rules of evidence, there are two main threshold questions that govern whether evidence will be admitted in a case. The first question: Is it relevant? FRE 401, which provides the test for relevant evidence, states that evidence is admissible if it (a) "has any tendency to make a fact more or less probable than it would without the evidence; and (b) the fact is of consequence in determining the action." The relevance of any evidence may change based on the specific proceeding. For example, the school records for a 45-year-old man who is not arguing any form of mental health or behavioral defense are likely not relevant to determining guilt in a homicide case (although it may be relevant to sentencing). Alternatively, mental health records are relevant to a pretrial competency hearing; however, once the defendant is determined competent to proceed, they may not be relevant to the case-in-chief. Article IV of the FRE covers the rules and limitations relating to relevancy.

Whereas the relevancy question is relatively straightforward, the second threshold question of evidence—Is it admissible?—requires a more complex analysis. Admissibility refers to a larger determination of whether it is fair or acceptable to let the evidence into court proceedings. Specific admissibility standards for expert testimony will be discussed in detail in Chapters 5 and 6. For the purposes of the following discussion regarding the foundation of expert testimony, it is necessary only to understand that the following rules and standards provide guidance for what is considered admissible.

It can be helpful to think of each of the rules of evidence as a series of nets, catching and screening out evidence that, for a variety of reasons, should not be included in a legal proceeding. The evidence that is "caught" is generally labeled inadmissible. Each net (i.e., rule) utilizes its own reasoning and has its own basis for catching evidence before it is introduced into the proceeding. The first net is relevancy, discussed previously. The remaining nets are broadly categorized as other admissibility rules. These rules are designed to assist the fact finder in weighing the importance of including the relevant evidence (its probative value) against any adverse impact or inefficiency created by its inclusion (its prejudicial effect) (see FRE 403).[8] For any piece of evidence to be determined admissible and therefore introduced at the proceeding, it must successfully pass through every layer of the interlocking nets. This issue is particularly salient (and often confusing) when it comes to expert testimony.

Witnesses: Lay and Expert

Witnesses offer evidence in legal proceedings. The content and scope of what they say are considered evidence and is thus subject to the applicable rules of evidence. The FRE discussing witness testimony can be found in Article VI

("Witnesses") and, most relevantly, Article VII ("Opinions and Expert Testimony"). Witness testimony is divided into two categories depending on the type of witness: lay witness and expert witness. The distinction between these two types of witnesses has important implications for the role of experts in legal proceedings.

Lay Witnesses

Lay witnesses, also referred to as fact witnesses (or sometimes ordinary witnesses or percipient witnesses), testify based on their firsthand knowledge of a fact relevant to the case. They require no additional specialized knowledge or training, and there is virtually no minimum bar for being a lay witness, other than the relevance of their testimony and their competency to testify. Thus, the accuracy and credibility of their testimony is established not through their credentials but by the testimony itself as presented during direct examination and cross-examination. In addition, because they are not "hired" to testify, but called based on their firsthand knowledge of something in the case, lay witnesses, unlike expert witnesses, are not typically paid for their time and/or testimony (although subpoenaed witnesses may receive a small witness fee [e.g., $5/day], depending on the state).

To counterbalance the low bar for service as a lay witness, the evidentiary rules greatly limit the scope of the testimony they can provide. A lay witness can only provide testimony about their personal observations and experience. In the case of a homicide where there is question regarding the defendant's sobriety, a bystander who saw the murder take place may be called as a witness to offer testimony about the time at which the events occurred, what they saw or heard, and any description of the actor(s). In narrow circumstances, a lay witness may offer evidence in the form of an opinion, but the opinion must be rationally based on the witness's perception, helpful in determining a fact in issue, and not based in scientific, technical, or other specialized knowledge better suited for expert testimony (see FRE 701).

Returning to the homicide example, the witness may be allowed to state their opinion that "the aggressor was acting strange," but would not be allowed to attribute the murder to the aggressor's inebriation. This second opinion would be reserved for an expert with specialized knowledge. Similarly, if the witness saw the defendant in motion, they may share the observation that the individual "looked unsteady on their feet" and "vomited," but they would likely not be able to say that the person in question "was drunk" or otherwise under the influence of substances because this opinion is not necessarily rationally based on their perception of the event and could be attributed to other factors (e.g., medical shock, trauma reaction). However, a second lay witness may be called to testify that they were at a local bar shortly before the murder where they saw the defendant consume 10 shots of alcohol within a 30-minute period, after which the defendant's speech was slurred and the defendant appeared intoxicated. Though the opinion offered is the same, it would likely be permitted here because it rationally follows from the lay observations of the latter witness, but not the former.

A mental health professional offering opinion testimony related to a defendant's mental state at the time of the offense could be called as an expert witness. The rules that are relevant to expert witnesses are discussed in the next section. It is also possible that another mental health professional who works as a therapist could be called as a fact witness to discuss the defendant's psychiatric diagnosis and course of mental health treatment. However, as noted, the fact witness should not be asked to offer, or spontaneously offer, an opinion relevant to the legal question before the court.

Expert Witnesses

As described earlier in the chapter, the Industrial Revolution and boom in science and technology necessitated the creation of a second class of witness: the expert. The expert witness is given more leeway to offer opinions to the court based on their specific area of knowledge. Coinciding with this added privilege is an additional set of restrictions and requirements. As previously mentioned, the legal basis for expert testimony lies in the FRE and associated case law; some of the rules and cases have been covered in this chapter, and others will be briefly mentioned and covered in more detail in later chapters.

An expert witness is defined in FRE 702 (2023):

> A witness who is qualified as an expert by knowledge, skill, experience, training, or education may testify in the form of an opinion or otherwise if the proponent demonstrates to the court that it is more likely than not that: (a) the expert's scientific, technical, or other specialized knowledge will help the trier of fact to understand the evidence or to determine a fact in issue; (b) the testimony is based on sufficient facts or data; (c) the testimony is the product of reliable principles and methods; and (d) the expert's opinion reflects a reliable application of the principles and methods to the facts of the case.

Notice that the first part of FRE 702 (i.e., what attributes must someone possess to be an expert) is disjunctive, which means a mental health professional does not need to have all of the attributes to be admitted as an expert. However, the lettered requirements of FRE 702 are conjunctive, which means that the expert and testimony must satisfy (a) through (d) to be admitted.[9]

FRE 702 provides a broad definition of "expertise" and allows for those in specialized fields (e.g., doctors, engineers, chemists), trades (e.g., contractors, architects, mechanics), and other professions (e.g., bankers, teachers, musicians) to lend their knowledge to the court, provided that their knowledge is relevant. Such a broad definition, however, begs the question: What exactly makes someone an "expert" for these purposes?

Whether a forensic mental health professional is admitted as an expert is a question for the judge in the court in which the expert will be asked to testify, and the judge's determination is made through a process called "qualifying" the witness, or *voir dire*. When the proffered expert is called to the stand, the retaining party will ask a series of questions that highlight the proffered expert's knowledge, skills, experience, training, and education—that is, the elements outlined in FRE 702. The opposing attorney is then given the opportunity to cross-examine the proffered expert to highlight any weaknesses in their qualifications. Alternatively, the parties may stipulate to the qualifications of the witness, in which case it is solely up to the discretion of the court whether the individual is admitted as an expert.[10]

There are no specific rules regarding what exactly makes an expert "qualified." They do not need to be the top person in their field, hold a specific license, or have any specific title or degree. The focus during the qualifying process is curating an argument that the person's specialized training or knowledge is enough to render them able to reliably and accurately assist the court in its decision-making. Functionally, the qualifying process often looks like a reading of the proposed expert's curriculum vitae (CV), which is also provided to the court and admitted as part of the record.[11] As demonstrated in the example above from *Hawthorne*, the process itself can be integral to whether the individual is eventually allowed to testify as an expert.

When an expert is accepted ("admitted") as an expert witness, the scope of their expertise is specified by the court. This sets limits for the testimony of the expert witness based on their qualifications and experiences. To provide a broad example, a psychiatrist with training in forensic issues may be admitted as an "expert in forensic psychiatry," whereas a psychologist with similar training may be admitted as an "expert in forensic psychology." Theoretically, the forensic psychiatrist would not be allowed to provide testimony on issues outside their scope (e.g., psychological testing) and the forensic psychologist would be likewise limited (e.g., medication recommendations). Some experts may be admitted to provide the court with information on a circumscribed issue, in which case their expertise on that particular issue will be vetted and specified during the qualification process. Depending on the case, an expert may be called based on their knowledge regarding a psychological measure (e.g., Psychopathy Checklist–Revised), an issue (e.g., competence to waive *Miranda* rights), a diagnosis (e.g., intellectual disability), or a population (e.g., juveniles). The scope of the expert's testimony, or if they testify in court at all, is also determined by the role they play in the case.

Roles of Experts

There are many ways individuals with specialized knowledge can be called to participate in a legal case. Defining the role the expert will play at the outset is important because some roles require objectivity (e.g., a testifying expert), while other roles permit some subjectivity (e.g., a consultant). The following provides a broad overview of each role and some of the associated legal considerations.

Consultants

Consultants offer their expertise to one of the parties in a case. Though not an exhaustive list, consultants can help attorneys decide if there is enough preliminary evidence for a particular psycholegal argument in the initial legal planning, identify other possible legal issues and avenues for argument, evaluate evidence and identify weaknesses, develop direct-examination or cross-examination questions, assist with juror selection, and prepare witnesses. The role of a consultant is not strictly objective (at least when compared to a testifying expert); consultants are retained specifically to assist a party to prevail in the case. Consultants may be present in the courtroom, but they are not expected to testify, and they are largely protected from compelled testimony at a pretrial hearing or trial. There are, however, exceptions. For example, according to the Federal Rules of Civil Procedure (FRCP), a consultant may be called to testify if there are "exceptional circumstances under which it is impracticable for the party to obtain facts or opinions on the same subject by other means" (FRCP 26(b)(4)(D)(ii)). A consultant's materials, if prepared in anticipation of litigation or trial, are typically protected from compelled disclosure, but they can be discovered (i.e., released) if there is a showing of substantial need (FRCP 26(b)(3)(A)(ii)).

Teaching Experts

Teaching experts take the stand to provide the court with general scientific or technical information. They still must be qualified and admitted to provide this testimony, but their familiarity with the specific case before the court is not required. Objectivity, however, is required. Though teaching experts may be retained by either party or the court, their duty is to the knowledge they possess. Returning to the homicide example from above, a teaching expert may provide general information about the impact of different substances on executive functioning and/or behavior, or the interaction of the defendant's prescribed medications with substances and the combined impact on decision-making and impulse control. In each case, the expert is speaking about the scientific basis or the medication and associated reaction itself, and not directly about the defendant.

Perhaps some of the most famous examples of teaching experts come from social science framework experts. Developed by Laurens Walker and John Monahan (1987), the social science framework asserts that experts can assist the court in summarizing social authority (e.g., scientific research) and applying social fact (e.g., those relevant to the case) to teach the fact finder about a relevant theory or construct (see Monahan & Walker, 2022). Social science has been presented and accepted as extremely persuasive to the court on a number of occasions that has effected significant change; for example, in the case of *Roper v. Simmons* (2005), where the Supreme Court of the United States relied heavily on social science when opining it unconstitutional to impose the death penalty upon minors.

Testifying Experts

The testifying expert is what most people think of as a stereotypical expert witness. Again, they must be qualified and admitted to the court to offer their testimony. In civil cases, testifying experts are required to submit a written report prior to their testimony that includes their opinions, the basis for their opinions, data considered in forming the opinions, exhibits that will be used, their compensation schedule, and their qualifications (e.g., CV to include all publications over the previous 10 years and testimony from the last 4 years) (FRCP 26(a)(2)(B)).

One controversy surrounding both teaching and testifying experts is the objectivity they realistically bring to the role, particularly when they are retained by one party. Justice Breyer voiced these concerns in an opinion piece, where he asked:

> Will the use of an independent expert in effect substitute that expert's judgment for that of the court? Will it inappropriately deprive the parties of control over the presentation of the case? Will it improperly intrude on the proper function of the jury? Where is one to find a truly neutral expert? After all, different experts, in total honesty, often interpret the same data differently. Will the search for the expert create inordinate delay or significantly increase costs? Who will pay the expert? (Breyer, 2000, p. 55).

The answer, at least in United States jurisprudence,[12] is the use of court-appointed experts.

Court-Appointed Experts

In the federal system, the court-appointed expert is regulated (partially) by FRE 706. The federal rules provide a fair amount of latitude in the appointment process: any party, or the court itself, can request the appointment of an expert witness. The parties can submit nominations or the court can choose from their own roster of experts. Regardless, the nominee must consent to the appointment. When the court appoints an expert (sometimes called a "706 expert"), and therefore they are not retained by any one party, either party can call the expert as their witness or participate in the cross-examination process, and both parties must get copies of any reports or findings. With these exceptions, the court-appointed expert functions, and operates under the same rules, as a party-retained expert.

In theory, having the court appoint an expert helps to reduce any potential retention biases or adversarial allegiances (see Murrie & Boccaccini, 2015). Additionally, it helps to reduce the likelihood that a party went "expert shopping" to find a "hired gun" who will go along with the conclusions the retaining attorney wants them to reach, rather than a more objective and possibly less flattering opinion based solely on the data (see Edens et al., 2012). The process of hiring a court-appointed expert may also help parties that would not otherwise be able to bear the cost of hiring an expert.

Despite the utility of court-appointed experts,[13] many judges are reluctant to appoint experts. Some judges view the appointment of experts as an extraordinary action that should rarely be used because it interferes with the adversarial process. The concern is that juries may ascribe too much weight to the court-appointed expert's testimony. There is also the potential for retention bias on the part of the court wherein the judge or other legal decision-maker places more weight in the testimony of "their" expert than a party-retained expert.[14]

Legal Bases for Expert Testimony

Once an expert has been identified, retained, and qualified, they can provide their testimony to the court. What they convey, and how they convey it, is guided by many different sources. For example, they must consider relevant ethical and practice-related guidance provided by the profession and (if applicable) state licensing board. The expert would also benefit from having a general understanding of the legal basis for their testimony, including the rules of evidence, court procedures, and any controlling case law. The following section outlines the legal basis for expert testimony and introduces some considerations that are further discussed in the next chapters.

Scope and Basis for Testimony

Unlike lay witnesses, experts can base their opinion on facts or data in the case that the expert has been made aware of or personally observed (see FRE 703). Typically, a forensic mental health professional would obtain their facts and data through a mental health evaluation, discovery, and other relevant case-specific sources. Whereas the testimony of lay witnesses cannot be based on inadmissible evidence, expert witnesses have more latitude (see DeMatteo et al., 2019). Per FRE 703: "If experts in the particular field would reasonably rely on those kinds of facts or data in forming an opinion on the subject, they need not be admissible for the opinion to be admitted." However, if the underlying facts or data would normally be inadmissible, they may only be disclosed to the jury if their probative value in helping the jury to evaluate the opinion substantially outweighs their prejudicial effect (see FRE 703).

To provide an example: a forensic mental health assessment and associated testimony may reference firsthand observation (e.g., mental status observations), record facts (e.g., prior court testimony), nonrecord facts (e.g., case file reviews), prior reports, and hearsay (e.g., interviews). As these sources are standard practice for a forensic mental health assessment, they will typically be allowed in court. However, if a forensic evaluator were to rely upon data from an interview with a medium who made contact with the deceased from beyond the grave, the facts or data from this interview would likely not pass the FRE 703 test and would be excluded. An in-depth discussion regarding this "reasonable" standard and how to determine if something is "reasonably relied" upon in the field can be found in the following chapters.

Contrary to what is expected in scientific writing and presentations, a testifying expert may state their opinion without first establishing the underlying facts or data (see FRE 705). The purpose of FRE 705 is to allow experts to state their conclusions or opinions at the beginning of their testimony, followed by an explanation, rather than having the expert set forth all of the data and methodological detail at the outset of their testimony. However, the methodological detail and supporting evidence may be raised on cross-examination, and so the expert must still be prepared to discuss the underlying facts and/or data in detail. It is also helpful to remember that testimony serves only as the final step in providing information to the court; a testifying expert will have also submitted a thorough report to the attorneys and court prior to their testimony (FRCP 26 and Federal Rule of Criminal Procedure 16). Therefore, all parties will have access to the opinion and underlying facts and data before the testimony begins.

Inclusion of Hearsay in Reports and Testimony

The rule of evidence that elicits the greatest ire from law students (and others new to the rules) is the rule against hearsay (FRE 802). Hearsay is an out-of-court statement used to prove the truth of the matter asserted (FRE 801). Essentially, hearsay is any communication (oral, written, or nonverbal) that was not made while testifying at the current trial or hearing under oath and that is accepted as the truth. Hearsay is generally inadmissible because it does not allow for cross-examination of the original statement, therefore creating an unfair assumption that a statement, without further justification or confirmation of its veracity, may play a role in a case without opposition. Outside of the context of court, hearsay statements are readily accepted and utilized, and, therefore, despite the rule on hearsay, the FRE offer more than 20 explicit exceptions that allow hearsay to be admitted (FRE 803, 804).[15]

Another possible exception to the rule against hearsay is FRE 703, which, again, permits experts to reasonably rely on otherwise inadmissible data in reaching their conclusions. This exception is crucial to forensic mental health testimony because the majority of underlying data in the forensic report come from inadmissible sources (e.g., defendant interviews, secondary observations and reports, collateral interviews). Additionally, the expert report *itself* could be considered hearsay by the court. One possible solution for the hearsay issue lies within FRE 703. As previously noted, the final sentence of FRE 703 states: "But if the facts or data would otherwise be inadmissible, the proponent of the ***opinion may disclose them*** to the jury only if their probative value in helping the jury evaluate the opinion substantially outweighs their prejudicial effect" (emphasis added). It follows, then, that one way around the hearsay issue during testimony is to disclose the source of the data (e.g., the interview) without disclosing any specific statements (hearsay).

Returning once more to the homicide example: the defendant has now made the argument that they were not, in fact, inebriated when the murder took place. They argue instead that they were experiencing psychosis and believed they saw the ghost of their late sibling who commanded them to attack the victim and *that hallucination*, not any alcohol-induced coordination and decision-making deficit, is the reason they killed the victim. A forensic evaluator has been called in to evaluate this claim. They read the arrest reports, watch the body-cam footage from the arresting officers, read available records from the jail, interview the defendant, interview the defendant's family and associates (i.e., collaterals), and conduct testing. They reach a conclusion regarding the defendant's mental state at the time of the offense and write a report. Every piece of data collected is considered hearsay, and the report is also considered hearsay.

According to FRE 703, and any state that has adopted this or similar language into their evidentiary code, the evaluator can testify generally to their conclusions and note their sources, even if each of those sources is inadmissible. They can provide further detail regarding the contents of those sources (e.g., quotes, detailed descriptions) only if their helpfulness substantially outweighs the possible negative impact. As the majority of states have adopted an evidentiary code that follows the federal rules, the majority of states allow experts to testify about their conclusions based on inadmissible evidence and the contents of the inadmissible evidence. A minority of states take a narrower approach and allow experts to rely on inadmissible evidence when coming to their conclusions, but they do not allow experts to refer to the contents of the evidence during testimony. Still other states offer more leniency than the federal rules, such as Pennsylvania, which *requires* disclosure of the facts or data on which opinion testimony is based (Pa. R. Evid. 705; *Boucher v. Pennsylvania Hospital*, 2003).

Other Inadmissible Evidence Possibly Allowed

One final consideration briefly mentioned here and discussed in depth in Chapter 7 is testimony that centers on the "ultimate issue." An ultimate issue for the purposes of testimony is one that is typically made by the fact finder. FRE 704(a) states that an opinion that "embraces" the ultimate issue is not automatically objectionable just because it does so. The hope is that the fact finder would come to their own conclusion based on the expert's testimony rather than deferring completely to the expert's opinion. However, the "ultimate issue issue" becomes more complicated in criminal cases. FRE 704(b) carves out an exception to 704(a) in the criminal context by prohibiting an expert from offering "an opinion about whether the defendant did or did not have a mental state or condition that constitutes an element of the crime charged or of a defense." For our defendant asserting what is essentially an insanity plea, the ultimate issue would be whether he was legally insane at the time of the offense. Thus, the forensic evaluator in the case will have to tread carefully in testimony. Further guidance on the subject can be found in Chapter 7 of this book.

Conclusion

Expert testimony as we know it in the United States today has developed slowly over the course of almost two millennia. Forensic mental health professionals who were previously barred from providing mental health testimony in court are now being relied on to opine on issues including matters of life and death (e.g., death penalty cases). Forensic mental health professional should exercise due diligence in familiarizing themselves with the legal bases for the process of being qualified as an expert, the scope of and limitations on expert testimony, and the relevant rules of evidence and court rules in their jurisdiction. These professionals should also seek to thoroughly understand their role in any given case (e.g., consultant, testifying expert) and comport themselves according to the ethical standards associated with that particular role. Additionally, while preparing testing materials and conducting interviews, a testifying expert should be aware of the rules surrounding the admissibility of such evidence in their relevant jurisdiction.

Chapter 5
Admissibility Standards for Expert Testimony—Part 1

Expert witnesses have extraordinary influence in the United States legal system. As discussed in Chapter 4, in most jurisdictions and in most legal contexts, expert witnesses can offer opinions on the ultimate legal issue and rely on inadmissible evidence (e.g., hearsay) in reaching their opinions (see DeMatteo et al., 2019). By contrast, lay or fact witnesses are limited to testifying about what they saw or heard, or matters of which they have personal knowledge, but they are generally precluded from offering an opinion. Given the testimonial "freedom" associated with being an expert witness, it is not surprising that expert witnesses can be highly influential on judicial decision-making (e.g., Jurs, 2016; Kovera & Austin, 2015; Krauss & Sales, 2001; Schauer & Spellman, 2013; Schweitzer & Saks, 2009).

As expert witnesses began to occupy a more prominent position in the legal system, courts and legislatures formulated legal frameworks for determining who should be recognized by a court as an expert and what types of expert evidence should be admitted into legal proceedings (see Monahan & Walker, 2022). Legal admissibility standards are premised on the idea that although United States courts use an adversarial system, the parties to an action do not fully control which evidence is admitted into the court proceedings (Slobogin et al., 2020). The broad purpose of these admissibility standards is to limit the introduction of expert testimony that is irrelevant, overly prejudicial, or of such low quality that it should not be used by the court (judge or jury) to reach a decision.

This chapter focuses on the admissibility standards for expert testimony used in the United States legal system. We begin with a discussion of the two primary admissibility standards—*Frye* and *Daubert*. As will be discussed, the role of trial court judges in making admissibility determinations in *Frye* and *Daubert* jurisdictions differs considerably. Next, we discuss the contours of the *Daubert* admissibility standard by examining several later Supreme Court cases, including the remaining cases in the so-called *Daubert* trilogy (*Joiner* and *Kumho Tire Co.*). This chapter provides the foundation for the in-depth discussion of admissibility standards for expert testimony found in Chapter 6.

Forensic Mental Health Practice and the Law. David DeMatteo, Daniel A. Krauss, Sarah Fishel, and Kellie Wiltsie, Oxford University Press. © Oxford University Press (2025). DOI: 10.1093/9780197686591.003.0005

The *Frye* Standard for Admissibility of Expert Testimony

One of the most important admissibility standards for expert testimony was first articulated in *Frye v. United States* (1923). However, before discussing *Frye*, it is instructive to examine how courts made admissibility decisions prior to *Frye*. Before *Frye* was decided in the early part of the 20th century, most courts used a simple "qualified" test for experts—that is, if the expert was qualified, the expert's testimony would be admitted in court (Faigman et al., 2022; Hilbert, 2019). An expert was considered qualified if they worked in a job or profession that required knowledge that was relevant to their proffered testimony. Faigman et al. (2022) refer to this evidentiary admissibility determination as the marketplace approach. If an expert could prosper in the marketplace, then the expert was considered qualified to provide expert testimony (Hilbert, 2019), particularly if the substantive focus of the testimony was outside the knowledge of the average juror. Of note, the pre-*Frye* admissibility marketplace approach only asked whether the expert was qualified; it did not require any examination of the validity of the proffered testimony (see Faigman et al., 2022, and Giannelli, 1980, for informative discussions). With this backdrop in mind, we now turn to a discussion of the *Frye* standard, which grew out of dissatisfaction with the common law approach to admissibility that many courts were using (see Jurs & DeVito, 2013).

The legal issue in *Frye v. United States* (1923) involved the admissibility of an early form of polygraph called the systolic blood pressure deception test. James Alfonso Frye pled not guilty to the murder of Dr. R. W. Brown, and his plea was supported by this polygraph evidence. The expert in *Frye*, Dr. William Moulton Marston, was a psychologist and a lawyer with an interest in lie detection,[1] and Dr. Marston invented the systolic blood pressure deception test at issue in *Frye*.[2] The prosecution objected to the introduction of the systolic blood pressure deception test, and the trial judge (Walter Irving McCoy) excluded Dr. Marston and his polygraph test from the proceedings. Defense counsel requested to have Dr. Marston conduct the polygraph test in front of the jury, but the trial judge rejected the request (*Frye*, 1923). Mr. Frye's two court-appointed defense lawyers, Mr. Richard Mattingly and Mr. Foster Wood, later reported that the trial judge excluded the novel polygraph evidence because it was not yet a matter of common knowledge (see Weiss et al., 2014, for an informative discussion). Mr. Frye was convicted of second-degree murder in 1922 and sentenced to life in prison.[3]

Mr. Frye appealed his conviction on the grounds that the novel polygraph evidence was erroneously excluded by the trial court. When addressing the admissibility standard that should apply to novel expert evidence, the United States Court of Appeals for the District of Columbia Circuit held that "the thing from which the deduction is made must be sufficiently established to have gained general acceptance in the particular field in which it belongs" (*Frye*, 1923, p. 1014). The admissibility standard articulated in *Frye* became known as the "general acceptance" test (see Slobogin et al., 2020). The appellate court acknowledged that it is not always easy to determine when a "scientific principle or discovery crosses the line between the experimental and demonstrable stages," and it noted that "[s]omewhere in this twilight zone the evidential force of the principle must be recognized" (*Frye*, 1923, p. 1014). Ultimately, the appellate court affirmed the decision of the trial court, holding that the trial court's exclusion of Dr. Marston and his polygraph test was appropriate because the test had not yet gained general acceptance in the relevant field (*Frye*, 1923). Specifically, Judge Van Orsdel stated:

> We think the systolic blood pressure deception test has not yet gained such standing and scientific recognition among physiological and psychological authorities as would justify the courts in admitting expert testimony deduced from the discovery, development, and experiments thus far made. (*Frye*, 1923, p. 1014)

Interestingly, although *Frye* is often heralded as representing a major shift in admissibility standards for expert testimony, Faigman et al. (1994, 2022) point out that the *Frye* decision garnered virtually no contemporaneous attention from courts, commentators, or scholars. *Frye* was such an unimportant decision that it went unnoticed for many years. *Frye* was even ignored in a later case decided the same day by the same judge who wrote the *Frye* opinion.[4] At that time, there were no law review articles written about *Frye* (Faigman et al., 2022), and *Frye* was not cited by any court for more than 10 years after it was decided (Faigman et al., 1994). *Frye* was not mentioned much even after other courts had become familiar with it. For example, *Frye* was cited only 13 times (8 federal cases and 5 state cases) in the 25 years after it was decided and only 83 times (54 federal cases and 29 state cases) over an additional 25 years (Faigman et al., 1994; Saks, 2009).

Although *Frye* did not result in a major paradigm shift in terms of admissibility standards for expert testimony, it led to several changes. First, Faigman et al. (2022) provide a useful conceptualization of *Frye* as being a version of the marketplace test but instead referencing a different market. Rather than looking to the commercial market, which was the approach pre-*Frye*, *Frye* looks to the field's marketplace to assess general acceptance. Before *Frye*, most courts were essentially using a variation of general acceptance test (couched in terms of the marketplace), and the admissibility decisions before *Frye* and after *Frye* would likely have been the same in most circumstances. Second, *Frye* recognized that there were two separate considerations relevant to a proffer of expert testimony—the expert and the body of knowledge. Per *Frye*, the expert must be qualified and there must also be a body of knowledge that is generally accepted in the relevant field (Faigman et al., 2022). Third, *Frye* clarified that the procedures used to obtain the scientific evidence, not the evidence itself, must be generally accepted in the relevant field. For example, an IQ score does not need to be generally accepted, but the procedure used to obtain the IQ score—"the thing from which the deduction is made" (*Frye*, 1923, p. 1014)—must be generally accepted in the relevant field (see Slobogin et al., 2020).

The *Frye* general acceptance test was the primary admissibility test for more than 100 years, so a lot has been written about it, both by supporters and detractors. The primary benefit of the *Frye* test is that it uses a bright-line rule—that is, proffered expert testimony that is generally accepted in the relevant field is admitted. Another benefit of *Frye* is that it does not require the court to have any particular substantive knowledge of the content area of the proffered expert testimony. Rather than having to develop some expertise in the content area, *Frye* employs the logical proposition that the most appropriate approach is to ask whether professionals in the relevant field generally accept the basis of the proffered testimony. Finally, only admitting expert testimony based on procedures that are generally accepted limits the introduction of "junk" science (see Neal et al., 2019).

Commentators have also criticized *Frye* on several grounds (see Faigman & Monahan, 2009). First, although seemingly straightforward, the *Frye* test leaves several open questions: How is general acceptance established? By whom must the procedures be accepted? How is the relevant field defined?[5] Is unanimity of acceptance required? (see Black, 1988, and Faigman et al., 2022, for useful discussions). Second, *Frye*'s perceived strength of not requiring the court to have substantive knowledge about the underlying content area means that the trial court judge is essentially abdicating review authority to the expert's field (Faigman & Monahan, 2009). Third, *Frye* can be both too conservative and too liberal. It can be too conservative because courts may exclude cutting-edge science until it is generally accepted in the relevant field (Giannelli, 1980), which deprives both the court and litigants of the science. However, *Frye* can be too liberal because if the relevant field accepts the basis of the proffered expert testimony, the testimony is admitted, even if there is little science to support it (see Melton et al., 2018). For example, phrenology was, at one time, accepted by the scientific community before later science discredited it. Finally, some have argued that the general relevance/prejudicial inquiry (à la Federal Rules of Evidence 401 and 403, 1975; see Chapter 4) is a "more sensitive tool" for determining admissibility of expert testimony (Slobogin et al., 2020, p. 529).

A final criticism of *Frye* strikes at the heart of what the *Frye* standard is intended to do—that is, prevent the introduction of unreliable science in court proceedings. Concluding that a scientific procedure is "generally accepted" does not necessarily equate with the procedure being correct, and many scientific procedures that are generally accepted are later found to be deficient.[6] In the classic text *The Structure of Scientific Revolutions*, philosopher Thomas Kuhn (1962) noted that science is never complete because it goes through predictable stages of evolution. Kuhn (1962) famously concluded that virtually all science is eventually found to be wrong and supplanted with new science; Kuhn popularized the phrase "paradigm shift" to capture this idea. Further, some commentators have documented *Frye*'s failure to exclude scientific evidence that was later found to be invalid (e.g., Giannelli, 1980; Kaye et al., 2010; see our prior mention of phrenology). Despite the criticisms of *Frye* and some empirical evidence that it was not achieving its intended purpose of excluding junk science, the *Frye* general acceptance test was the dominant approach for determining the admissibility of novel scientific evidence, and it remained relatively unchallenged for 70 years (see Green et al., 2017).

The *Daubert* Standard for Admissibility of Expert Testimony

Daubert v. Merrell Dow Pharmaceuticals (1993) involved a lawsuit brought by the parents of two minor children (Jason Daubert and Eric Schuller) who were born with serious birth defects.[7] The lawsuit alleged that the birth defects resulted from the mother's use of Bendectin, which was a morning sickness medication manufactured by Merrell Dow Pharmaceuticals. Merrell Dow filed a motion for summary judgment contending that Bendectin does not cause birth defects and that the plaintiffs would not be able to produce any credible evidence to the contrary.[8] Merrell Dow submitted an affidavit from Dr. Steven Lamm, who reviewed over 30 published studies involving more than 130,000 patients and concluded that Bendectin was not a human teratogen.[9] In response, the plaintiffs offered the testimony of eight experts who concluded that Bendectin causes birth defects. The plaintiffs' experts based their conclusion on animal studies that found a link between Bendectin and birth defects, chemical structure studies of Bendectin that showed similarities between the drug's structure and other substances that are known to cause birth defects, and a reanalysis of previously published epidemiological (human) studies.

The United States District Court for the Southern District of California granted Merrell Dow's motion for summary judgment (*Daubert v. Merrell Dow Pharmaceuticals*, 1989). Citing *Frye*, the court held that scientific evidence is admissible only if the principle upon which it is based is sufficiently established to have gained general acceptance in the field to which it belongs. The court held that the plaintiffs' evidence did not satisfy *Frye* and could not establish that Bendectin causes birth defects.

On appeal, the United States Court of Appeals for the Ninth Circuit affirmed the lower court's decision (*Daubert v. Merrell Dow Pharmaceuticals*, 1991). The Ninth Circuit held that expert testimony based on a scientific technique is inadmissible unless the technique is generally accepted as reliable in the relevant scientific community. The Ninth Circuit further stated that an expert opinion based on a methodology that diverges significantly from procedures accepted by recognized authorities in the relevant field cannot be shown to be generally accepted as a reliable technique. Ultimately, the Ninth Circuit concluded that the plaintiffs' evidence provided an insufficient foundation to allow admission of the proffered expert testimony that Bendectin caused their injuries and, accordingly, that the plaintiffs could not satisfy their burden of proving causation at trial.

The Supreme Court of the United States granted certiorari[10] to address the proper standard for admitting expert testimony in federal courts (*Daubert v. Merrell Dow Pharmaceuticals*, 1993). Specifically, the Court addressed whether *Frye* or the Federal Rules of Evidence (FRE; 1975)[11] governed the admissibility of expert testimony in federal courts. The plaintiffs argued that *Frye* had been superseded by the FRE, particularly FRE 702.[12] The Court held that FRE 702, not *Frye*, governed the admissibility of expert testimony. The Court offered three reasons in support of its holding: (1) FRE 702 does not incorporate general acceptance as an absolute prerequisite to admissibility; (2) the drafting history of FRE 702 does not mention *Frye* or general acceptance, so there is no indication that Federal Rules of Evidence intended to incorporate a general acceptance standard; and (3) the FRE are intended to be construed liberally, and a rigid general acceptance test would be "at odds" (*Daubert*, 1993, p. 588) with the "liberal thrust" of the FRE (*Beech Aircraft Corp. v. Rainey*, 1988, p. 169) and their intended approach of relaxing the traditional barriers to expert testimony (*Daubert*, 1993).

Given these considerations, the Court held that *Frye*'s "austere standard" of general acceptance is incompatible with the FRE and should not be used as the admissibility standard for expert testimony in federal courts (*Daubert*, 1993, p. 589). *Daubert* effectively ended the use of general acceptance as the sole criterion for determining the admissibility of proffered expert testimony. However, the Court suggested that general acceptance of the expert's method or technique is still a valid consideration in admissibility determinations as long as other admissibility criteria are used (discussed below). It is undeniable that the *Daubert* holding "deepened and expanded the trial judge's responsibilities" over proffered expert evidence (Faigman et al., 2022, p. 28).

The Court then turned to an analysis of the admissibility standard contained in FRE 702 (*Daubert*, 1993). The Court began by noting that the starting point is that FRE 702 applies to "scientific knowledge," which it defined as being derived by the "scientific method" (*Daubert*, 1993, p. 590); the Court viewed the requirement that an expert's testimony pertain to scientific knowledge as establishing a standard of evidentiary reliability.[13] The Court noted that in addition to being reliable, the proffered expert evidence must assist the trier of fact to understand the evidence or determine a fact in issue—that is, it must be relevant. The Court described this "helpfulness" criterion of FRE 702 as being one of "fit" (*Daubert*, 1993, p. 591). Specifically, the Court stated that FRE 702 "requires a valid scientific connection to the pertinent inquiry as a precondition to admissibility" (*Daubert*, 1993, p. 592). In summary, when a trial judge is faced with a proffer of expert scientific evidence, the trial judge must determine "whether the expert is proposing to testify to (1) scientific knowledge that (2) will assist the trier of fact to understand or determine a fact in issue" (*Daubert*, 1993, p. 592). Accomplishing this requires a "preliminary assessment of whether the reasoning or methodology underlying the testimony is scientifically valid and of whether that reasoning or methodology properly can be applied to the facts in issue" (*Daubert*, 1993, pp. 592–593).[14] In a later case, the Court emphasized that the purpose of the *Daubert* standard is to ensure that any expert "employs in the courtroom the same level of intellectual rigor that characterizes the practice of an expert in the relevant field" (*Kumho Tire Co. v. Carmichael*, 1999, p. 152).

Next, the Supreme Court noted that "many factors will bear on the inquiry" of whether proffered expert scientific evidence is admissible (*Daubert*, 1993, p. 593). However, the Court specifically articulated four criteria to assist trial judges in their gatekeeping function: (1) whether the theory or technique has been (and can be) tested (this is commonly referred to as "falsifiability"); (2) whether the theory or technique has been subjected to peer review and publication; (3) the known or potential rate of error of the scientific technique; and (4) general acceptance in the relevant scientific field (à la *Frye*). We discuss each criterion in detail in Chapter 6. The Court noted that the district court and appellate court focused almost exclusively on general acceptance and, as such, it vacated the appellate court's decision and remanded the case back to the appellate court. Upon remand, the United States Court of Appeals for the Ninth Circuit, in its new gatekeeper role, rejected the plaintiffs' proffered expert testimony as failing to satisfy the *Daubert* criteria and other indica of reliability (*Daubert v. Merrell Dow Pharmaceuticals*, 1995).

Almost immediately, courts began expressing concern about the new gatekeeping function imposed on trial court judges by *Daubert*, and this even occurred in the *Daubert* opinion itself. In his dissent, Chief Justice Rehnquist stated:

> I defer to no one in my confidence in federal judges; but I am at a loss to know what is meant when it is said that the scientific status of a theory depends on its "falsifiability," and I suspect some of them will be, too. I do not doubt that Rule 702 confides to the judge some gatekeeping responsibility in deciding questions

> of the admissibility of proffered expert testimony. But I do not think it imposes on them either the obligation or the authority to become amateur scientists in order to perform that role. I think the Court would be far better advised in this case to decide only the questions presented, and to leave the further development of this important area of the law to future cases. (*Daubert*, 1993, pp. 600–601)

In the Ninth Circuit's decision after the case was remanded, Judge Kozinski—in a section of the opinion titled Brave New World—stated:

> [T]hough we are largely untrained in science and certainly no match for any of the witnesses whose testimony we are reviewing, it is our responsibility to determine whether those experts' proposed testimony amounts to "scientific knowledge," constitutes "good science," and was "derived by the scientific method" . . . [W]e take a deep breath and proceed with this heady task. (*Daubert*, 1995, p. 1316)

Many commentators have addressed the gatekeeping function imposed on trial court judges by the *Daubert* decision (e.g., DeMatteo et al., 2019; Faigman et al., 2016, 2022; Neal et al., 2019). The issue of whether judges can effectively apply *Daubert* is an empirical question, and we return to that topic in Chapter 6.

Before finishing our discussion of *Daubert*, there are three points worth emphasizing. First, *Daubert* only pertains to the FRE in federal court, so state courts are not required to adopt the *Daubert* standard. Nevertheless, *Daubert* has been adopted by the majority of states (see Faigman et al., 2022; Harlan & Routh, 2016; Slobogin et al., 2020, and Table 5.1 for the admissibility standard used in each state). Second, the Supreme Court emphasized that "the inquiry envisioned by Rule 702 is . . . a flexible one" (*Daubert*, 1993, p. 594), and the focus "must be solely on principles and methodology, not on the conclusions that they generate" (*Daubert*, 1993, p. 595).[15] As will be discussed in Chapter 6, many courts have adopted other "*Daubert*" criteria for determining the admissibility of expert testimony. Third, in contrast with the *Frye* standard, which required little to no judicial oversight and instead asked trial court judges to look to the relevant field for guidance, *Daubert* places a heavy burden on trial court judges, who must be familiar with concepts such as validity, reliability, and the scientific method (see Cole, 2008; Faigman et al., 2022; Slobogin et al., 2020). As a final note, 7 years after *Daubert* was decided, the United States Congress amended FRE 702 to be more consistent with the Supreme Court's decision in *Daubert* (Melton et al., 2018; Slobogin et al., 2020). As stated by Faigman et al. (2022), "Thus, the Federal Rules were amended in 2000 to state more plainly the plain meaning the Court had ascribed to them in 1993" (pp. 22–23).[16]

Table 5.1 Admissibility Standards by State

State	Standard	Citation
Alabama	*Daubert* (with exceptions)	Ala. R. Evid. 702
Alaska	*Daubert*	Ak. R. Evid. 703 (Commentary) *State v. Coon*, 974 P.2d 386 (Alaska 1999)
Arizona	*Daubert*	Ariz. R. Evid. 702
Arkansas	*Daubert*	*Farm Bureau Mut. Ins. Co. of Arkansas, Inc. v. Foote*, 14 S.W.3d 512 (Ark. 2000)
California	Own standard, based on *Frye* and *Daubert*	*People v. Kelly*, 17 Cal.3d 24 (Cal. 1976). *Sargon Enterprises, Inc. v. University of Southern California*, 55 Cal. 4th 747 (2012)
Colorado	*Daubert* (with additions)	Colo. R. Evid. 702 *People v. Shreck*, 22 P.3d 68 (Colo. 2001)
Connecticut	*Daubert*	Conn R. Evid. 7–2 (Commentary) *State v. Porter*, 241 Conn. 57 (Conn. 1997)
Delaware	*Daubert*	Del. R. Evid. 702
District of Columbia	*Daubert*	F.R.E. 702 *Motorola Inc. v. Murray*, 147 A.3d 751 (D.C. 2016)
Florida	*Daubert*	Fla. Stat. 90.702 *In re: Amendments to the Florida Rules of Evidence* (Fla. 2019)
Georgia	*Daubert*	Ga. Code 24-7-702
Hawaii	Own standard	Haw. Rev. Stat. 702 *State v. Vliet*, 95 Haw. 94 (Haw. 2001)
Idaho	Own standard	*Walker v. American Cyanamid Co.*, 130 Idaho 824 (Idaho 1997)
Illinois	*Frye*	Ill. R. Evid. 702 (Commentary)
Indiana	Consider *Daubert*	Ind. R. Evid. 702 *Smith v. Yang*, 829 N.E.2d 624 (Ind. App. 2005)
Iowa	Consider *Daubert*	*Leaf v. Goodyear Tire & Rubber Co.*, 590 N.W.2d 525 (Iowa 1999)
Kansas	*Daubert*	Kan. Stat. 60–456(b)
Kentucky	*Daubert*	K.R.E. 702 *Mitchell v. Commonwealth*, 908 S.W.2d 100 (Ky. 1995)
Louisiana	*Daubert*	La. Code Evid. art. 702

Continued

Table 5.1 *Continued*

State	Standard	Citation
Maine	Own standard	Me. R. Evid. 702 (and notes) *State v. Williams*, 388 A.2d 500 (Me. 1978) *Searles v. Fleetwood Homes of Pennsylvania*, 878 A.2d 509 (Me. 2005)
Maryland	*Daubert*	Md. R. Evid. 5–702 *Rochkind v. Stevenson*, 471 Md. 1 (2020)
Massachusetts	*Daubert*	Mass. Guide to Evid. 702 *Commonwealth v. Lanigan*, 419 Mass. 15 (1994)
Michigan	*Daubert*	Mich. R. Evid. 702
Minnesota	*Frye-Mack*	Minn. R. Evid. 702
Mississippi	*Daubert*	Miss. R. Evid. 702
Missouri	*Daubert*	MO Rev Stat 490.065
Montana	Sometimes *Daubert*	M. R. Evid. 702 *Hulse v. State*, 289 Mont. 1 (Mont. 1998)
Nebraska	*Daubert*	Neb. Rev. Stat. 27–702 (and Annotations)
Nevada	Own standard	N.R.S. 50.275 *Higgs v. State of Nevada*, 222 P.3d 648 (Nev. 2010)
New Hampshire	*Daubert*	N.H. R. Evid. 702
New Jersey	*Daubert*	N.J. R. Evid. 702 *State v. Olenowski*, 253 N.J. 133 (N.J. 2023)
New Mexico	*Daubert-Alberico* (modified *Daubert*)	N.M. R. Evid. 11–702 *Parkhill v. Alderman-Cave Milling*, 245 P.3d 585 (N.M. Ct. App. 2010)
New York	*Frye*	Guide to NY Evid. *Rule 7.01(2) Opinion of Expert Witness* (and Note)
North Carolina	*Daubert*	N.C. Gen. Stat. 702(a) *State v. McGrady*, 368 N.C. 880 (N.C. 2016)
North Dakota	Own standard	N.D. R. Evid. 702 *State v. Hernandez*, 707 N.W.2d 449 (N.D. 2005)
Ohio	*Daubert*	Ohio R. Evid. 702 *Watkins v. Affinia Grp.*, 54 N.E.3d 174 (Ohio Ct. App. 2016)
Oklahoma	*Daubert*	Okla. Stat. tit. 12 Sec. 2702 *Christian v. Gray*, 65 P.3d 591 (Okla. 2003)

State	Standard	Citation
Oregon	*Daubert*	ORS Sec. 40.410–702 *State v. O'Key*, 321 Or. 285 (Or. 1995)
Pennsylvania	*Frye*	225 Pa. Code Sec. 702 (and Comments)
Rhode Island	*Daubert*	R.I. R. Evid. 702 *Raimbeault v. Takeuchi Manufacturing*, 772 A.2d 1056 (R.I. 2001)
South Carolina	Own standard (similar to *Daubert*)	S.C. R. Evid. 702 *State v. Council*, 335 S.C. 1 (S.C. 1999)
South Dakota	*Daubert*	S.D. Codified Laws Sec. 19–19-702 *State v. Hofer*, 512 N.W.2d 482 (S.D. 1994)
Tennessee	*Daubert*	Tenn. R. Evid. 702 (and Comments)
Texas	*Daubert*	Tex. R. Evid. 702 *E.I. du Pont de Nemours Co. v. Robinson*, 923 S.W.2d 549 (Tex. 1995)
Utah	Own standard	Utah R. Evid. 702 and Notes *State v. Sheehan*, 273 P.3d 417 (Utah Ct. App. 2012)
Vermont	*Daubert*	Vt. R. Evid. 702
Virginia	Own standard (but not opposed to *Daubert*)	Va. R. Sup. Ct. 2:702(a) *John v. Wong Shik Im*, 263 Va. 315 (Va. 2002) *Billips v. Commonwealth*, 274 Va. 805, 652 S.E.2d 99 (Va. 2007)
Washington	*Frye*	Wash. R. Evid. 702 *State v. Copeland*, 130 Wn. 2d 244 (Wash. 1996)
West Virginia	*Daubert*	W.Va. R. Evid. 702 (and Commentary) *Wilt v. Buracker*, 191 W. Va. 39 (W. Va. 1993)
Wisconsin	*Daubert*	Wi. Stat. 907.02 (and Comments)
Wyoming	*Daubert*	Wy. R. Evid. 702

Post-*Daubert* Admissibility Cases

Daubert established the admissibility standard for expert testimony in federal courts, but there were still some unanswered questions. Some of those questions were addressed by the Supreme Court of the United States in the two remaining cases from the so-called *Daubert* trilogy: *General Electric Co. v. Joiner* (1997) and *Kumho Tire Co. v. Carmichael* (1999). We focus primarily on *Joiner* and *Kumho*, although we mention another case that provided additional guidance for those jurisdictions that use the *Daubert* admissibility standard.

General Electric Co. v. Joiner (1997)

The second case in the *Daubert* trilogy is *General Electric Co. v. Joiner* (1997). In *Joiner*, an electrician, Robert Joiner, sued General Electric Company (and other entities) alleging that he developed small-cell lung cancer after being exposed to polychlorinated biphenyls (PCBs) that were in some of the fluid in the city's electrical transformers. The United States District Court for the Northern District of Georgia excluded the testimony of the plaintiff's experts and granted the defendants' motion for summary judgment because the experts failed to establish a link between exposure to PCBs and the subsequent development of lung cancer (*Joiner v. General Electric Co.*, 1994). The United States Court of Appeals for the Eleventh Circuit reversed the district court, holding that a "particularly stringent standard of review" is required when reviewing a trial court's exclusion of expert testimony (*Joiner v. General Electric Co.*, 1996, p. 529). Applying that standard, the Eleventh Circuit held that the lower court erred in excluding the testimony of the plaintiff's experts because the "Federal Rules of Evidence governing expert testimony display a preference for admissibility" (*Joiner*, 1996, p. 529).

The Supreme Court of the United States granted certiorari to determine what standard an appellate court should apply when reviewing a trial court's decision to admit or exclude proffered expert testimony under *Daubert* (*General Electric Co. v. Joiner*, 1997). This was a question left unanswered by the Court in *Daubert*, but of striking importance to litigants who rely on expert testimony.[17] The Court held that a trial court's determination regarding the admissibility of expert evidence should be reviewed on appeal using an abuse of discretion standard. The Court noted that the abuse of discretion standard applies to all questions of evidentiary admissibility, which highlights its applicability in reviewing admissibility determinations of expert evidence in a *Daubert* context.

The Court also disagreed that a higher standard of review, such as the "stringent standard" applied by the Eleventh Circuit, was appropriate. In contrast with a de novo standard of review, which occurs when a court decides an issue without reference to the trial court's decision, the abuse of discretion standard provides great deference to trial court determinations regarding the admissibility of expert evidence, which means that trial court admissibility determinations will rarely be overturned on appeal. The Court stated that the Eleventh Circuit's "stringent standard" of review "failed to give the trial court the deference that is the hallmark of abuse-of-discretion review" (*Joiner*, 1997, p. 143). Using the abuse of discretion standard, the Court reversed the decision of the Eleventh Circuit and held that the District Court did not abuse its discretion in excluding the plaintiff's proffered expert evidence.[18]

Kumho Tire Co. v. Carmichael (1999)

Daubert v. Merrell Dow Pharmaceuticals (1993) addressed the admissibility standard for *scientific* expert testimony in federal courts. But not all expert testimony can be conceptualized as scientific. Even the FRE recognize different types of expert testimony. Specifically, FRE 702, which is the admissibility rule for expert evidence, mentions scientific, technical, and other specialized knowledge. As such, in the years following *Daubert*, there was uncertainty among courts, attorneys, and litigants regarding whether *Daubert* applied to all expert testimony or only scientific expert testimony.

Most relevant for our purposes, several commentators expressed concern that a strict application of *Daubert* would exclude proffered expert testimony from mental health professionals, which is often not considered by courts to be "scientific" (see Gottesman, 1994, for a brief discussion). In an article published 1 year after the Court decided *Daubert*, Michael Gottesman, the attorney who represented the families of Jason Daubert and Eric Schuller, stated that the Supreme Court's opinion in *Daubert* if "read literally . . . would dictate the end of the receipt of psychiatric and psychological testimony in federal courts" (Gottesman, 1994, p. 875; see Graham, 1994). Following *Daubert*, some courts conceptualized mental health testimony as "specialized knowledge" (see FRE 702), which meant that *Daubert* did not apply (see Melton et al., 2018). In *United States v. Rouse* (1996), the United States Court of Appeals for the Eighth Circuit addressed the application of *Daubert* to the "soft" sciences. In *Rouse*, the Eighth Circuit stated:

> Application of *Daubert* criteria to behavioral and social science evidence, particularly psychological syndromes, is problematic for two reasons: (1) judges' level of understanding of scientific principles and methodology may ill prepare them to evaluate science, including social science, as now required by *Daubert* and (2) the nature of certain social and behavioral science theories may be inherently inconsistent with *Daubert* criteria such as "falsifiability" and "error rates." (*Rouse*, 1996, p. 568; quoting Richardson et al., 1995, pp. 10–11)

The Eighth Circuit in *Rouse* acknowledged that *Daubert* applies to soft sciences, but it concluded that some "social science . . . cannot have the exactness of the hard science methodologies" (*Rouse*, 1996, p. 567).

Fortunately, in *Kumho Tire Co. v. Carmichael* (1999), the Supreme Court addressed some of the unanswered questions regarding the scope and applicability of *Daubert* when trial court judges are faced with a proffer of nonscientific expert testimony. In *Kumho*, the plaintiffs sued Kumho Tire Company alleging that a defective tire resulted in a fatal accident. In July 1993, Patrick Carmichael was driving a minivan when the right rear tire blew out, which resulted in an accident that killed one passenger and severely injured several other passengers. In their civil lawsuit against the tire company, the Carmichaels relied on the testimony of an expert in tire failure analysis, Dennis Carlson, Jr., who concluded that a defect in the manufacture or design of the tire caused the tire failure.

The United States District Court for the Southern District of Alabama granted Kumho Tire Company's motion to exclude Carlson's testimony on the grounds that his methodology failed FRE 702's requirement of reliability (*Carmichael v. Samyang Tires, Inc.*, 1996a). The plaintiffs appealed the exclusion of their expert on the grounds that the District Court's application of the *Daubert* factors was too inflexible.[19] On appeal, the United States Court of Appeals for the Eleventh Circuit reversed the lower court's decision, holding that *Daubert* only applies to scientific knowledge (*Carmichael v. Samyang Tires, Inc.*, 1997). The Eleventh Circuit concluded that Carlson's testimony, which was not based on scientific knowledge but rather on professional experience, fell outside the scope of *Daubert*. Accordingly, the Eleventh Circuit remanded the case back to the lower court for further non-*Daubert* consideration of Carlson's testimony under FRE 702.

The Supreme Court of the United States granted Kumho Tire Company's petition for certiorari to address the question of whether *Daubert* applies to all expert testimony or only scientific expert testimony (*Kumho Tire Co. v. Carmichael*, 1999). After discussing its earlier decision in *Daubert*, the Court concluded that the *Daubert* gatekeeping function applies to all expert testimony. The Court held that the Eleventh Circuit was incorrect in concluding that *Daubert* only applied to scientific expert testimony and, accordingly, it reversed the Eleventh Circuit's decision.[20]

In an opinion by Justice Breyer, the Court in *Kumho* offered three reasons in support of its conclusion that *Daubert* applies to all expert testimony. First, the language of FRE 702 does not make any meaningful distinction between "scientific" knowledge and "technical" or "other specialized" knowledge, which means that a plain reading of FRE 702 indicates that it applies to scientific, technical, *and* other specialized knowledge. The *Daubert* decision only addressed the admissibility standard for scientific knowledge (and not the other types of knowledge mentioned in FRE 702) because that was the nature of the expertise at issue in the case. Second, given the testimonial latitude that is available to expert witnesses, the rationale underlying *Daubert*'s gatekeeping function—that is, to prevent the introduction of invalid or unreliable science into court proceedings—is not limited to scientific knowledge. Because the FRE grant a high degree of testimonial freedom to all types of expert witnesses, not just scientific experts, the *Daubert* gatekeeping function should apply to all types of expert testimony. Finally, the Court questioned whether trial court judges could reliably distinguish among the three types of knowledge mentioned in FRE 702: "[I]t would prove difficult, if not impossible, for judges to administer evidentiary rules under which a gatekeeping obligation depended upon a distinction between 'scientific' knowledge and 'technical' or 'other specialized' knowledge. There is no clear line that divides the one from the others" (*Kumho Tire Co.*, 1999, p. 148).

Weisgram v. Marley (2000)

Although not part of the *Daubert* trilogy, the Supreme Court's decision in *Weisgram v. Marley Co.* (2000) deserves comment. *Weisgram* involved a wrongful death action brought by the son of Bonnie Weisgram (on behalf of Ms. Weisgram and her heirs), who died of carbon monoxide poisoning in a fire allegedly caused by a defective baseboard heater manufactured by the defendant. At trial, the plaintiffs proffered three experts (fire captain, fire investigator, and metallurgist) who opined that a faulty heater led to the fire that resulted in Ms. Weisgram's death. The defendant objected that the expert testimony was unreliable and, therefore, inadmissible under FRE 702 and *Daubert*, and it moved for judgment as a matter of law. The United States District Court for the District of North Dakota admitted the expert testimony and denied the defendant's motion for judgment as a matter of law, and the jury returned a verdict for the plaintiff. On appeal, the United States Court of Appeals for the Eighth Circuit vacated the District Court's judgment (*Weisgram v. Marley Co.*, 1999). However, instead of remanding the case for a new trial, the Eight Circuit directed judgment as a matter of law for the defendant. The Eighth Circuit concluded that judgment as a matter of law in favor of the defendant was appropriate because the expert testimony introduced by the plaintiffs was "speculative and not shown to be scientifically sound" and "incompetent to prove Weisgram's case" (*Weisgram v. Marley Co.*, 2000, p. 445). The Eighth Circuit further stated:

> We reject any contention that we are required to remand for a new trial because our failure to do so would deny the plaintiffs the opportunity to reopen discovery and identify additional witnesses who might testify to their theory of liability. . . . Although Federal Rule of Civil Procedure 50(d) certainly gives this Court the discretion to remand for a new trial, we can discern no reason to give the plaintiffs a second chance to make out a case of strict liability. . . . This is

> not a close case. The plaintiffs had a fair opportunity to prove their claim and they failed to do so. (*Weisgram v. Marley Co.*, 1999, p. 517)[21]

The Supreme Court of the United States granted certiorari to address a split among federal courts of appeal on the question of whether Federal Rule of Civil Procedure 50 permits an appellate court to direct the entry of judgment as a matter of law when it determines that (a) evidence was erroneously admitted at trial and (b) the remaining properly admitted evidence is insufficient to constitute a submissible case (*Weisgram v. Marley Co.*, 2000). Stated differently, the Court phrased the legal question as concerning the "respective authority of federal trial and appellate courts to decide whether, as a matter of law, judgment should be entered in favor of a verdict loser" (*Weisgram v. Marley Co.*, 2000, p. 443). In essence, the Court was addressing whether a federal appellate court can simply direct a judgment against a party, or whether the appellate court must remand the case to the lower court and permit the lower court to decide whether to enter judgment for a party or order a new trial.

The Court upheld the power of federal appellate courts to find expert testimony (or other evidence) inadmissible as matter of law and direct entry of a judgment for the losing party without remanding for a new trial (*Weisgram v. Marley Co.*, 2000). In the specific context of the *Weisgram* case, the Court held that the Eighth Circuit did not abuse its discretion in directing entry and judgment for the defendant, given that the plaintiffs' expert testimony failed to satisfy the requirements of FRE 702 and *Daubert*. In the Court's unanimous opinion, Justice Ginsburg stated:

> Since *Daubert* . . . parties relying on expert evidence have had notice of the exacting standards of reliability such evidence must meet. [citations omitted] It is implausible to suggest, post-*Daubert*, that parties will initially present less than their best expert evidence in the expectation of a second chance should their first try fail. (*Weisgram*, 2000, p. 455)

Justice Ginsburg further stated that the Court was not persuaded by "Weisgram's fears that allowing courts of appeals to direct the entry of judgment for defendants will punish plaintiffs who could have shored up their cases by other means had they known their expert testimony would be found inadmissible" (*Weisgram*, 2000, pp. 455–456).

Daubert Versus *Frye*

The *Daubert* and *Frye* admissibility standards differ in important respects. Whereas *Frye* looks to the relevant field to assess whether the expert's scientific procedures are generally accepted, *Daubert* requires a more judicially active approach to determine if the proffered expert testimony is based on valid and reliable science. Further, *Daubert* applies to all proffered expert evidence, whereas *Frye* was limited to novel techniques, methods, or procedures. Many commentators assumed that *Daubert* set a lower threshold than *Frye* for the admissibility of expert evidence (see Faigman et al., 2022, for a discussion). After all, in *Daubert* (1993), the Supreme Court concluded that *Frye*'s "austere standard" (p. 589) of general acceptance was "at odds" (p. 588) with the liberal thrust of the FRE. Further, in *Joiner* (1997), the Supreme Court stated that "the Federal Rules of Evidence allow district courts to admit a somewhat broader range of scientific testimony than would have been admissible under *Frye*" (p. 142).[22]

As Hilbert (2019) noted, whether *Daubert* is actually less stringent than *Frye* is a complicated question, as reflected in that "both sides of the debate—plaintiff's and defense counsel—claimed victory after the decision" (p. 791). Further, Jurs and DeVito (2013) stated: "The question of whether *Daubert v. Merrell Dow Pharmaceuticals, Inc.* adopted a more lenient or more stringent standard for testing the reliability of expert evidence has dogged academics, practitioners, and researchers for twenty years" (p. 677 [footnotes omitted]). Some researchers concluded that *Daubert* was much more stringent and resulted in the exclusion of more expert testimony (e.g., Flores et al., 2010; Jurs & DeVito, 2013; Krafka et al., 2002), while others concluded that *Daubert* had no meaningful effect on admissibility rates (e.g., Billauer, 2016; Cheng & Yoon, 2005; Groscup et al., 2002).

Some have even questioned whether *Frye* and *Daubert* lead to different admissibility results (see Faigman et al., 2022, for a useful discussion). For example, Saks and Faigman (2005) suggest that application of *Frye* or *Daubert* would lead to the same result in most contexts:

> That which has a strong scientific foundation usually will be generally accepted; that which has a weak scientific foundation usually will not be widely accepted. In either situation, both tests should lead to the same decision to admit or to exclude. (p. 119)

They note, however, that there are circumstances in which the trial judges' determination of admissibility may differ:

> When a scientific proposition is sound but not generally accepted, *Daubert* should admit while *Frye* should exclude. . . . But when a scientific proposition has not been shown to be sound yet nevertheless has gained general acceptance in its field, then *Daubert* excludes even though *Frye* admits. (Saks & Faigman, 2005, p. 119)

So what effect has *Daubert* had on the admissibility of expert evidence? Although there is mixed evidence, we draw three broad conclusions.

First, attorneys are more likely to challenge expert testimony, at least in civil cases. These challenges typically take the form of a pretrial motion *in limine*,[23] or objections at trial to limit or exclude expert testimony (Flores et al., 2010; Hilbert, 2019; Krafka et al., 2002). When these challenges are successful, they may lead to a motion for summary judgment. Flores et al. (2010) addressed the effects of *Daubert* on federal civil cases: "*In limine* challenges have grown in frequency, and the bases of these challenges are now based heavily on substantive grounds, including the *Daubert* standards" (p. 563). Further, Krafka et al. (2002) noted that motions *in limine* "are in much greater use than they were prior to *Daubert*, so it is not surprising to find that judges are holding more pretrial *Daubert-like* hearings than previously" (p. 330).

Interestingly, post-*Daubert*, challenges to admissibility of expert evidence increased dramatically in civil cases (Flores et al., 2010), but hardly at all in criminal cases (Groscup et al., 2002). Risinger (2000) found that approximately 90% of *Daubert* challenges in federal courts were in civil cases (and raised by defendants against the plaintiff's expert evidence), and less than 10% of all *Daubert* challenges in federal courts were in criminal cases. Further, Dixon and Gill (2001) found that the exclusion of challenged expert evidence in federal civil cases rose from 50% pre-*Daubert* to 70% post-*Daubert*, and Krafka et al. (2002) reported figures of 25% pre-*Daubert* and 41% post-*Daubert*.

There are also some interesting data regarding which party is more likely to win a *Daubert* challenge. For example, Risinger (2000) reported that civil defendants win their *Daubert* challenges a majority of the time, whereas criminal defendants virtually always lose their *Daubert* challenges. In a more recent analysis, Cicchini (2021) examined all *Daubert* appellate cases in Wisconsin since that state adopted *Daubert*. In 68 criminal cases consisting of 134 judicial decisions across all levels of the Wisconsin court system, the defense never won a *Daubert* decision, regardless of the type of case or type of expert (Cicchini, 2021).

Saks and Faigman (2005) and Faigman et al. (2022) offer several potential explanations for the widely discrepant rates of successful *Daubert* challenges in criminal and civil cases, including differences in the quality of the underlying science being proffered and in the quality of the attorney advocacy. Faigman et al. (2022) also suggested one other possibility: "[A]s a general proposition, judges disfavor civil plaintiffs and criminal defendants and, are more likely to rule against them than against their opposites even when presenting equivalent evidence or arguments" (p. 152).

Second, after *Daubert*, attorneys are taking more care in choosing their experts and preparing their experts for trial (Hilbert, 2019; Krafka et al., 2002). *Daubert* (and *Weisgram*) put attorneys on notice that they need to carefully choose their experts or risk having their expert excluded and/or being on the wrong side of a summary judgment motion. As one article concluded:

> Perhaps in response to the increasingly active role of the judges in excluding or limiting testimony, attorneys reported more closely scrutinizing the credentials of their own experts. . . . They also reported greater involvement in the preparation of their expert's testimony. (Krafka et al., 2002, p. 330)

Finally, and perhaps most importantly, *Daubert* focused attention on the risks associated with bad science (Hilbert, 2019; Vickers, 2005). *Daubert* imposed a gatekeeping role on trial court judges that requires them to assess the validity of the science underlying the proffered expert testimony. They no longer had the luxury of deferring to the relevant field to see if the science was generally accepted. As stated by Vickers (2005): "To the extent [*Daubert*] had a real effect on admissibility, it did so primarily by informing judges that they should function as gatekeepers to ensure that bad science does not make its way into the courtroom" (p. 140). In other words, *Daubert* "sounded a clarion cry that evidence was being too hastily and inappropriately admitted" (Billauer, 2016, p. 22), and "*Daubert*'s most important contribution to the development of evidentiary standards has more to do with *Daubert*'s educative function than with its doctrinal text" (Vickers, 2005, p. 147).

Conclusion

Given the documented influence of expert testimony and the testimonial latitude enjoyed by experts, courts have developed standards for determining who qualifies as an expert, what constitutes expert evidence, and how courts should make admissibility decisions. The *Frye* standard uses general acceptance of the scientific procedures underlying the proffered expert testimony as the sole criterion for determining admissibility. However, *Daubert* requires trial court judges to become sophisticated consumers of science to determine whether a proffered expert will testify about scientific knowledge that will assist the trier of fact. A subsequent Supreme Court case clarified that *Daubert* applies to all expert testimony, not just testimony based on scientific knowledge. In contrast with the relatively passive role of the trial judge in *Frye* jurisdictions, the *Daubert* standard requires trial judges to assess the reliability of the underlying science. We address this important role shift in the next chapter.

Chapter 6

Admissibility Standards for Expert Testimony—Part 2

As discussed in Chapter 5, expert witnesses occupy a unique and privileged position in the United States legal system. The testimonial latitude afforded to expert witnesses and the well-documented persuasiveness of expert testimony have resulted in the development of court rules and case law that seek to regulate experts and the testimony they provide (see DeMatteo et al., 2019). Following is a summary of the key cases discussed in Chapter 5:

- *Frye v. United States* (1923): The United States Court of Appeals for the District of Columbia Circuit established the "general acceptance" test for the admissibility of novel scientific expert evidence—that is, the thing from which scientific evidence is deduced "must be sufficiently established to have gained general acceptance in the particular field in which it belongs" (*Frye*, 1923, p. 1014)
- *Daubert v. Merrell Dow Pharmaceuticals* (1993): The Supreme Court of the United States held that *Frye* had been superseded by Federal Rule of Evidence (FRE) 702 as the admissibility standard for expert testimony in all federal courts. To be admissible, proffered expert evidence must assist the trier of fact, and the basis for the expert's opinion must be valid and reliable. The Court identified four criteria to assist federal trial court judges in their new gatekeeping role: (1) testing, (2) peer review and publication, (3) known error rate, and (4) general acceptance. The Court noted that the FRE 702/*Daubert* inquiry is flexible, which means that trial courts are not required to use the *Daubert* criteria.
- *General Electric Co. v. Joiner* (1997): The Supreme Court of the United States held that the appellate standard of review of trial court decisions regarding the admissibility of expert testimony is "abuse of discretion," which is a highly deferential standard. As such, trial court decisions regarding the admissibility of proffered expert evidence are rarely overturned on appeal.
- *Kumho Tire Co. v. Carmichael* (1999): The Supreme Court of the United States held that *Daubert* applies to all expert testimony, not just scientific expert testimony.

Forensic Mental Health Practice and the Law. David DeMatteo, Daniel A. Krauss, Sarah Fishel, and Kellie Wiltsie, Oxford University Press. © Oxford University Press (2025). DOI: 10.1093/9780197686591.003.0006

- *Weisgram v. Marley* (2000): The Supreme Court of the United States upheld the power of appellate courts to find expert testimony inadmissible as a matter of law and to direct the entry of a verdict for the other party (without holding a new trial).

Many other cases have added complexity and nuance to the interpretation and application of *Daubert* in admissibility contexts, but a review of all such cases is beyond the scope of this chapter.

Daubert Examined

Daubert only pertains to the FRE (1975) in federal court, so state courts are not required to adopt the *Daubert* standard. Nevertheless, *Daubert* has been adopted by most states (Faigman et al., 2022; Harlan & Routh, 2016; Slobogin et al., 2020; see Table 5.1 in Chapter 5). Given that *Daubert* is the admissibility standard in all federal courts and the primary admissibility standard used across states, it is important to take a closer examination of what it requires.

Daubert applies to all expert testimony (per *Kumho Tire Co. v. Carmichael*, 1999),[1] which places a substantial burden on trial court judges. Expert testimony covers an extremely wide range of content areas in both criminal and civil contexts, ranging from accident reconstruction and fire investigations to fraudulent accounting and the insanity defense (see Constanzo et al., 2007). However, in all contexts, *Daubert* requires three things: the proponent of the expert testimony bears the burden of demonstrating by a preponderance of the evidence that the expert is qualified, the proffered testimony is relevant to the dispute (i.e., will assist the trier of fact), and the basis for the expert's opinion is valid and reliable. The trial court may hold a preliminary hearing pursuant to FRE 104(a) to fulfill this gatekeeping mandate. FRE 104(a) states: "(a) In General. The court must decide any preliminary question about whether a witness is qualified, a privilege exists, or evidence is admissible. In so deciding, the court is not bound by evidence rules, except those on privilege." Of note, although some courts hold these *Daubert*/FRE 104(a) hearings, other courts do not. In contexts in which no *Daubert*/FRE 104(a) hearing is held, the relevant admissibility determinations are made during the trial itself. However, the failure to hold a *Daubert*/FRE 104(a) hearing may constitute an abuse of discretion and result in the reversal of the trial court's admissibility determination (e.g., *Padillas v. Stork-Gamco, Inc.*, 1999). According to Faigman et al. (2022), appellate courts are increasingly insisting that trial courts create a sufficient record when they do not hold a *Daubert*/FRE 104(a) hearing so that the basis for the trial court's admissibility decision can be reviewed on appeal if necessary.

As noted, the trial court determines whether the proponent of the expert testimony has demonstrated by a preponderance of the evidence that the expert is qualified, the proffered testimony is relevant to the dispute, and the basis for the expert's opinion is valid and reliable. In addition to vetting the expert, the court must determine whether the proffered expert evidence satisfies the admissibility rules that govern all evidence—that is, FRE 401 (Test for Relevant Evidence) and FRE 403 (Excluding Relevant Evidence for Prejudice, Confusion, Waste of Time, or Other Reasons). If it satisfies the FRE 401/403 relevance/prejudice hurdle, the trial court looks to the rules (e.g., FRE 702) and cases (e.g., *Daubert*) that are specifically applicable to expert witnesses/testimony. In the sections that follow, we address the trial court's determinations related to expert qualifications, the relevance of the proffered expert testimony, and whether the basis for the expert's opinion is valid and reliable.

Expert Qualifications

The standard for being recognized as an expert witness in federal courts is in FRE 702 (2023):

> A witness who is qualified as an expert by knowledge, skill, experience, training, or education may testify in the form of an opinion or otherwise if the proponent demonstrates to the court that it is more likely than not that (a) the expert's scientific, technical, or other specialized knowledge will help the trier of fact to understand the evidence or to determine a fact in issue; (b) the testimony is based on sufficient facts or data; (c) the testimony is the product of reliable principles and methods; and (d) the expert's opinion reflects a reliable application of the principles and methods to the facts of the case.[2]

Of note, this version of FRE 702 took effect on December 1, 2023, when several FRE were amended. For comparison purposes, here is the version of FRE 702 (1975) that was in effect prior to December 1, 2023:

> A witness who is qualified as an expert by knowledge, skill, experience, training, or education may testify in the form of an opinion or otherwise if: (a) the expert's scientific, technical, or other specialized knowledge will help the trier of fact to understand the evidence or to determine a fact in issue; (b) the testimony is based on sufficient facts or data; (c) the testimony is the product of reliable principles and methods; and (d) the expert has reliably applied the principles and methods to the facts of the case.

There are two key differences between the older and current version of FRE 702. First, amended FRE 702 makes it clear that the proponent of the expert testimony must meet the FRE 702 standards for admissibility by demonstrating to the court that it is "more likely than not" the testimony meets the admissibility requirements in FRE 702. The phrase "more likely than not" is essentially synonymous with the standard of proof referred to as preponderance of the evidence (see Chapter 1). Second, the revision of clause (d) in amended FRE 702 makes it clear that an adequate basis for the proffered expert testimony is a prerequisite for admissibility. The idea that the basis of the proffered expert testimony only goes to the weight, not admissibility, of the expert testimony is no longer applicable. The revised language of clause (d) was intended to safeguard against overstated conclusions by experts by directing trial court judges to ensure that the experts' opinions result from reliable methodologies that are reliably applied.

The FRE 702 standard addresses expertise in broad terms, so it is helpful to examine the bases upon which courts are admitting or excluding experts. In general, proffered experts are excluded for two reasons. First, some proffered experts are excluded because they lack the basic credentials or necessary experience to testify on the subject for which the expert is being offered. A proffered expert may be excluded, for example, for not having a sufficient educational background, a required professional license, or sufficient relevant experience. Second, some proffered experts are excluded because although the proffered expert is qualified in one area or qualified as a generalist, they lack sufficient expertise on the specific subject matter at issue before the court. Given the increased specialization in many fields, including mental health, the second basis is likely the more common reason that proffered experts are excluded (see Faigman et al., 2022, for a discussion). For example, it is conceivable that a psychologist would be excluded as an expert if the case calls for more specialized psychological expertise (e.g., neuropsychology). With that said, some courts are permissive and hold that if a proponent demonstrates the expert's general competency, questions regarding expertise in a specific subdiscipline are a matter of weight, not admissibility.

Nevertheless, in fields with lots of specializations (e.g., medicine, mental health, engineering), courts seem to prefer specific expertise that is relevant to the issue before the court. Courts are increasingly concluding that the *ipse dixit* of the expert,[3] no matter how well qualified, is not sufficient for admitting the expert. A court's decision to admit or exclude a mental health professional from the proceedings based on the proffered expert's qualifications may hinge on several factors, including how far off the mental health professional's expertise is from the issue before the court, whether there are more qualified mental health professionals in the immediate geographic area, and whether the party proffering the expert has the necessary means to hire a mental health professional with more specific expertise. The determination of whether the proffered expert has sufficient qualifications is a fact-based preliminary inquiry (per FRE 104) that is only overturned on appeal if there is an abuse of discretion. We return to FRE 104 later in this chapter.

Relevance (or Fit)

The second *Daubert* requirement is demonstrating that the proffered expert testimony is relevant to the dispute. As you may recall from Chapter 4, all evidence—expert or lay—must be relevant (per FRE 401). For expert evidence, FRE 702 also requires that the testimony will assist the trier of fact to understand the evidence or to determine a fact in issue. The Supreme Court noted that this requirement of FRE 702 "goes primarily to relevance," and it described the consideration as one of "fit" (*Daubert*, 1993, p. 591). The *Daubert* Court further stated: "Rule 702's 'helpfulness' standard requires a valid scientific connection to the pertinent inquiry as a precondition to admissibility" (*Daubert*, 1993, pp. 591–592). Regardless of the validity of the proffered expert evidence, it must pertain to a disputed fact in the case. As the Supreme Court emphasized in *General Electric Company v. Joiner* (1997):

> But nothing in either *Daubert* or the Federal Rules of Evidence requires a district court to admit opinion evidence that is connected to existing data only by the *ipse dixit* of the expert. A court may conclude that there is simply too great an analytical gap between the data and the opinion proffered. (p. 146)

FRE 401 essentially employs a logical proposition when describing relevance: Does knowing X (evidence) make Y (material fact) more or less probable? Relevance/fit raises questions about the applicability of findings in the specific case before the court. It may also pertain to external validity—that is, whether research generalizes in a useful way outside of the scientific field and in the specific context of the case. The attorney offering the expert bears the burden of demonstrating that the proffered expert's testimony is relevant to an issue before the court. Although most courts merely require that the expert evidence assist the trier of fact, some state admissibility rules also require that the expert's knowledge be "beyond that possessed by the average layperson" (e.g., PA Rule of Evidence 702) (see Faigman et al., 2022).

Validity/Reliability

The final requirement of *Daubert* is that the basis for the expert's opinion is valid and reliable (*Daubert*, 1993; see Faigman et al., 2016).[4] The core part of *Daubert* is the Supreme Court's interpretation that FRE 702 requires the proponent of expert evidence to demonstrate by a preponderance of the evidence (per FRE 104) that the basis for the proffered opinion is valid and reliable. *Daubert* is not concerned with the validity of the expert's opinions, but with the methods and procedures by which the expert's opinions were derived. As discussed in Chapter 5, the Supreme Court in *Daubert* articulated four criteria to assist trial judges in their gatekeeping function of assessing whether the basis for a proffered expert opinion is valid: (1) whether the theory or technique has been (and can be) tested; (2) whether the theory or technique has been subjected to peer review and publication; (3) the known or potential rate of error of the scientific technique; and (4) general acceptance in the relevant scientific field (see Bernstein & Lasker, 2015; Fournier, 2016; Garrett & Fabricant, 2018; Neal et al., 2019). We discuss each *Daubert* criterion below (for further discussion of each *Daubert* criterion, see DeMatteo et al., 2024).

Testing

In *Daubert*, the Supreme Court noted that testing is the basis of scientific knowledge in many fields. The Court stated: "Ordinarily, a key question to be answered in determining whether a theory or technique is scientific knowledge that will assist the trier of fact will be whether it can be (and has been) tested" (*Daubert*, 1993, p. 593). As one federal appellate court stated: "An untestable scientific theory is all theory and no science" (*United States v. Gissantaner*, 2021, p. 463). It is important to note the foundational status of this criterion—that is, without testing, there is typically no peer review and publication, known error rates, or general acceptance.

The Court in *Daubert* equated testing with the scientific concept of falsifiability (or refutability), which is the idea that something must be capable of being proven wrong for it to be considered true science. The use of falsifiability as the criterion of scientific status can be traced back to the work of Austrian-British philosopher Karl Popper (2002a, 2002b) in the early to mid-20th century. Popper (2002a) spoke about falsifiability—predictions that can be falsified—as being the demarcation between science and pseudoscience. For the testing criterion, some relevant considerations include whether theory or technique can be tested, whether it was actually tested, how it was tested, the degree of error, and the analyses. Further, for this criterion to be meaningfully applied, trial court judges must recognize that not all testing is equal, with some tests having more or less rigor. There are notable differences, for example, between correlational studies and randomized controlled trials. As Faigman et al. (2022) stated:

> If *Daubert* is not to become a dead letter, judges must develop sufficient scientific literacy to recognize research designed to truly test a hypothesis as compared to research designed merely to supply impressive looking graphs and imposing numbers to a researcher's theory. In other words, judges (and lawyers) must be able to distinguish the methods of science from those methods that imitate science. (p. 68)

It is also important for courts to realize that some fields do not use testing, which (again) supports a flexible approach to applying the *Daubert* criteria. The research, albeit limited, suggests that trial court judges do not often rely on the testing criterion when making admissibility decisions (Dahir et al., 2005; Groscup et al., 2002). In Dahir et al.'s (2005) survey of state trial court judges, they found that only 1 of 216 judges mentioned testing/falsifiability first in terms of their admissibility considerations, and only 2 of 216 judges mentioned testing/falsifiability in their top four factors they consider when making admissibility determinations. In earlier research, Groscup et al. (2002) examined state and federal cases decided 5.5 years pre-*Daubert* and 5.5 years post-*Daubert* to assess whether *Daubert* changed how judges make admissibility decisions. They found that the amount of discussion devoted to the testing criterion in judicial opinions did not significantly increase after *Daubert* was decided (Groscup et al., 2002).

DeMatteo et al. (2024) offer several implications related to the use or nonuse of the testing/falsifiability criterion in admissibility decisions. First, judges must remember to focus on the testability/falsifiability of the theory or technique underlying the proffered expert evidence as opposed to the conclusions generated from the theory or technique. In *Daubert*, the Court stated that the "focus, of course, must be solely on principles and methodology, not on the conclusions that they generate" (*Daubert*, 1993, p. 595). The trial judge's focus on the "scientific validity—and thus the evidentiary relevance and reliability—of the principles that underlie" proffered expert testimony, as opposed to the expert's conclusions, illustrates the distinction between admissibility and weight (*Daubert*, 1993, pp. 594–595). Second, judges should recognize that good science, which necessarily incorporates the concept of testing/falsifiability, is not dependent on the facts of the specific case or the expert's conclusions. As DeMatteo et al. (2024) stated:

> Although the specific theory or technique that underlies the expert testimony may differ from case to case, judges must resist the urge to 'reinvent the wheel'

in each case by developing a *fact-specific analysis* of whether the proffered expert evidence constitutes good science. Whether something constitutes good science relates solely to the validity and reliability of the method or technique that underlies the preferred expert testimony, not the facts of the case or the expert's conclusions. (p. 148)

Peer Review and Publication

Peer review is thought to be the hallmark of good science. In *Daubert*, the Court stated that "submission to the scrutiny of the scientific community is a component of 'good science,' in part because it increases the likelihood that substantive flaws in methodology will be detected" (p. 593). In most branches of science, peer review is the primary mechanism for quality control (Bornmann, 2011), and the usefulness of peer review lies in vetting a manuscript's methodology, analyses, and conclusions to prevent the publication of poor science (Lee et al., 2013).

However, in *Daubert*, the Court also recognized that there are limits to relying on peer review and publication when determining the admissibility of proffered expert evidence. For example, the Court noted that "[p]ublication (which is but one element of peer review) is not a *sine qua non* of admissibility" and "does not necessarily correlate with reliability" (*Daubert*, 1993, p. 593). The Court also noted that "in some instances well-grounded but innovative theories will not have been published" and that "some propositions, moreover, are too particular, too new, or of too limited interest to be published" (*Daubert*, 1993, p. 593). Despite these caveats, the Court stated that peer review and publication is "a relevant, though not dispositive, consideration in assessing the scientific validity of a particular technique or methodology on which an opinion is premised" (*Daubert*, 1993, p. 594).[5]

There are a few considerations that are relevant to this criterion (see DeMatteo et al., 2024). First, the peer review process is not always effective in identifying bad science. For example, several researchers sent a purposefully flawed manuscript to 221 reviewers for the *British Medical Journal*, and reviewers only identified a mean of approximately two (out of eight) clear weaknesses in design, analysis, or interpretation (Godlee et al., 1998). Moreover, no reviewer identified more than five errors, and 16% of the reviewers (n = 35) did not identify any of the eight weaknesses. In a systematic analysis on the effects of peer review, Jefferson et al. (2002) raised concerns about whether peer reviewers (a) are adept at identifying methodological errors in scientific work and (b) inappropriately rely on their own biases in making publication recommendations. Relatedly, a notable concern is that reviewers of the same manuscript frequently disagree in their assessments of the manuscript's merits. For example, in a study examining consecutive manuscript submissions to two scientific journals, researchers found that rates of reviewer agreement were little better than what would be expected by chance (Rothwell & Martyn, 2000).

Second, there are many peer-reviewed journals, and they are not equal in terms of the quality and rigor of the studies they publish. In 2003, it was estimated that there were 80,000 to 100,000 scientific journals in the world, with an annual growth rate of more than 3% (Mabe, 2003). According to a more recent estimate from WordsRated, an international research data and analytics group, there were 46,736 academic journals worldwide as of 2020 (Curcic, 2023). WordsRated also reported that the number of academic journals has grown by 28.7% in the past 10 years, with an average annual growth rate of 2.56%, and that more than 5.1 million academic articles are published per year (Curcic, 2023). Some journals require extremely rigorous scientific methodologies and data analyses, with very high rejection rates (over 90%), while other journals are much less selective in terms of the articles they publish. This highlights the Supreme Court's caution in *Daubert* that peer review and publication "does not necessarily correlate with reliability" (*Daubert*, 1993, p. 593). Relatedly, the number of peer-reviewed publications on a topic does not necessarily equate with reputable science (e.g., astrology).

Error Rate

In *Daubert* (1993), the Supreme Court provided no discussion of the error rate criterion beyond simply noting that trial court judges "ordinarily should consider the known or potential rate of error" of the scientific technique, method, or procedure that underlies the proffered expert's testimony (p. 594). Unfortunately, the Court did not define error rate, clarify under what conditions error rate should result in the exclusion of proffered expert evidence, specify which error rates are acceptable, or provide any examples of error rates. In addition to receiving little attention from the Supreme Court, this criterion has received little attention from scholars (see Meixner & Diamond, 2014). As a result, trial court judges have not been provided with much guidance in terms of understanding and applying this criterion, and empirical results (discussed later in this chapter) support the conclusion that trial court judges lack a sufficient understanding of error rates and rarely rely on that criterion when making admissibility determinations (e.g., Gatowski et al., 2001; Haug & Baird, 2011).

Error is a natural part of most science, and it can result from a variety of sources, including imperfect assessment tools (arguably all of them) and human error. A key consideration, therefore, is the level of error that is acceptable for a technique or procedure to be considered valid and reliable (Faigman et al., 2022). There are also several complicating considerations. First, error rates may refer to several types of variability, including the aggregate error rate for a specific technique or errors made by a specific expert (Meixner &

Diamond, 2014). Second, there are several kinds of errors that may be relevant, including random errors, systematic errors, and errors related to false positives (Type I), false negatives (Type II), sensitivity, specificity, positive predictive values, and negative predictive values (see DeMatteo et al., 2024). Using the language of *Daubert*, Meixner and Diamond (2014) distinguish between "known error rate" (e.g., known error rate among the Wechsler family of IQ tests) and "potential error rate" (e.g., errors that result in a biased sample). Third, not all errors have the same consequences because the analysis of error rates is context-specific.

Do trial court judges pay attention to this criterion? Some research suggests that judges do not rely on known error rates when making admissibility decisions. For example, Groscup et al. (2002) found no significant increase in judicial discussion of error rates from pre-*Daubert* to post-*Daubert* cases. In another study, Haug and Baird (2011) reviewed federal trial and appellate cases that cited *Daubert* and mentioned error rates in the written opinions. They found that error rate was the least analyzed *Daubert* factor among 101 trial court cases and that only 33 of 200 experts who were challenged on the admissibility of their evidence were asked about error rate (Haug & Barid, 2011). They also found that appellate court reversals of trial court decisions decreased when error rate was mentioned in the trial court, which suggests that appellate judges may be reluctant to address error rates and instead prefer to defer to trial court decisions (Haug & Baird, 2011). Other research, however, suggests that judges are indeed relying on this criterion when making admissibility decisions. In a 2014 study of 208 federal district court cases, Meixner and Diamond found that judges rely on error rate far more commonly than other research suggests. They also found that the trial court judges' discussion of the potential error rate of a procedure, technique, or method was predictive of the admissibility decision (Meixner & Diamond, 2014). Specifically, Meixner and Diamond (2014) found that detailed discussions of error rate were associated with higher rates of rejection, while less detailed analyses of error rate were associated with a higher likelihood of admission.

DeMatteo et al. (2024) identified several implications for trial court judges in *Daubert* contexts. First, the importance of error rates lies in its ability to inform a judge's perception of whether a method or technique is valid and reliable (i.e., good science) and, in turn, whether the method or technique will assist the trier of fact. Unfortunately, some lawyers inaccurately claim that the error rate criterion is satisfied when a *p* value is below .05 (conventional cut-off for statistical significance) (Haug & Baird, 2011). Second, the Supreme Court in *Daubert* suggested that knowing the error rate is important in terms of making an admissibility determination, but the error rate should arguably go more to the weight of the expert evidence as opposed to the admissibility. Along these lines, some have noted that the error rate of a procedure, method, or technique that underlies proffered expert testimony must simply be known or potentially knowable, which means that even a high error rate would not necessarily be grounds for excluding the evidence (e.g., Schauer & Spellman, 2013).

General Acceptance

The fourth *Daubert* factor is general acceptance, which is a nod to *Frye*, although the Supreme Court had just overruled *Frye* and did not mention *Frye* when discussing this criterion. When discussing general acceptance in *Daubert* (1993), the Court stated that "[w]idespread acceptance can be an important factor in ruling particular evidence admissible," and that a technique that has only attracted minimal support with the relevant field "may properly be viewed with skepticism" (p. 593). As discussed in Chapter 5, general acceptance is the sole criterion for admissibility under *Frye*, but it should be viewed in combination with other factors in a *Daubert* jurisdiction (see Monahan & Walker, 2022, and Slobogin et al., 2020, for useful discussions).

DeMatteo et al. (2024) highlight several implications for trial court judges considering the general acceptance criterion in *Daubert* jurisdictions. First, it is useful to define what is meant by general acceptance. The Supreme Court in *Daubert* did not define general acceptance, but taken at face value, one can reasonably assume that general acceptance means that the procedure, technique, or method that resulted in the expert's opinion has sufficient support within the relevant field (see Stern & Horvitz, 2002). There is, however, some nuance to the meaning of general acceptance. For example, Neal et al. (2019) noted that there is no consensus on "what must be generally accepted, the scope of the 'field' that must generally accept it, and how acceptance is to be measured" (p. 140). Faigman (2013) notes that courts often seek input from narrow professional groups, even though such groups may not fairly be considered the relevant field. Also, as noted in Chapter 5, a long-standing concern is that judges may exclude valid but emerging science because it has not yet become generally accepted in the relevant field (see Giannelli, 1980). Interested readers can consult Chapter 5 for discussion of additional considerations and concerns related to general acceptance.

Do Judges Understand *Daubert*?

When the Supreme Court determined that FRE 702 was the appropriate test for the admissibility of expert testimony, it entrusted trial court judges with a gatekeeping role (*Daubert v. Merrell Dow Pharmaceuticals*, 1993). The *Daubert* decision shifted determinations of admissibility of expert testimony from the consensus of experts (*Frye*) to the decisions of individual judges based on their assessment of the underlying science. A synthesis of the *Daubert* trilogy indicates that trial court judges in *Daubert* jurisdictions are expected to apply fairly sophisticated concepts when evaluating scientific validity and reliability to make admissibility decisions about a wide range of expert evidence (see *Kumho Tire Co. v. Carmichael*, 1999), and their admissibility decisions will be upheld on appeal unless the decision was an abuse of discretion (see *General Electric Co. v. Joiner*, 1997).

As discussed in Chapter 5, the *Daubert* decision sparked immediate concern among some judges, including Chief Justice Rehnquist in his dissenting opinion in *Daubert*, about whether judges could function as effective gatekeepers of expert testimony. Specifically, Chief Justice Rehnquist was concerned that *Daubert* requires trial court judges to become "amateur scientists" when making admissibility decisions (*Daubert*, 1993, p. 601). Also, upon remand, the United States Court of Appeals for the Ninth Circuit expressed similar concern about its new gatekeeping role: "[T]hough we are largely untrained in science and certainly no match for any of the witnesses whose testimony we are reviewing, it is our responsibility to determine whether those experts' proposed testimony amounts to 'scientific knowledge,' constitutes 'good science,' and was 'derived by the scientific method'" (*Daubert v. Merrell Dow Pharmaceuticals*, 1995, p. 1316). Many commentators and scholars have also addressed the gatekeeping function imposed on trial court judges by the *Daubert* decision (e.g., DeMatteo et al., 2019; Faigman et al., 2016; Neal et al., 2019).

Fortunately, the question of whether trial court judges understand the *Daubert* criteria is an empirical one, although the data are limited (see Jurs, 2012). In an often-cited study conducted nearly a decade after *Daubert* was decided, Gatowski et al. (2001) asked a large sample of state trial court judges (N = 400) about the utility of the *Daubert* criteria and their understanding of those criteria. They found that 55% of the judges believed *Daubert* had great value, 91% believed that performing a gatekeeping function was appropriate for judges, 62% reported taking an active role in the admissibility process, and 52% felt adequately prepared based on their education, training, and experience to handle a wide range of expert evidence (Gatowski et al., 2001). The judges also overwhelmingly believed that the four *Daubert* criteria were useful in determining the admissibility of proffered expert evidence: testing (88%), error rate (91%),[6] peer review and publication (92%),[7] and general acceptance (93%). The results were more variable, however, when looking at how well the judges understood the *Daubert* criteria. Although 82% of the judges had a sufficient understanding of general acceptance[8] and 71% understood peer review and publication, only 6% understood testing[9] and only 4% understood error rate (Gatowski et al., 2001). It is worth noting that the judges demonstrated the lowest level of understanding for the two *Daubert* criteria that relate most directly to scientific merit.

In Kovera and McAuliff's (2000) study of 144 state court judges regarding their knowledge of research design and methodology, they found that 92% of the judges failed to identify a major methodological flaw in a research study (i.e., missing control group), and 83% of the judges mistakenly concluded that a high-quality, flaw-free study should be excluded. As such, the judges were both highly likely to (a) admit invalid expert evidence (flawed studies) and (b) exclude valid expert evidence (good studies/science) (Kovera & McAuliff, 2000). Although these results are concerning, it is fair to point out that there was no cross-examination or competing experts to highlight the methodological flaws for the judges.

Given the state of the research, DeMatteo et al. (2019) concluded: "Obviously, those who do not understand the [*Daubert*] criteria cannot be expected to apply them properly" (p. 130). Fortunately, there are several ways to potentially improve judicial decision-making in *Daubert* contexts (see DeMatteo, 2024, for a discussion). For example, judges could become more informed consumers of general scientific methodology. To accomplish this goal, given that some law students will eventually become judges, law schools could offer a course on the basics of science and scientific research, and current lawyers (some of whom may become judges) and judges could take relevant Continuing Legal Education seminars or seek out other opportunities to learn about the scientific method, epistemology, statistics, and related considerations. Federal judges can refer to the *Reference Manual on Scientific Evidence* (National Research Council, in press). The first edition of the *Reference Manual on Scientific Evidence* (Federal Judicial Center, 1994) was published soon after the Supreme Court decided *Daubert* with the express purpose of assisting federal judges to handle difficult issues involving scientific testimony. The *Reference Manual* is now in its fourth edition. Finally, given the age of some of the empirical research discussed in this chapter, newer research on judges' admissibility decisions in *Daubert* jurisdictions would be informative to judges, lawyers, experts, and litigants.

There are also some mechanisms in the FRE that could prove useful for judges in *Daubert* jurisdictions. For example, judges can appoint their own experts, following one of two approaches—independent expert or technical advisor. Under FRE 706,[10] judges can appoint an independent expert. A court-appointed independent expert, sometimes called a Rule 706 expert, is a neutral (i.e., not party-retained) expert who assists the court to, among other functions, assess the weight that should be given to expert evidence proffered by one or both parties. Although judges have been reluctant historically to appoint 706 experts (see Faigman et al., 2022, for a discussion), concerns about bias among party-retained experts may lead some courts to take advantage of 706 experts. Per FRE 706, these court-appointed independent experts are subject to the ordinary rules of discovery, which means they can testify in court and be cross-examined by one or both parties.

Federal judges also have the option of appointing a technical advisor to assist them in making admissibility decisions when faced with a proffer of expert evidence. The FRE (mostly FRE 104(a)) provide judges with the inherent authority to appoint a technical advisor. Technical advisors do not assist the jury in assessing the weight that should be given to expert evidence; they exclusively assist the judge (not the jury), and they are not subject to the adversarial procedures of discovery and cross-examination.

Other "*Daubert*" Criteria

As previously noted, the analysis of the admissibility of proffered expert evidence in *Daubert* jurisdictions is flexible. In *Daubert* (1993), the Supreme Court noted that "the inquiry envisioned by Rule 702 is . . . a flexible one" (p. 594). Later, in *Kumho Tire Company v. Carmichael* (1999), the Court stated: "But as the Court stated in *Daubert*, the test of reliability is 'flexible,' and *Daubert*'s list of specific factors neither necessarily nor exclusively applies to all experts or in every case" (p. 141). Given this latitude, several commentators and state and federal courts have developed other "*Daubert*" criteria to assist trial court judges in their gatekeeping function.

It did not take long for courts to develop other "*Daubert*" criteria. After the Supreme Court decided *Daubert* and remanded the case back to the appellate court, the United States Court of Appeals for the Ninth Circuit developed the first two other "*Daubert*" criteria—that is, (1) preparation/creation for purpose other than litigation and (2) whether the specific science at issue in the case has been published (as opposed to publications more generally on the topic) (*Daubert v. Merrell Dow Pharmaceuticals*, 1995). When articulating the former criterion, the Ninth Circuit stated:

> One very significant fact to be considered is whether the experts are proposing to testify about matters growing naturally and directly out of research they have conducted independent of the litigation, or whether they have developed their opinions expressly for purposes of testifying. (*Daubert*, 1995, p. 1317)

With respect to the litigation conducted in the *Daubert* case, the Court noted that "none of the experts based his testimony on preexisting or independent research . . . none claims to have studied the effect of Bendectin on limb reduction defects before being hired to testify in this or related cases" (*Daubert*, 1995, p. 1317). In terms of the second criterion, the Ninth Circuit stated that if the proffered expert testimony is not based on independent research, as was the case in *Daubert*, the proffering party "must come forward with other objective, verifiable evidence that the testimony is based on 'scientifically valid principles'" (*Daubert*, 1995, p. 1318). The Ninth Circuit indicated that a party could satisfy this criterion by showing that the "proffered conclusions have been subjected to normal scientific scrutiny through peer review and publication" (*Daubert*, 1995, p. 1318). When applying this criterion, the Ninth Circuit noted that none of the plaintiffs' experts had published their work on Bendectin in a scientific journal. Based on these considerations, the Ninth Circuit concluded that the plaintiffs' proffered expert testimony was not admissible.

As noted in Chapter 5, the United States Congress amended FRE 702 in 2000 to be more consistent with the Supreme Court's decision in *Daubert*. The Commentary to the 2002 amendments for FRE 702 notes that courts both before and after *Daubert* have identified other factors for trial courts to consider when making admissibility decisions, including whether the expert is testifying about matters "growing naturally and directly" out of research conducted independent of the litigation, whether the expert has unjustifiably extrapolated from an accepted premise to an unfounded conclusion, whether the expert has adequately accounted for obvious alternative explanations, whether the expert exercises the same care as they would in their professional work outside of litigation, and whether the field of expertise claimed by the expert is known to reach reliable results for the type of opinion the expert is providing.

Several commentators have discussed alternative "*Daubert*" criteria, with some overlap with courts and other commentators in their identification of relevant admissibility considerations. Here are some of the alternate "*Daubert*" factors that have been identified (e.g., Malone & Zwier, 2014; McCormick, 1982; see Faigman et al., 2022):

- Existence and maintenance of standards governing use of the method, procedure, or technique
- Presence of safeguards in the characteristics of the technique
- Extent to which the basic data are verifiable by the court and jury
- Analogy to other scientific techniques that are admissible
- Nature and breadth of the inferences adduced
- Clarity and simplicity with which the technique or theory can be described
- Availability of other experts to test and evaluate the technique
- Probative significance of the evidence in the circumstances of the case
- Care with which the technique was employed
- Adequacy to explain important empirical data (i.e., the expert's methodology should either consider existing empirical data related to the expert's science or explain why there was no need to consider such existing data)

- Basis in quantitatively sufficient data (e.g., a sufficiently large and representative sample)
- Basis in qualitatively acceptable data (i.e., the expert must show that the data on which the expert relied are relevant to the specific litigation)
- Methodological consistency (i.e., methodology should produce consistent results)
- Consistency in the specific application of the methodology (i.e., use of the same methodology with the same case-specific data should lead to consistent results)
- Recognition in a body of literature (i.e., whether a body of quality literature recognizes the expert's method, technique, or procedure)
- The precision of the results generated by the methodology (i.e., whether the methodology leads to precise results or broad and nonspecific results)
- Deviation from accepted approaches (i.e., deviation for generally accepted methods, techniques, and procedures)
- Comparison with established methods, techniques, and procedures

McCormick (1982) concluded that the alternate *Daubert* criteria "require examination of the characteristics of the evidence, the foundation for the proffer, and the context of the proffer" (p. 912).

The use of other "*Daubert*" criteria in making admissibility decisions is consistent with the Supreme Court's indication that the four factors identified in *Daubert* were not exhaustive and that the *Daubert* analysis should be flexible. However, it raises the questions of whether these alternative "*Daubert*" criteria actually help judges to assess the validity and reliability of the science (which is the primary charge of *Daubert*) and whether the judges have an adequate understanding of these factors. Ultimately, those are empirical questions that await future research.

Effectuating *Daubert* Through Other Means

This chapter addressed the admissibility of expert evidence under *Daubert*. An express goal of *Daubert* is to limit the introduction of poor science into court proceedings. However, as noted in other parts of this chapter, there is an important distinction between admissibility (i.e., whether evidence is admitted into court proceedings) and weight (i.e., how much credibility the judge/jury affords to evidence that has been admitted). It is possible, of course, that some proffered expert evidence will satisfy FRE 702 and be admitted into court proceedings but nevertheless be of relatively low quality. It is also possible that some juries may place too much weight on such testimony.

Fortunately, there are some options to minimize the impact of weak but admissible expert evidence. The Supreme Court of the United States provided some guidance on this issue in *Daubert* (1993): "Vigorous cross-examination, presentation of contrary evidence, and careful instruction on the burden of proof are the traditional and appropriate means of attacking shaky but admissible evidence" (p. 596). This chapter focused on the admissibility of expert evidence, so a detailed discussion of these postadmission strategies is beyond the scope of this chapter. However, some empirical evidence suggests these three strategies are not particularly effective safeguards against shaky but admissible expert evidence (e.g., McAuliff & Groscup, 2009).

In *Daubert* (1993), the Supreme Court offered some additional guidance when courts and parties are faced with "shaky but admissible" expert evidence:

> Additionally, in the event the trial court concludes that the scintilla of evidence presented supporting a position is insufficient to allow a reasonable juror to conclude that the position more likely than not is true, the court remains free to direct a judgment, Fed. Rule Civ. Proc. 50(a), and likewise to grant summary judgment, Fed. Rule Civ. Proc. 56. (p. 596)

Directed verdicts are rulings entered by a trial judge after determining that there is no legally sufficient evidentiary basis for a reasonable jury to reach a different conclusion. Directed verdicts are available in both criminal and civil contexts. The trial court can grant a directed verdict on its own initiative (referred to as *sua sponte*) or upon a motion by either party. A party who files a motion for summary judgment, or judgment as a matter of law, is asking the court to enter a judgment based on the merits of the case without holding a trial because there is no reasonable dispute of fact.

Conclusion

In *Daubert* (1993), the Supreme Court of the United States imposed a gatekeeping function on trial court judges when they are faced with a proffer of expert testimony. Rather than solely asking if the theory, technique, or method that underlies the expert's opinion is generally accepted in the relevant field (à la *Frye*), trial court judges must determine if the proffered testimony is relevant to the dispute (i.e., will assist the trier of fact) and whether the basis for the expert's opinion is valid and reliable. The Court offered four criteria to assist trial court judges in their gatekeeping function: whether the theory or technique has been (and can be) tested, whether the theory or technique has been subjected to peer review and publication, the known or potential rate of error of the scientific technique, and general acceptance in the relevant scientific field. In the years following *Daubert*, courts have developed other "*Daubert*" criteria. Unfortunately, there is some evidence that trial court judges may not possess a sufficient understanding of some of the original four *Daubert* criteria, and there is a lack of research on whether judges understand the other "*Daubert*" criteria.

Chapter 7
Considerations Related to Expert Testimony

In offering expert opinions to courts, mental health professionals and other types of experts are often regulated by the legal system in what they *can* explicitly state in their testimony (Grisso, 1986, 2003). These rules governing the testimonial language of mental health professional experts vary by jurisdiction, and it is incumbent on those serving as experts to understand how various legal regulations (i.e., statutes, rules of evidence, common law) interact with their profession's ethical obligations. For example, Guideline 2.04 of the American Psychological Association's *Specialty Guidelines for Forensic Psychology* states that forensic psychologists should possess "a fundamental and reasonable level of knowledge and understanding of the legal and professional standards laws, rules, and precedents that govern their participation in legal proceedings" (American Psychological Association, 2013, p. 9).

Although knowledge of legal rules and precedents is important, this does not absolve mental health professionals from other ethical obligations, such as their ethical obligations to (a) take reasonable steps to correct or minimize the misuse or misrepresentation of their work (*Ethical Principles of Psychologists and Code of Conduct* [EPPCC] Standard 1.01; American Psychological Association, 2017), (b) base their opinions and testimony on sufficient data (EPPCC 2.04 & 9.01; American Psychological Association, 2017), and (c) make reasonable attempts to resolve conflicts between their ethics and the law even if they eventually follow the law (EPPCC 1.02; American Psychological Association, 2017). These ethical directives are not limited to psychologists, as the *Ethics Guidelines for the Practice of Forensic Psychiatry* provide similar guidance (American Academy of Psychiatry and the Law, 2005). These ethical constraints may differ from the limits on mental health expert testimony imposed by courts. In other words, they may dictate what a forensic expert *should* opine regardless of what legal regulations allow.

This chapter focuses on two of the most common and debated legal and professional restrictions on mental health expert's testimony: (1) the use of the phrase "reasonable scientific [or psychological or medical or insert discipline] certainty"[1] related to the admissibility of their expert opinions; and (2) prohibitions on mental health experts' proffering "ultimate issue" testimony,

Forensic Mental Health Practice and the Law. David DeMatteo, Daniel A. Krauss, Sarah Fishel, and Kellie Wiltsie, Oxford University Press. © Oxford University Press (2025). DOI: 10.1093/9780197686591.003.0007

which occurs when experts specifically offer expert opinions on questions at the heart of legal disputes. The chapter will trace the origins of these rules and prohibitions, highlight developments of these rules over time, and make recommendations as to how experts should proceed in an ethically and legally appropriate manner.

"Reasonable Degree of Scientific Certainty"

Legal History of "Reasonable Degree of Scientific Certainty"

At some point, most forensic mental health professionals have been asked if their opinion is being expressed to a "reasonable degree of certainty" (RSC) (National Committee on Forensic Science (NCFS), 2016; Otto et al., 2014). Yet most experts, mental health or otherwise, have little idea what this phrase means and what level of certainty it connotes when they are asked to use it (Drogin et al., 2012; Fox et al., 2022). In the scholarly literature, RSC is often compared to other standards of proof, but depending on jurisdiction and common law practices it can mean anything from "preponderance of evidence" to "beyond a reasonable doubt," and "[n]o consensus exists among judges, attorney, or academic commentators as to whether 'reasonable medical certainty' means 'more probable than not' or 'beyond a reasonable doubt' or something in between" (Lewin, 1998, p. 310). More specifically, with regard to RSC use and meaning by mental health experts offering testimony, RSC occurs frequently in case law but is rarely defined. In an examination of appellate court cases involving sexually violent predator (SVP) decisions from 1996 to 2019, the phrase "reasonable degree of certainty" appeared in 84 cases. Yet in only one of those cases was the level of proof associated with this terminology defined, and in that case, *In re Detention of Twining* (1995), it was defined as "more likely than not" (Fox et al., 2022).

Scholarly commentators have been critical of the nebulousness of this phrase and its continued use in the legal system. Kaye (2010) summarizes this concern, stating it is "legal mumbo jumbo derived from archaic cases in which lawyers discovered that if a medical doctor did not utter the incantation 'to a reasonable degree of medical certainty' his testimony might be excluded" (p. 82). A comprehensive review of the origin of this terminology indicates that "reasonable medical certainty" seems to have originated in Illinois courts in the early 20th century (Lewin, 1998). Although originally developed as a phrase necessary for expert opinions related to substantive proof for future damages in civil cases, it eventually became widely used as an admissibility standard for many different types of expert testimony (Lewin, 1998).

The exact published case in which this terminology first appears is disputed, with Lewin (1998) tracing its origins to an Illinois Supreme Court decision, *Fellows-Kimbrough v. Chicago City Railway Company* (1916). In that case, the court examined a hypothetical question involving a man who was injured when two trains collided, and he was thrown to the ground. The expert's opinion on the medical conditions that resulted from the accident are offered in reply to a question from his attorney "as a medical man, and based upon reasonable certainty, as to what was the cause of the neurasthenia in the hypothetical patient?" (*Fellows-Kimbrough v. Chicago City Ry. Co.*, 1916, p. 502). The Illinois Supreme Court prohibited the hypothetical question of the expert and remanded the case back to the trial court. The remand, however, was not because of the use of term "reasonable certainty," but rather because the hypothetical question contained the phrase "was the cause" of the injury (Lewin, 1998); this language was at odds with the "ultimate issue" rule in effect in Illinois with the court prohibiting such a definitive causal statement when the cause of the injury was the main issue in the dispute. This is a point we will return to later in the chapter when we discuss "ultimate issue" expert testimony.

Other scholars point to the origin of the phrase RSC to a later case in Illinois, *Herbst v. Levy* (1935) (NCFS, 2016; Weiss & LaPorte, 2018). In that case, the prosecution expert, Fred Ludoph, was "asked whether he could determine with reasonable scientific certainty the cause of the capsizing boat" (*Herbst v. Levy*, 1935, p. 358). Regardless of the exact origins of RSC, the phrase eventually found itself recommended in several trial advocacy manuals published by an Illinois attorney, Irving Goldstein, with the popularity of his books further propagating its use across many types of experts and court proceedings (Lewin, 1998). By the 1970s, RSC had become a commonplace precursor to admissibility of expert testimony in several jurisdictions (Lewin, 1998; NCFS, 2016).

Current Admissibility of "Reasonable Degree of Scientific Certainty"

However, many in the legal and psychological fields have continually argued that RSC confuses rather than clarifies the expert's opinion and offers a level of certainty that may be misleading to the trier of fact (DeMier & Otto, 2017). As one scholar highlights:

> The term "reasonable medical certainty" has no scientific meaning. Its legal meaning is at best ambiguous, at worst misleading. It is not required by the Federal Rules of Evidence nor any evidence code. More importantly, the term

> ("scientific certainty") is problematic for a different reason—misleading the jury and should be excluded under Federal Rule 403 for that reason alone. (Gianelli, 2010, pp. 40–41)

Critiques of the use of RSC led a number of jurisdictions (e.g., Hawaii, Ohio, Nebraska—see Table 7.1 for state requirements regarding use of RSC) to either not require its use for admissibility of expert testimony or prohibit its use. In 2016, the National Commission on Forensic Science issued a report calling for an end to the use of the phrases "reasonable scientific certainty" and/or "to a reasonable degree of [discipline] certainty" (NCFS, 2016). It should be noted that this report was directed at forensic science expert testimony broadly (e.g., fingerprints, DNA analysis, ballistic matching) and was not specifically aimed at mental health professional expert testimony. This critique is, however, equally relevant to mental health professionals proffering expert opinions.

The NCFS report highlighted many of the issues with RSC, including (1) the explicit terms have no scientific meaning, (2) the language is not routinely used in scientific disciplines; (3) the phrase does not have any consensual definition in either law or science; (4) the words are not required by any state evidence code or the Federal Rules of Evidence (FRE); (5) the verbiage may confuse the trier of fact by suggesting a higher degree of certainty associated with the expert opinion than is warranted by the underlying science; and (6) the language may be difficult for the trier of fact to use when combined with other probabilistic evidence common in many legal proceedings (i.e., how should "reasonable certainty" be combined when it used with other probabilities, such as "to a reasonable degree of scientific certainty" that X was *probably* the cause of the injury) (NCFS, 2016). Taken together, a strict legal analysis of these criticisms suggests that the probative value of RSC terminology with regard to expert testimony may be substantially outweighed by its danger of unfair prejudice, confusion, or misleading the jury (see FRE 403).

Based on the NCFS report, the U.S. Attorney General and the Department of Justice adopted several NCFS recommendations. Further, the Attorney General issued a memorandum in which he instructed the following:

> Department forensic laboratories will review their policies and procedures to ensure that forensic examiners are not using the expressions "reasonable scientific certainty" or "reasonable [forensic discipline] certainty" in their reports or testimony. Department prosecutors will abstain from use of these expressions when presenting forensic reports or questioning forensic experts in court unless required by a judge or applicable law. (U.S. Department of Justice, 2016, p. 1)

Table 7.1 States That Require Expert Testimony to a "Reasonable Degree of Scientific Certainty"

State	Required/Permitted	Citation
Alabama	Likely required	*Vrocher v. State*, 813 So.2d 799 (Ala. Crim. App. 2001); *Keaton v. State*, 375 So.3d 44 (Ala Crim. App. 2021)
Alaska	Permitted	*Smith v. State*, 229 P.3d 221 (Alaska Ct. App. 2010); *State v. Alexander*, 364 P.3d 458 (Alaska Ct. App. 2015)
Arizona	Permitted	*State v. Romero*, 236 Ariz. 451 (Ct. App. 2014)
Arkansas	Permitted	*Drake v. State*, 2019 Ark. App. 9 (Ct. App. 2019)
California	Permitted	*People v. Cordova*, 62 Cal. 4th 104 (2015); *People v. Cua*, 191 Cal. App. 4th 582 (2011)
Colorado	Permitted	*Clark v. People*, 232 P.3d 1287 (Colo. 2010); *People v. Holmes*, 2014 Colo. Dist. LEXIS 2073
Connecticut	Permitted	*State v. Patterson*, 344 Conn. 281 (2022); *Fedorka v. Billy Wilson's, LLC*, 2014 Conn. Super. LEXIS 380
Delaware	Cannot require	*Barriocanal v. Gibbs*, 697 A.2d 1169 (Del. 1997); *Town of Townsend v. Grassbusters, Inc.*, 2019 Del. Super. LEXIS 363
District of Columbia	Cannot require	*Clifford v. United States*, 532 A.2d 628 (D.C. 1987); *Robinson v. United States*, 50 A.3d 508 (D.C. 2012); *Coates v. United States*, 558 A.2d 1148 (D.C. 1989)
Florida	Cannot require	*Delap v. State*, 440 So.2d 1242 (Fla. 1983)
Georgia	Cannot require	*Layfield v. Dept. of Transp.*, 280 Ga. 848 (2006); *Early v. Morgan Fleet Servs., Inc.*, 368 Ga. App. 175 (2023)
Hawaii	Cannot require	*State v. DeLeon*, 131 Hawai'i 463 (2014)
Idaho	Permitted	*State v. Hall*, 163 Idaho 744 (2018)
Illinois	Likely required	*Torres v. Midwest Dev. Co.*, 383 Ill. App. 3d 20 (2008); *Dominguez v. St. John's Hosp.*, 260 Ill. App. 3d 591 (1993)
Indiana	Cannot require	*Noblesville Casting Div. of TRW, Inc. v. Prince*, 438 N.E.2d 722 (1982); *Sophia Myers v. Conway*, 2021 Ind. App. Unpub. LEXIS 88 (2021)

State	Required/Permitted	Citation
Iowa	Cannot require	*Des Moines Pub. Sch. v. Hildreth*, 2021 Iowa App. LEXIS 481 (2021); *Johnson v. Knoxville Cmty. Sch. Dist.*, 570 N.W.2d 633 (Iowa 1997); *State v. Berry*, 2005 Iowa App. LEXIS 28 (2005)
Kansas	Permitted	*State v. Denney*, 545 P.3d 1058 (Kan. Ct. App. 2024)
Kentucky	Permitted	*Commonwealth v. Hardin*, 528 S.W.3d 342 (2017)
Louisiana	Permitted	*State v. Miller*, 295 So. 3d 443 (La. Ct. App. 2020)
Maine	Cannot require	*State v. Mitchell*, 390 A.2d 495 (Me. 1978)
Maryland	Cannot require	*Lyles v. State*, No. 1536, 2020 Md. App. LEXIS 1033 (App. Oct. 21, 2020)
Massachusetts	Cannot require	*Commonwealth v. Ronchi*, 491 Mass. 284 (2023)
Michigan	Permitted with limitations	*People v. McMillen*, No. 332089, 2017 Mich. App. LEXIS 1378 (Ct. App. Aug. 24, 2017); *People v. Coy*, 243 Mich. App. 283 (2000); *People v. Urban*, 504 Mich. 950 (2019)
Minnesota	Permitted	*State v. Dixon*, 822 N.W.2d 664 (Minn. Ct. App. 2012); *Pfeiffer ex rel. Pfeiffer v. Allina Health Sys.*, 851 N.W.2d 626 (Minn. App. 2014); *Lanoue v. Better Water Indus., Inc.*, No. A17-1963, 2018 Minn. App. Unpub. LEXIS 460 (June 4, 2018)
Mississippi	Likely required	*Willie v. State*, 274 So.3d 934 (Miss. App. 2018); *Easterling v. Mississippi*, 306 So.3d 808 (2020); *Thomas v. State*, 249 So.3d 331 (Miss. 2018)
Missouri	Cannot require	*State v. Buchli*, 152 S.W.3d 289 (Mo. Ct. App. 2004); *State v. Bowman*, 337 S.W.3d 679 (Mo. 2011)
Montana	Permitted	*State v. Ingraham*, 290 Mont. 18 (1998)
Nebraska	Sometimes required	*State v. Koch*, No. A-15-959, 2016 Neb. App. LEXIS 102 (Ct. App. May 24, 2016); *Ewers v. Saunders Cty.*, 298 Neb. 944 (2018)
Nevada	Permitted	*Las Vegas Metro. Police Dep't v. Yeghiazarian*, 129 Nev. 760 (2013)

Continued

Table 7.1 *Continued*

State	Required/Permitted	Citation
New Hampshire	Permitted	*State v. Decato*, 165 N.H. 294 (2013)
New Jersey	Cannot require	*State v. Howard-French*, 259 A.3d 322 (N.J. Super. Ct. App. Div. 2021); *State v. Penix*, No. A-0265-20, 2022 N.J. Super. Unpub. LEXIS 1093 (Super. Ct. App. Div. June 21, 2022)
New Mexico	Permitted	*State v. Chavez*, 2020 N.M. Unpub. LEXIS 2; *State v. Lovett*, 286 P.3d 265 (N.M. 2012)
New York	Permitted	*People v. John*, 27 N.Y.3d 294 (2016)
North Carolina	Permitted	*State v. Brennan*, 203 N.C. App. 698 (2010)
North Dakota	Permitted	*Gaddie v. Barrera (In re Barrera)*, 744 N.W.2d 744 (N.D. 2008)
Ohio	Cannot require	*State v. Benner*, 533 N.E.2d 701, 535 N.E.2d 315 (Ohio 1988); *Stinson v. England*, 633 N.E.2d 532 (Ohio 1994); *State v. Thompson*, 23 N.E.3d 1096 (Ohio 2014); *State v. Westley*, 2017-Ohio-7717 (Ct. App.); *State v. Fannon*, 2018-Ohio-5242 (Ct. App.)
Oklahoma	Permitted	*Taylor v. State*, 889 P.2d 319 (Okla. Crim. App. 1995)
Oregon	Permitted	*Interstate Roofing, Inc. v. Springville Corp.*, 221 Or. App. 604 (2008)
Pennsylvania	Permitted	*Commonwealth v. Brooks*, 122 A.3d 1120 (Pa. Super. Ct. 2015); *Commonwealth v. Stallworth*, 566 Pa. 349 (2001)
Rhode Island	Cannot require	*State v. Howard*, No. K1-2017-0564A, 2020 R.I. Super. LEXIS 14 (Super. Ct. Feb. 17, 2020); *State v. Bertram*, 591 A.2d 14 (R.I. 1991)
South Carolina	Permitted	*State v. Bell*, 430 S.C. 449 (Ct. App. 2020)
South Dakota	Permitted	*State v. McDonald*, 421 N.W.2d 492 (S.D. 1988)
Tennessee	Cannot require	*State v. Shaffighi*, No. E2022-00525-CCA-R3-CD, 2023 Tenn. Crim. App. LEXIS 502 (Crim. App. Dec. 15, 2023)
Texas	Permitted	*Alvarez v. State*, No. 04–17-00449-CR, 2018 Tex. App. LEXIS 5945 (Tex. App. Aug. 1, 2018)

State	Required/Permitted	Citation
Utah	Permitted	*State v. Miller*, 740 P.2d 1363 (Utah Ct. App. 1987)
Vermont	Permitted	*State v. Tester*, 185 Vt. 241 (2009)
Virginia	Permitted	*Castillo v. Commonwealth*, 70 Va. App. 394 (2019); *Thorpe v. Commonwealth*, 223 Va. 609 (1982)
Washington	Permitted	*State v. Mitchell*, 997 P.2d 373 (Wash. Ct. App. 2000); *State v. Atsbeha*, 16 P.3d 626 (Wash. 2001); *State v. Crute*, No. 50366-2-II, 2019 Wash. App. LEXIS 390 (Ct. App. Feb. 20, 2019)
West Virginia	Likely required	*State v. Wakefield*, 236 W. Va. 445 (2015); *State ex rel. Boggs v. Sallaz*, No. 18–1105, 2020 W. Va. LEXIS 407 (June 18, 2020); *State v. Stewart*, 228 W. Va. 406 (2011); *State v. Steele*, 359 S.E.2d 558 (W. Va. 1987)
Wisconsin	Permitted	*State v. Miller*, No. 2022AP1755-CR, 2023 Wisc. App. LEXIS 1296 (Ct. App. Dec. 13, 2023); *State v. Wind*, 208 N.W.2d 357 (Wis. 1973); *State v. Stank*, 708 N.W.2d 43 (Wis. Ct. App. 2005)
Wyoming	Permitted	*Anderson v. State*, 317 P.3d 1108 (Wyo. 2014)

Several aspects of the Attorney General's statement are noteworthy. It instructs both those employed by the Department of Justice in forensic laboratories and prosecutors who work for the Department of Justice to no longer use RSC. It, however, leaves open the terminology's use if it is required by the judge or applicable law. Additionally, it should be noted that this directive does not apply to state-funded forensic laboratories, to attorneys employed by those states, or to most forensic mental health professionals who rarely work directly for the Department of Justice.

It is likely, however, that the NCFS's report and the U.S. Attorney General's adoption of those recommendations will have far-reaching implications outside the Department of Justice because the NCFS report will serve as persuasive authority for attorneys and judges to reconsider this terminology in other situations and jurisdictions (Weiss & LaPorte, 2018). For example, in *J.H. v. Cruz* (2023), the United States District Court for the District of Tennessee prohibited a Tennessee Bureau of Investigations employee's report from using the phrase "within [or with] a reasonable degree of scientific certainty" (p. 12) with regard to his conclusions regarding DNA analysis. The court explicitly relied on both the NCFS report and the U.S. Attorney General's directive, concluding, "Due to the phrase's lack of precision and the likelihood of confusing the jury, the court holds that Fort, in presenting his testimony, may not use the phrase 'to a reasonable degree of scientific certainty'" (*J.H. v. Cruz*, 2023, p. 17). Other courts may well follow this example across a broad array of expert testimony, including those offered by mental health professional experts.

Most recently, FRE 702 (Testimony by Expert Witnesses) was revised to further instruct federal judges on proper application of their "gatekeeping" role in admitting expert testimony in court, and it also advised against the use of RSC by testifying experts (see generally Chapter 5 of this book). The commentary to revised FRE 702 explicitly states: "The amendment is especially pertinent to the testimony of forensic experts in both criminal and civil cases. Forensic experts should avoid assertions of absolute or one hundred percent certainty—or to a reasonable degree of scientific certainty—if the methodology is subjective and thus potentially subject to error" (Advisory Committee Notes, FRE 702, 2023). This statement is a further indication that experts employing the term "reasonable scientific certainty" will face significant scrutiny in the admissibility of their testimony and may have their testimony not admitted at trial. Yet, as noted in previous chapters, only federal courts are bound the FRE, and even in state jurisdictions that have adopted FRE 702, the advisory committee notes are instructive but not definitive to state courts' interpretation of the rule.

Going Forward: Mental Health Experts and "Reasonable Psychological Certainty"

In addition to the other noted problems with RSC, Melton et al. (2018) highlight that it often turns a probabilistic statement by a mental professional expert into a legal fact. When experts use this phrase, they are no longer testifying about what *may* be true but rather opining about what they are *certain* is true. This provides a heightened level of confidence with the expert opinion that is often not supported by the science underlying the statement. As such, it raises clear ethical concerns regarding an expert's use of RSC and the likelihood such statements will result in misuse, misunderstanding, and an inappropriate level of confidence in the expert's judgment by legal actors. Clearly, RSC has the potential to confuse or mislead the trier of fact in a legal proceeding, although to date no empirical study has directly examined this issue (Weiss & LaPorte, 2018).

Some commentators have suggested that many of the issues associated with the phrase would be resolved if it was specifically defined as equivalent to "clear and convincing evidence" and uniformly applied by courts and mental health experts (Fox et al., 2022). This assumes that judges, jurors, and mental health experts have a consensual definition of "clear and convincing evidence" that they can uniformly apply to RSC. Unfortunately, research on lay understanding of the "clear and convincing evidence" standard suggests this proposal's assumptions are dubious. For example, in one simulated SVP trial, 274 jury-eligible individuals demonstrated limited ability to consistently understand and apply "clear and convincing evidence" as a standard of proof (Krauss & Scurich, 2014). These jurors showed wide and significant individual variations in the probabilities they associated with their own "clear and convincing" certainty estimates, nonsignificant mean differences in their confidence estimates when compared to jurors who received a "beyond a reasonable doubt" standard (clear and convincing $M = 82.6\%$; beyond a reasonable doubt $M = 83.4\%$), and no significant difference in eventual verdicts regardless of the standard of proof they received in the case. As a result, there seems to be little reason to believe that equating RSC to the more commonly used "clear and convincing evidence" standard will ameliorate the problems with the former's vague definition, inexact application, and potential for misunderstanding.

Given its unusual origination, development, and evolution, it appears more appropriate to side with the NCFS report, the advisory committee notes to FRE 702, and U.S. Attorney General's directive and remove this phrase from its continued use by mental health experts. There is nothing unique or special about this phrase, and it is not required for expert admissibility in *Frye* jurisdictions and is explicitly now advised against in those that follow the newly adopted FRE 702 (i.e., many *Daubert* jurisdictions) (Advisory Committee Notes, FRE 702, 2023; NCFS, 2016). RSC's continued use seems to be more a result of its commonplace usage by attorneys, judges, and experts with little thought to how it might confuse rather than clarify issues.

How then should mental health professional experts proceed when directed to use this phrase? Oftentimes, simply explaining the difficulties with RSC will lead attorneys to reconsider its use as well as investigating whether it is actually required by legal authority rather than just commonly employed in legal proceedings. Hopefully, this additional scrutiny will lead to RSC's wholescale removal or replacement in mental health professionals' expert testimony.

How should an expert proceed in a jurisdiction that requires it or when a judge demands the use of RSC? Based on APA's Ethics Standard 1.02, it would seem prudent for the mental health professional expert to detail the many problems associated with the terminology, especially those raised in the NCFS report and those highlighted by other critiques. Given RSC's potential for confusion, misunderstanding, and prejudice as well as the importance of the legal interests often at stake in proceedings where it is employed, the expert should further state that several professional ethical guidelines caution against such definitive statements without clearer guidance. Some direction on RSC's use might be available in case law in the particular jurisdiction, but that appears less than likely for many areas of mental health expert testimony (e.g., SVP evaluations; Fox et al., 2022). At that point, the mental health expert can ask or determine if the court or judge is willing to provide sufficient guidance that would resolve the ethical issues for the expert raised in this section. If this is not done to the expert's satisfaction, they can choose to refrain from testifying using this phrase until courts are willing to provide further direction. This will hopefully motivate courts from continuing to employ this archaic and problematic terminology. Another option in this scenario is for the expert to provide their own definition of the phrase. For example, the expert could state that they equate RSC with an evaluation that was conducted using recognized best practices in the field of forensic mental health assessment.

"Ultimate Issue" Expert Testimony

In addition to the controversy associated with use of the phrase RSC, there are legal and ethical debates about whether mental health professionals can testify to the "ultimate issue" in a particular case. In other words, should experts be permitted to conclude dispositively whether the legal standard at issue in a dispute is met or unmet? For example, *can* and *should* a mental health expert testify to whether a defendant is "sane," "incompetent to stand trial," or "committable," or whether one specific custodial arrangement would be in the "best interest of a child" in a custody dispute (Melton et al., 2018)? Similar to our previous discussion, what the law allows and what professional ethics suggest can come into conflict in these matters.

Several issues lie at the heart of this debate. First, there is a concern that opinions on the legal "ultimate issues" lie outside the expertise of mental health professionals; that is, "such opinions are founded on analysis that involves social and moral policy in addition to clinical data and therefore are outside the prefecture of scientific inquiry" (Dvoskin & Guy, 2008, p. 211). These opinions fundamentally require moral, normative, or legal judgments that are not based in science, and mental health experts do not possess any specific training or expertise in determining such issues. For example, the exact point at which criminal defendants should be found not culpable for their crime due to a mental illness based upon a legally created definition of insanity is not a psychiatric or psychological decision, but rather a moral one.

Second, the legal field is concerned that the trier of fact may be adversely or unduly affected by such expert opinions, and that the trier of fact will not independently evaluate, assess, and analyze other evidence in these matters to reach their own conclusions (Slobogin, 1989). The American Psychiatric Association summarized these concerns aptly in discussing the insanity defense:

> When . . . 'ultimate issue' questions are formulated by the law and put to the expert witness who then must say 'yea' or 'nay', then the expert witness is required to make a leap of logic. He no longer addresses himself to medical concepts but instead must infer or intuit what is in fact unspeakable, namely, the *probable relationship* between medical concepts and legal or moral constructs. . . . These impermissible leaps in logic made by the expert witnesses confuse the jury. (American Psychiatric Association, Statement on the Insanity Defense, 1983, p. 681)

How the law has regulated this controversy has changed over time with the insanity defense being singled out for idiosyncratic treatment (Melton et al., 2018).

Legal History of "Ultimate Issue" Expert Testimony

From the latter half of the 19th century to the first half of the 20th century, courts generally did not allow expert testimony on the "ultimate issue" in legal cases (Braswell, 1987). Although the exact published origin of the rule is somewhat unclear, it appears to have originated in a Vermont Supreme Court case, *Davis v. Fuller* (1840). In that case, an expert's opinion on what created a backwater in a river was prohibited by the court because it answered the ultimate question in the case, and thus "usurped" or "invaded" the province of the jury (Cohen, 1988, p. 543). This is the same rationale that the Illinois Supreme Court used to prohibit expert testimony in *Fellows-Kimbrough v. Chicago City* (1916) discussed earlier in this chapter. In that case, a medical expert was explicit in testifying to what "caused" the plaintiff's injury instead of using less definitive language such as "may have caused" or "could have caused" (Lewin, 1998). It was not until the 1930s and 1940s that many jurisdictions began questioning the "ultimate issue" rule. They often determined that such expert opinions could aid the jury because jurors could still independently evaluate the credibility of experts and decide to accept or reject experts' conclusions (Braswell, 1987; Cohen, 1988).

By the 1960s, the majority of U.S. courts had rejected the "ultimate issue" rule for experts, with it being explicitly abolished in federal courts by the 1975 passage and adoption of the FRE (Advisory Committee Notes, Federal Rule of Evidence 704, 1975; Braswell, 1987). The FRE were generally viewed as more favorable toward the admissibility of evidence, assuming that the trier of fact could evaluate the quality of evidence and that common adversarial procedures (i.e., cross-examination, competing experts, judicial instructions) would aid them in making such evaluations (Krauss et al., 2009). The initial version of FRE 704 stated: "Testimony in the form of an opinion or inference otherwise admissible is not objectionable because it embraces an ultimate issue to be decided by the trier of fact" (Federal Rule of Evidence 704, 1975). The advisory committee notes to this rule highlighted that the prohibition on "ultimate issue" expert testimony limited useful information that the trier of fact might need in deciding the case, and that it was difficult for judges to apply the "ultimate issue" rule consistently (Advisory Committee Notes, Federal Rule of Evidence 704, 1975).

Yet the scope of this rule would change following the controversial trial of John Hinckley. Hinckley attempted to assassinate then-President Ronald Reagan in 1981, and he offered an insanity defense at trial. There was disagreement among the mental health experts involved in the case about Hinckley's psychiatric diagnosis and whether his resulting impairment rendered him not culpable for his actions under the federal insanity standard. Following Hinckley's acquittal on grounds that he was not guilty by reason of insanity and the substantial public outrage at the verdict, Congress enacted a number of changes to the federal insanity defense standard and FRE 704 (Braswell, 1987; Cohen, 1988). Beyond modifying the insanity standard's language, shifting the burden of proof to the defense, and adopting the "clear and convincing evidence" standard of proof in determining insanity, Congress was particularly concerned by the "battle of experts" in the Hinckley case and how the experts' divergent and confident opinions on insanity may have confused the jury. As a result, in 1984, the passage of the Insanity Defense Reform Act (IDRA) led FRE 704 to be modified so that it included two separate provisions. Rule 704 now reads:

> 704(a). Except as provided in subdivision (b), testimony in the form of an opinion or inference otherwise admissible is not objectionable because it embraces an ultimate issue to be decided by the trier of fact.
>
> 704(b). No expert witness testifying with respect to the mental state or condition of a defendant in a criminal case may state an opinion or inference as to whether the defendant did or did not have the mental state or condition constituting an element of the crime charged or of a defense thereto. Such ultimate issues are matters for the trier of fact alone.

This modified version of FRE 704 remains the current one applied by federal courts, with many state courts adopting a similar provision (e.g., Melton et al., 2018). However, the scope of these new provisions of Rule 704 and other legal interpretations related to "ultimate issue" expert testimony require further discussion.

Current Admissibility of "Ultimate Issue" Expert Testimony

What is notable about Rule 704 is that it specifically continues to allow "ultimate issue" expert testimony in most cases but prohibits its use in cases involving "mental state" or "condition constituting an element of the crime." While 704(b) was clearly intended to restrict definitive conclusions by experts about whether a defendant was "sane" or "insane" in federal insanity cases, if it were interpreted more broadly, it could provide limitations on mental health expert testimony outside these specific legal confines, such as in cases involving diminished capacity, sentencing, or other forensic issues (Braswell, 1987). Further, the prohibition contained in Rule 704(b) is limited to testimonial statements made by forensic mental professionals at trial. The United States Code specifically requires that reports in insanity cases include a conclusion regarding a defendant's "ultimate" sanity:

> (c) Psychiatric or Psychological Reports.—A psychiatric or psychological report ordered pursuant to this chapter shall be prepared by the examiner designated to conduct the psychiatric or psychological examination, shall be filed with the court with copies provided to the counsel for the person examined and to the attorney for the Government, and shall include—
>
> (1) the person's history and present symptoms;
> (2) a description of the psychiatric, psychological, and medical tests that were employed and their results;
> (3) the examiner's findings; and
> (4) the examiner's opinions as to diagnosis, prognosis, and—
>
> (B) if the examination is ordered under section 4242, *whether the person was insane at the time of the offense charged.* (18 USC §4247, emphasis added)

In other words, this statute does not bar and, in fact, seems to require a recommendation concerning insanity in the report completed by the forensic examiner, which is sent to the judge and attorneys in the case. Rule 704(b) only requires that the expert cannot offer such "ultimate issue" opinions in testimony at trial. This appears to suggest a much more limited prohibition on expressed "ultimate issue" testimony than was envisioned by the federal courts and Congress.

Yet, even if this bar is limited to testimonial "ultimate issue" expert testimony, what language, opinions, or statements from the expert does Rule 704 specifically prohibit? A strict interpretation of Rule 704(b) could limit the bar to expert testimony that specifically proffers an opinion concerning whether a defendant is "insane" or "sane." However, should it apply to what Slobogin (1989) refers to as the penultimate issue in a federal insanity trial—whether the defendant "at the time of the commission of the acts constituting the offense, the defendant, as a result of a severe mental disease or defect, was unable to appreciate the nature and quality or the wrongfulness of his acts" (18 USC § 17)? If a conclusion using this verbiage runs afoul of Rule 704(b), can attorneys, in questioning the expert, paraphrase the standard into language that resembles the legal standard but is not the "ultimate issue" in an insanity case? In other words, can an expert answer the question of whether "as a result of a mental illness the defendant had considerable difficulty understanding his acts were wrong"? In fact, Slobogin (1989) offered a hierarchy of possible levels of inference an expert could employ regarding insanity that speaks to whether the expert is addressing the "ultimate legal" issue:

1. application of meaning (perception) to a behavioral image (e.g., "he was wringing his hands")
2. perception of general mental state (e.g., "he appeared anxious")
3. "formulation" of the perception of general mental state to fit into theoretical constructs or the research literature and/or to synthesize observations (e.g., "his anxiety during the interview was consistent with a general obsession")
4. diagnosis (e.g., "his behavior on interview and reported history are consistent with a generalized anxiety disorder")
5. relationship of formulation or diagnosis to legally relevant behavior (e.g., "at the time of the offense, his anxiety was so overwhelming that he failed to reflect upon the consequences of his behavior")
6. elements of the ultimate legal issue (e.g., "although he was too anxious at the time of the offense to reflect upon the consequences of his behavior, he was aware of the wrongfulness of his acts")
7. ultimate legal issue (e.g., "he was sane at the time of the offense"). (Slobogin, 1998, p. 265)

Most courts would hold that levels 1 through 4 of such mental health expert testimony in an insanity trial would be allowed by Rule 704(b) and the "ultimate issue" rule, but greater controversy and interpretation surrounds the admittance of expert testimony at levels 5 through 7 (Melton et al., 2018). Courts and judges could easily disagree on what exactly constitutes "ultimate issue" testimony in such instances, and this judicial application and consistency concern is another reason the more general rule against "ultimate issue" expert testimony was initially abandoned (Cohen, 1988).

Further, although the FRE have been largely adopted by many state court jurisdictions, not every rule has been adopted or interpreted in the same manner as the federal ones, with considerable variation existing with regard to FRE

704(a) and 704(b) (e.g., Imwinkelried, 1994). As a result, it is necessary for forensic mental health professionals to be aware of whether the jurisdiction where they are testifying has adopted FRE 704(a) and 704(b), and if they have, what specific language and testimony by mental health professionals is prohibited and allowed by that jurisdiction's interpretation and precedence related to "ultimate issue" expert testimony (see Table 7.2 for state rules regarding ultimate opinion evidence).

Table 7.2 State Adoption of the Federal Rule Regarding Ultimate Opinion Evidence

State	Similarity to Federal Rules of Evidence	Citation
Alabama	None	Ala. R. Evid. 704
Alaska	704(a)	Alaska R. Evid. 704
Arizona	704(a) and (b)	Ariz. R. Evid. 704
Arkansas	704(a)	Ark. R. Evid. 704
California	704(a) and allows opinions regarding sanity	Cal. Evid. Code 805 Cal. Evid. Code 870
Colorado	704(a)	Colo. R. Evid. 704
Connecticut	704(a) and (b)	Conn R. Evid. 7–3
Delaware	704(a)	Del. R. Evid. 704
District of Columbia	704(a)	*Lampkins v. United States*, 401 A.2d 966 (D.C.1979) *Jackson v. United States*, 76 A.3d 920 (D.C. 2013)
Florida	704(a)	Fla. Stat. 90.703
Georgia	704(a) and (b)	Ga. Code 24-7-704
Hawaii	704(a)	Haw. Rev. Stat. 704
Idaho	704(a)	Idaho R. Evid. 704
Illinois	704(a)	Ill. R. Evid. 704
Indiana	704(a) and (b)	Ind. R. Evid. 704
Iowa	704(a)	Iowa R. Evid. 5.704
Kansas	704(a)	Kan. Stat. 60–456(d)
Kentucky	None	*Stringer v. Commonwealth*, 956 S.W.2d 883 (Ky. 1997)
Louisiana	704(a) and (b) (sort of)	La. Code Evid. Art. 704

Continued

Table 7.2 *Continued*

State	Similarity to Federal Rules of Evidence	Citation
Maine	704(a)	Me. R. Evid. 704
Maryland	704(a)	Md. R. Evid. 5–704
Massachusetts	704(a)	Mass. Guide to Evid. 704
Michigan	704(a)	Mich. R. Evid. 704
Minnesota	704(a)	Minn. R. Evid. 704
Mississippi	704(a)	Miss. R. Evid. 704
Missouri	704(a) and (b)	Mo. Rev. Stat. 490.065 (2)(3)
Montana	704(a)	Mont. R. Evid. 704
Nebraska	704(a)	Neb. Rev. Stat. 27–704
Nevada	704(a)	N.R.S. 50.295
New Hampshire	704(a)	N.H. R. Evid. 704 (and 2016 N.H. R. Evid Update Committee Note)
New Jersey	704(a)	N.J. R. Evid. 704
New Mexico	704(a)	N.M. R. Evid. 11–704
New York	704(a)	Guide to NY Evid. *Rule 7.01(3) Opinion of Expert Witness*
North Carolina	704(a)	N.C. Gen. Stat. 704
North Dakota	704(a)	N.D. R. Evid. 704
Ohio	704(a)	Ohio R. Evid. 704
Oklahoma	704(a)	Okla. Stat. tit. 12 Sec. 2704
Oregon	704(a)	ORS Sec. 40.420 Rule 704
Pennsylvania	704(a)	225 Pa. Code Sec. 704 (and Comments)
Rhode Island	704(a)	R.I. R. Evid. 704
South Carolina	704(a)	S.C. R. Evid. 704
South Dakota	704(a)	S.D. Codified Laws Sec. 19–19-704
Tennessee	704(a) and does not allow for opinions regarding sanity	Tenn. R. Evid. 704 (and Comments)
Texas	704(a)	Tex. R. Evid. 704
Utah	704(a) and (b)	Utah R. Evid. 704
Vermont	704(a)	Vt. R. Evid. 704

State	Similarity to Federal Rules of Evidence	Citation
Virginia	No (but allows for discussion of mental health and hypothetical impact)	Va. R. Sup. Ct. 2:704
Washington	704(a)	Wash. R. Evid. 704
West Virginia	704(a)	W.Va. R. Evid. 704
Wisconsin	704(a)	Wi. Stat. 907.04
Wyoming	704(a) and (b)	Wy. R. Evid. 704

Going Forward: Mental Health Experts and "Ultimate Issue" Testimony

The legal field has largely adopted a permissive stance toward "ultimate issue" expert testimony offered by mental health professionals across a wide variety of forensic areas. The only legal limitation on such testimony is the explicit language used by mental health professionals in their opinions during insanity trials (in federal courts). However, several scholarly commentators have argued for greater caution in proffering such expert opinions because it is not clear that mental health experts *should* be providing such testimony even if it is permitted by courts (e.g., Bonnie & Slobogin, 1981; Melton et al., 2018). Stephen Morse (1978), the most critical of these commentators, argues that mental health professionals should be treated as fact witnesses. Because they lack the necessary expertise and are likely to adversely affect the trier of facts decision-making, he contends that mental health professionals should be prohibited from expressing conclusions relevant to legal standards across a broad array of possible forensic outcomes (Morse, 1978). Morse posits that (1) the trier of fact is competent to make decisions regarding mental illness issues; (2) mental health legal cases involve primarily moral not scientific issues; (3) reliance on mental health experts encourages the law to pretend these moral decisions are scientific ones; and (4) mental health experts should more readily recognize their inability to address many of these questions based upon their scientific expertise (Morse, 1978).

Although not as critical, Melton et al. (2018) argue against treating mental health "ultimate issue" expert testimony on insanity differently than other areas of forensic testimony and practice. More specifically, they highlight that overreaching by experts in child custody proceedings is frequent. Common mental health expert testimony in this arena opines directly as to the "best interest of the child" in terms of a custodial arrangement, and it may be more problematic than "ultimate issue" testimony in insanity cases because of its limited scientific basis, likelihood of including personal values, and potential to confuse the trier of fact (Melton et al., 2018). In terms of the level of expert testimony inference they support with regard to addressing "ultimate issues" across forensic contexts, they specifically caution against offering expert testimony for any forensic area at level 7 of Slobogin's hierarchy. Additionally, they suggest that level 6 expert testimony may be problematic unless the expert sufficiently explains the legal terminology contained in the standard and how it is being interpreted by the expert in their opinion (Melton et al., 2018).

Other commentators' ethical advice concerning "ultimate issue" expert testimony focuses on the transparency of reasoning underlying the mental health expert's "ultimate" opinion. While not contending that such expert testimony should be banned per se, they suggest that "the basis of an expert's opinion should be communicated clearly to the trier of fact, which involves showing one's work and not asking the court to trust the expert blindly and take their word for it" (Dvoskin & Guy, 2008, p. 208). In other words, it is important for the expert to convey to the trier of fact exactly how the expert arrived at their final opinion regarding the legal standard. This testimony should include (1) what alternative hypotheses or conclusions the expert considered; (2) what evidence led the expert to reject those alternatives; and (3) what evidence led the expert to the conclusion they offered at trial. Testifying at this level of detail allows the juror or judge to rationally decide whether to accept or reject the expert's opinion as well as the evidence that serves as the basis of that "ultimate" conclusion (Dvoskin & Guy, 2008).

Taken together, these commentaries offer some useful ethical advice for mental health professionals who are considering testifying about "ultimate issues" in legal proceedings. First, the mere fact that the legal system does not prohibit experts from testifying concerning a forensic issue and offering an opinion on an "ultimate issue" does not mean that the expert *should* do so without further thought. Clearly, some legal regulations related to "ultimate issue" expert testimony are idiosyncratic and arbitrary, such as prohibiting "ultimate issue" expert testimony in federal insanity proceedings but not in other forensic areas and/or prohibiting testimonial "ultimate issue" expert testimony on insanity, but requiring it in forensic reports submitted to the federal courts.

Ethically, mental health professionals should consider whether the legal standard they are addressing and the conclusions they are offering are scientific ones or ones that rely to a greater degree on moral or normative judgments. The balance between these interests may vary by the legal standard being addressed, with some requiring greater leaps of logic, less scientific underpinnings to testimony, and greater likelihood of personal values affecting "ultimate" conclusions. For example, "ultimate issue" expert testimony about a specific custodial placement that will be in the best interest of a child during a custody proceeding is more likely to involve moral, normative, and personal judgments than scientific ones (e.g., Krauss & Sales, 2000).

Mental health professionals should also thoughtfully consider what level of "ultimate issue" expert testimony they are comfortable offering based upon Slobogin's (1989) hierarchy. This decision should be partially based upon (1) what level of testimony their jurisdiction allows and prohibits on "ultimate issues"; (2) how the jurisdiction defines and applies important legal terms relevant to addressing the "ultimate issue"; and (3) what guidance case law and precedent provides in understanding "ultimate issue" expert testimony in their jurisdiction. This determination, however, should also be based on ethical concerns related to the scientific basis of their opinions and conclusions (see EPPCC Standards 2.04 & 9.01; APA, 2017). Regardless, of the exact testimonial language the expert presents on the "ultimate issue," mental health professionals should also "show their work" concerning how they reached their eventual decision. This transparency will allow courts, judges, attorneys, and the trier of fact to determine for themselves how much weight to grant the expert's opinion in reaching their own "ultimate" determination. Additionally, such transparency will lessen the likelihood of the mental health professional's testimony being misused or misunderstood by legal actors (EPPCC Standard 1.02; APA, 2017).

Conclusion

The legal system has explicit rules that govern what mental health professionals can express in their role as experts to the courts. Yet legal regulation and requirements concerning the phrase "reasonable degree/level of scientific certainty" and legal prohibitions and allowances of expert testimony on "ultimate issues" have generated controversy and ethical conflict within the disciplines. These debates center on what mental health experts *can* and *should* say in testimony with regard to these issues. While the legal system allows and sometimes even requires experts to possess RSC for their expert testimony to be admissible at trial, the tide seems to be shifting against its use. Moreover, mental health professionals' ethical concerns argue against most instances of employing such confident language in conclusions. Such statements suggest a level of certainty to legal actors that is not based upon scientific knowledge or expertise, and they raise concerns that the expert's opinion will be misunderstood or misused in important decisions. These concerns have led to scientific recommendations to remove this phrase from expert testimony in a number of forensic areas. As a result, mental health experts should be cautious and thoughtful in using this phrase even when the phrase is encouraged or required by courts and other legal actors.

The legal field also currently allows mental health experts to offer "ultimate issue" expert testimony on a wide variety of forensic questions. There are, however, specific legal prohibitions (at the federal level and in states that have adopted a similar standard) against expert testimony related to a defendant's mental state due to concerns that this testimony in this specific area will unfairly influence jury decisions. Yet, even in instances where courts allow expert testimony on "ultimate issues" in forensic areas, mental health experts should be ethically thoughtful concerning the legal contexts in which they are willing to do so. Additionally, if mental health professionals decide to offer such conclusions, then these experts should be ethically cautious in what language they use to deliver their opinions, so they do not adversely affect legal decisions. Those that decide to offer such testimony must be willing to transparently provide the reasoning and evidence that led to their "ultimate" decision. This "showing of their work" will allow legal actors to make their own independent determinations about experts' opinions and allow them to reach their own legal decisions.

Chapter 8
Legal and Ethical Requirements and Considerations Relevant to Forensic Practice

The importance of legal and ethical guidance for mental health professionals has been clear since Milgram's 1963 study on obedience and Zimbardo's 1971 Stanford prison experiment (Haney et al., 1973). Although all mental health professionals are subject to some combination of laws, ethics codes, and professional guidelines that apply to research and practice, forensic mental health professionals often face unique ethical and legal challenges. For example, there are often questions relating to the various roles and relationships assumed by forensic mental health professionals, how to manage multiple roles and responsibilities, the applicability of confidentiality and its limits, and the operation of informed consent.

There are numerous books and chapters discussing the ethics of forensic psychology and forensic psychiatry (e.g., Bush et al., 2020; Griffith, 2018; Igoumenou, 2020; Jackson & Roesch, 2016; Melton et al., 2018; Otto et al., 2017; Pirelli et al., 2017). This chapter adds to the existing literature by synthesizing authorities by topic area, discussing guidance for both forensic psychiatrists and psychologists, and offering solutions for common ethical dilemmas in forensic practice. This chapter serves as a primer that provides a relatively broad discussion of several key topics under the umbrella of forensic ethics, but comprehensive coverage of all relevant topics is beyond the scope of the chapter. There are many important and timely ethical topics that would have been suitable for inclusion in this chapter, including test security and third-party observers, so we had to be selective in our coverage.[1] In the interest of brevity, this chapter focuses on select legal and ethical guidance as it applies to the practice of forensic psychology and forensic psychiatry. After discussing the professions of psychology and psychiatry, including training, licensure, and certification, this chapter provides a discussion of legal authority and persuasive guidance for forensic mental health professionals. We then discuss common ethical issues that arise in forensic practice, and we conclude with a discussion of expert witness liability and immunity.

Forensic Mental Health Practice and the Law. David DeMatteo, Daniel A. Krauss, Sarah Fishel, and Kellie Wiltsie, Oxford University Press. © Oxford University Press (2025). DOI: 10.1093/9780197686591.003.0008

Licensure and Certification

The pathways into forensic psychiatry and forensic psychology differ considerably. These nuances are discussed below.

Psychiatry

Although the field of psychiatry has existed in the United States since the late 1830s, the era of what we now know as forensic psychiatry began in 1969 with the creation of the American Academy of Psychiatry and Law (AAPL) (Sadoff, 2015). Prior to the creation of AAPL, there had been various forensic psychiatry departments at academic institutions, but no formal process for recognition or certification. For multiple decades, AAPL attempted to create uniform standards for the competent practice of forensic psychiatry, but these standards were not recognized nationally until the early 1990s (Frierson, 2020).

The practice of psychiatry in general is governed by state law (see Slobogin et al., 2020, for a useful discussion). In most states, any licensed physician, regardless of training, can practice psychiatry. However, as a practical matter, the practice of psychiatry is limited to those who have received specialized training in psychiatry. Most third-party payors restrict the practice of psychiatry to physicians who completed a psychiatric residency program approved by the American College of Graduate Medical Education (ACGME), and most hospitals only provide psychiatric treatment privileges to physicians who completed an accredited psychiatric residency (Slobogin et al., 2020).

To specialize in forensic psychiatry, students must complete medical school followed by a residency in psychiatry, which typically involves 4 years of supervised clinical practice. The psychiatric residency focuses on psychiatry-specific training, including psychopharmacology. The amount of exposure to forensic psychiatry that residents receive varies widely depending on the individual program (Sadoff, 2015). ACGME does not specify a required amount of time that residents must spend accruing forensic experience; rather, it specifies that residents "experience evaluating patients' potential to harm themselves or others, appropriateness for commitment, decisional capacity, disability, and competency" (ACGME, 2023, p. 29). ACGME first recognized forensic psychiatry as a subspecialty in the early 1990s (Frierson, 2020).

Following the first year of residency, residents take Part 3 of the United States Medical Licensing Examination (USMLE) and, after passing, can apply for medical licensure in the state in which they intend to practice. After completing their 4-year residency, psychiatrists who wish to become certified in forensic psychiatry must next complete a 1-year fellowship (Sadoff, 2015). There are currently 51 ACGME-accredited forensic psychiatry fellowships in the United States. Completion of a fellowship in forensic psychiatry is required for board certification by the American Board of Psychiatry and Neurology (ABPN) (Frierson, 2020). To become a board-certified forensic psychiatrist, applicants must first be board-certified in general psychiatry, complete a 1-year forensic psychiatry fellowship, and pass a board-certification examination. The ABPN board-certification examination is multiple choice, and the 2023 ABPN Annual Report reflects a 91% pass rate for those who took the forensic psychiatry initial certification examination (ABPN, 2023). Although becoming board certified is not a requirement per se for the practice of forensic psychiatry, many third-party payors use board certification as a criterion for determining which psychiatrists should be admitted to panels of clinicians that are authorized to receive reimbursement (Slobogin et al., 2020).

Psychology

Forensic psychologists who engage in clinical practice, such as the assessment and/or treatment of justice-involved individuals, must be licensed as psychologists. By contrast, forensic psychologists who exclusively conduct research are not required to be licensed because they do not provide direct clinical services. The two primary mechanisms that govern psychological practice are licensure and certification. Although both licensure and certification are designed to protect the public, the manner by which they accomplish that goal differs.

Licensure limits the performance of certain activities or the provision of certain services to a designated class of people, and it also limits the use of certain professional titles (e.g., psychologist) to those with the appropriate qualifications (Slobogin et al., 2020). States restrict the acquisition of a license to individuals who meet established qualifications. In contrast to the licensure model, some states utilize a certification model. Certification restricts the use of certain titles to individuals who meet the enumerated training and experience requirements in that jurisdiction (Slobogin et al., 2020). The key difference is that licensing limits *both* the performance of certain activities *and* the use of certain titles, while certification only limits the use of specific titles. For example, in certification states, individuals can engage in activities that may be typically associated with psychologists, such as counseling, without running afoul of state regulations as long as they do not refer to themselves as "psychologists." In some states, individuals with master's degrees are permitted to engage in the practice of psychology while under the direct supervision of a licensed psychologist. Similarly, it is common practice for graduate students seeking their doctoral degree in psychology to engage in activities typically reserved for psychologists; these individuals are viewed as operating under the license of their direct supervisor (Slobogin et al., 2020).

All 50 states currently require psychologists to be licensed by the state in which they intend to practice, and some states require both licensure and certification of psychologists (DeMatteo et al., 2020).[2] In addition, some states that only require licensure for psychologists (e.g., Massachusetts, Virginia) may have additional requirements for the practice of forensic psychology.[3] Generally, individuals are eligible to be licensed as psychologists if they earned a doctoral degree in psychology, amassed a sufficient number of supervised practice hours, passed the Examination for Professional Practice in Psychology (EPPP), and completed necessary procedural steps (e.g., paperwork, fees) (DeMatteo et al., 2020). The EPPP, which is a national licensing exam designed by the Association of State and Provincial Psychology Boards (ASPPB), consists of 225 multiple-choice questions covering eight topic domains relevant to psychological practice (Association of State and Provincial Psychology Boards, 2024).[4] In addition to the EPPP, some jurisdictions require individuals to pass a state-specific examination that covers state-specific laws governing the practice of psychology.[5]

As of 2024, 11 jurisdictions require individuals seeking to become licensed psychologists to have attended an APA-accredited doctoral program.[6] APA accreditation serves as a certification to state licensing boards that the educational program meets basic curriculum and training requirements. In addition to the requirements outlined above, some states require that an individual attend an APA-accredited internship (Slobogin et al., 2020). Once an individual has become a licensed psychologist, they must maintain their license in good standing. Licenses in psychology must be renewed on a regular basis (typically every 1–3 years, depending on the jurisdiction). License renewal often involves completing a minimum number of continuing education credits, with some states specifying a specific number of continuing education hours on specific topics (e.g., ethics, child abuse reporting) (DeMatteo et al., 2020).

Forensic psychologists interested in demonstrating heightened competence (beyond licensure) may seek board certification. There are various boards that offer certification for forensic psychologists, but the oldest and most respected is the American Board of Professional Psychology (ABPP) (DeMatteo et al., 2020).[7] ABPP was founded in 1947 and functions as the governing body of separately incorporated specialty examining boards (American Board of Professional Psychology, 2024).[8] Currently, there are 17 specialty boards and 1 subspecialty board. Each specialty board functions independently and, therefore, has separate requirements for certification (American Board of Professional Psychology, 2024).

ABPP has a specialty board for forensic psychology, which is the American Board of Forensic Psychology (ABFP). ABFP was established in 1978 with the goal of protecting the consumer of forensic psychological services by establishing, promoting, and revising the standards and qualifications for those who practice forensic psychology (American Board of Forensic Psychology, 2021). There are several steps to becoming board certified by ABFP, including application and credential review for ABPP and the specialty-specific requirements for ABFP, passing a written examination, submitting two practice samples, and passing an oral examination (American Board of Forensic Psychology, 2021).

Unlike some other professions, board certification in psychology is voluntary, and only a small percentage of licensed psychologists (3–4%) are board certified by ABPP (Khaddouma, 2023; Page et al., 2024). With that said, some employers (e.g., Veteran's Affairs) provide a salary increase for psychologists who are board certified by ABPP, and other employers (e.g., Federal Bureau of Prisons) encourage board certification. There are multiple benefits to becoming board certified, such as being distinguished on the job market, enhanced licensure mobility, and access to resources for referrals and networking. The next section discusses the sources of authority and guidance that forensic mental health professionals should be aware of to engage in competent and ethical practice.

Sources of Authority and Guidance

Forensic mental health professionals' work, whether clinical, research, or consulting, is shaped by a variety of sources, including laws, professional ethics codes, and specialty guidelines. It is important to note the key difference among sources of authority and guidance. Laws are binding authority that must be followed to avoid exposure to potential liability. In contrast, ethics codes may or may not be binding on psychologists (depending on the jurisdiction), and practice guidelines are typically aspirational in nature, constitute "best practices" in the field, and are (typically) not legally enforceable.

In 2015, the American Psychological Association (APA) published guidance for psychologists on the difference between guidelines and standards:

> *Guidelines* differ from *standards*. *Standards* are mandatory and, thus, may be accompanied by an enforcement mechanism; *guidelines* are not mandatory, definitive, or exhaustive. *Guidelines* are aspirational in intent. They aim to facilitate the continued systematic development of the profession and to promote a high level of professional practice by psychologists. A particular set of *guidelines* may not apply to every professional and clinical situation within the scope

> of that set of guidelines. As a result, *guidelines* are not intended to take precedence over the professional judgments of psychologists that are based on the scientific and professional knowledge of the field. (p. 824)

However, several courts, licensing boards, and employers may incorporate practice guidelines into statutes, regulations, or standards of practice, which effectively establishes an *enforceable* standard of care based on an *aspirational* set of guidelines (Otto, 2023). Regardless of whether the source is binding or aspirational, competent practice requires mental health professionals to be familiar with relevant sources of authority (Otto, 2023). The next few sections will discuss each of the sources of authority and guidance.

Laws and Regulations

The laws that govern forensic practice are varied and depend on a number of factors, including the jurisdiction, the legal topic(s) at issue, and the specialty area (e.g., clinical, research) in which the professional is working. Laws are an example of binding authority, which providers *must* be aware of and follow. Awareness is important because ignorance is not a valid defense to violating a law.[9] Examples of the types of laws that forensic mental health professionals should be aware of include federal and state codes (e.g., Federal Rules of Evidence, Pennsylvania Code), relevant case law from the Supreme Court of the United States, and relevant federal and state case law. If federal and state law conflict on a particular topic, federal law typically preempts state law.[10]

Laws are specific to each jurisdiction, and it is imperative for a forensic mental health professional to understand which jurisdiction they are practicing in to ensure they are conforming their conduct appropriately. For example, a forensic mental health professional practicing in Philadelphia, Pennsylvania, could be subject to both state and federal law, including the Pennsylvania Code, case law from the Supreme Court of the United States, and case law from both the Pennsylvania Supreme Court and the United States Court of Appeals for the Third Circuit. A Philadelphia-based psychologist may be hired to serve as an expert witness or consultant on cases that are taking place in a Pennsylvania state court *or* the federal jurisdiction that "sits" in that geographic portion of Pennsylvania. Therefore, the forensic psychologist must be familiar with both state and federal laws if they intend to take cases from both jurisdictions. Differences in laws in these jurisdictions may include the rules of evidence governing expert testimony, or definitions of key legal and psychological concepts, such as insanity or intellectual disability (Otto, 2023). Of note, forensic mental health professionals who are operating in a clinical role are subject both to the laws governing nonforensic clinical practice (e.g., mandated reporting laws) and laws specific to working with individuals involved in the justice system.

For forensic psychologists and psychiatrists, both clinical and consulting practice are also governed by state licensing boards. State boards enact regulations that govern the behavior of psychologists in that state, and boards can impose sanctions on psychologists who violate these administrative regulations, although there are limits on the sanctions a psychologist can receive (Otto, 2023). For example, state licensing boards can impose fines and restrict the ability of a psychologist to practice in that state (DeMatteo et al., 2020).

In addition to the laws that impact forensic clinical and consulting practice, there are a variety of laws that govern forensic research.[11] Importantly, the Code of Federal Regulations requires that prisoners and other vulnerable populations (e.g., children, individuals with impaired decision-making capacity) be given special consideration in research due to concerns about exploitation and coercion. The category of "prisoners" is defined broadly to include individuals who are involuntarily confined or detained, which includes individuals who are court-mandated to correctional, psychiatric, residential, or treatment settings (Pirelli et al., 2017; Protection of Human Subjects, 2009). Research participants may also be considered vulnerable based on other factors, including some specific to the individual (e.g., individuals with intellectual disabilities) or the setting (e.g., state hospital) (Pirelli et al., 2017). This is an important consideration for forensic practitioners because individuals with either intrinsic or extrinsic vulnerability factors tend to be overrepresented in forensic settings compared to the general population (Chen et al., 2011). Thus, forensic researchers seeking to conduct studies that include or impact these groups must be aware of the laws that govern their research and understand how to mitigate the risk to these populations by working with their institutional review board (IRB).

Professional Ethics Codes

Professional ethics codes represent another form of binding legal authority (in many jurisdictions, but not all), as many ethics codes have been integrated into state law.

Psychiatry

In 1973, the American Psychiatric Association (ApA) published the first ethics code specific to the practice of psychiatry: *The Principles of Medical Ethics with Annotations Especially Applicable to Psychiatry* (American Psychiatric Association, 2013). Prior to 1973, psychiatrists were governed by the ethics code published by the American Medical Association (AMA), with its inception dating back to 1847. However, ApA published its own ethics code because the AMA's guidelines were difficult to interpret for psychiatrists. Specifically, ApA notes that "while psychiatrists have the same goals as all physicians, there are special ethical problems in psychiatric practice that differ in coloring and degree from ethical problems in other branches of medical practice, even though the basic principles are the same" (American Psychiatric Association, 2013, pp. 1–2). ApA also states that all members of the association are bound by *The Principles of Medical Ethics with Annotations Especially Applicable to Psychiatry*, which incorporates the AMA ethics code (American Psychiatric Association, 2013).

The ApA ethics code includes annotations to the nine sections of the AMA ethics code, and it has been updated 18 times since its original edition in 1973 (American Psychiatric Association, 2013). The code covers competent practice (including respect for human dignity and rights), professionalism, respect for the law, confidentiality and privacy, continuing education, physician autonomy, improving the community, responsibility to the patient, and access to medical care. The annotated ethics code does not directly reference the practice of forensic psychiatry, but many subsections address topics relevant to forensic psychiatry, including limits of confidentiality and involuntary treatment (American Psychiatric Association, 2013). Forensic psychiatrists are often encouraged to utilize the AAPL's specialty-specific ethics guidelines, which will be discussed in a later section (Candilis et al., 2014).

Psychology

The American Psychological Association (APA) was established in 1892 and is the only U.S.-based broad membership organization of psychologists that has published an ethics code (Otto, 2023). The APA Committee on Ethical Standards for Psychologists, which was convened in 1947, solicited practicing psychologists to describe morally and ethically challenging scenarios they had personally experienced or were otherwise made aware of (Pirelli et al., 2017). The APA ethics code, known as the *Ethical Principles of Psychologists and Code of Conduct* (EPPCC),[12] was published in 1953 and has been amended multiple times, with its most recent amendment occurring in 2017 (American Psychological Association, 2017). The initial version of the EPPCC consisted of solely aspirational principles and case studies, but it shifted in 1992 to providing both aspirational guidelines and enforceable standards (Pirelli et al., 2017). The EPPCC consists of a preamble, general principles, and ethical standards. The general principles are the aspirational portion, while the ethical standards are the more specific and enforceable rules that address several domains, including competence, human relations while functioning a professional role, privacy and confidentiality, public statements, recordkeeping and fees, education and training, research and publication, assessment, and therapy (American Psychological Association, 2017).

The EPPCC governs the practice of psychologists regardless of the type of services they are providing. As a condition of membership, psychologists affiliated with the APA are bound by the EPPCC, which means they can be sanctioned if they deviate from the principles outlined in the ethics code. Sanctions can include a reprimand, censure, expulsion from APA, or required resignation from APA (DeMatteo et al., 2020). However, psychologists are not required by law to be members of APA. So, what ethics code applies to psychologists who are not affiliated with the APA? Fisher's (2017) analysis of jurisdictions in the United States estimated that over half of the psychology practice acts directly reference the EPPCC and require licensed psychologists to abide by the code. This means that although psychologists are not required to be members of APA and therefore may not be subject to the EPPCC via that membership, they are still bound by the ethics code via licensure if they are licensed in a state that has adopted the EPPCC through state regulation.

The EPPCC purports to be intentionally vague so as to apply to a variety of situations and a broad range of activities in which psychologists may engage (Pirelli et al., 2017). However, the EPPCC's broad focus and lack of specificity also represent its greatest weakness in that it can often be too vague, confusing, or inconsistent when psychologists attempt to apply the standards to their daily practice (Otto, 2023). Another major criticism of the EPPCC is that it focuses heavily on the obligations of psychologists who are providing therapeutic clinical services, as opposed to psychologists who provide services that are clinical but not therapeutic (e.g., forensic assessment) (Otto, 2023). Therapeutic and forensic services differ (and outright conflict) in many ways (see Chapter 2), and this gap in guidance by the EPPCC left forensic psychologists in search of "best practice" guidance.

Specialty Guidelines

The lack of specific application to forensic practice in the ethics codes for psychology and psychiatry prompted discussion about the need for best-practice guidance in forensic psychology. Historically, best practices in forensic psychology and forensic psychiatry were established through a review of the professional literature (Otto, 2023). Professionals could also consult directly with acknowledged experts on a particular topic. However, the early 2000s saw a shift toward the creation of practice guidelines that are (typically) sponsored by an organization with a specialty in the field. The sponsoring organization would empanel a group of experts to publish aspirational guidelines that represent competent practice with a specific population, activity, or condition (Otto, 2023).[13]

Ethics Guidelines for the Practice of Forensic Psychiatry

In forensic psychiatry, the leading guidance is the AAPL *Ethics Guidelines for the Practice of Forensic Psychiatry* (AAPL, 2005). These guidelines were initially developed in 1987 and revised in 2005. The AAPL notes that it is an organization dedicated to the "highest standards of practice in forensic psychiatry," which alludes to the guidelines' aspirational nature (AAPL, 2005, p. 1). The guidelines also note that they are meant as a supplement to *The Principles of Medical Ethics with Annotations Especially Applicable to Psychiatry* (American Psychiatric Association, 2013). The guidelines address five main (limited) topic areas: confidentiality, consent, honesty and striving for objectivity, qualifications, and procedures for handling complaints of unethical conduct (AAPL, 2005). The last section reiterates that the AAPL does not adjudicate ethics complaints, and that all ethics complaints must be handled by the American Psychiatric Association or state licensing board.

In a commentary on how the AAPL's aspirational guidelines and the binding professional ethics code for psychiatrists work in conjunction, Candilis et al. (2014) argue that the ApA ethics code does not adequately encompass ethical dilemmas that arise in forensic psychiatry practice. Further, Candilis et al. (2014) argue that while rendering the AAPL aspirational guidelines entirely enforceable would cause more problems than it solves, more integration of the subspecialty into the professional ethics code is needed to adequately protect both forensic psychiatrists as well as those filing complaints against psychiatrists with the ethics board.

Specialty Guidelines for Forensic Psychology

In forensic psychology, the leading source of guidance is the *Specialty Guidelines for Forensic Psychology* (SGFP) (American Psychological Association, 2013).[14] Although the subspecialty of forensic psychology was first recognized by the APA in 2001, the *Specialty Guidelines for Forensic Psychologists* were initially published in 1991, with an updated revision published in 2013. The goals of the SGFP are to "improve the quality of forensic psychological services; enhance the practice and facilitate the development of forensic psychology; encourage a high level of quality in professional practice; and encourage forensic practitioners to respect the rights of those they serve" (American Psychological Association, 2013, p. 7). Of note, the SGFP are APA-approved guidelines that are intended to be national in scope and consistent with state and federal law (American Psychological Association, 2013).[15] The SGFP address 11 topic areas: responsibilities; competence; diligence; relationship; fees; informed consent, notification, and assent; conflicts in practice; privacy, confidentiality, and privilege; methods and procedures; assessment; and professional and other public communications (American Psychological Association, 2013).

As guidelines, the SGFP were intended to provide aspirational, rather than enforceable, guidance for the practice of forensic psychology. The SGFP specifically state that they "are not intended to serve as a basis for disciplinary action or civil or criminal liability" (American Psychological Association, 2013, p. 8). However, some states (e.g., Pennsylvania) have adopted the SGFP into state law, which means that psychologists in those jurisdictions may be held legally responsible if they fail to adhere to the SGFP requirements (DeMatteo et al., 2020). Although it is desirable to want psychologists to serve the public using best practices, there are significant concerns that arise with psychologists being required to adhere to aspirational guidelines. Specifically, enforcement of aspirational guidelines could result in inconsistent and confusing application by the courts, leaving psychologists to question what conduct will subject them to liability. Further, because the authors of the aspirational guidelines did not contemplate their use as the foundation for disciplinary action, the guidelines do not provide guidance on proper and proportionate disciplinary sanctions. To date, there has been no case law that specifically raises the question of whether a psychologist can be held liable for violating the SGFP if their conduct does not violate the EPPCC.

In sum, when forensic mental health professionals are determining how to interpret and incorporate practice guidance into their professional practice, they should first turn to the laws and enforceable ethics codes in their jurisdiction. However, as noted above, there are multiple circumstances in which the professional ethics codes may leave practitioners confused or in need of more guidance. At that point, forensic mental health professionals should consult relevant specialty-specific practice guidelines. When deciding which practice guidelines to consult, forensic mental health professionals should first look at the process in which an organization develops and adopts these documents, including the stated need for the proposed guidelines, opportunity for comment, and formal peer review (Otto, 2023). Competent forensic mental health professionals will not only familiarize themselves with the relevant laws in their jurisdiction and professional ethics codes but also "best practice" guidance in the form of practice guidelines for their specific topic areas and specialties.

Common Ethical Issues

Forensic mental health professionals are often faced with ethical dilemmas, including challenging conflicts among the demands of the law, ethics codes, and practice guidelines. This section addresses key ethical considerations and common issues that arise for forensic mental health professionals in the clinical, consulting, and research domains, including the nature of the relationship, multiple roles, confidentiality, objectivity, and informed consent.

Nature of the Relationship

In most cases, professionals providing forensic services owe duties to multiple people, including their employer (e.g., prison, state hospital), the individual they are evaluating or treating, and the individual or organization that retains them (e.g., attorney, court). The duty that a forensic mental health professional owes to each of these individuals or entities depends on the nature of the relationship and the role played by the forensic mental health professional. As mentioned previously, most clinical services that mental health professionals provide are therapeutic in nature. However, when working in forensic contexts, mental health professionals may not be assuming a therapeutic role.

In forensic mental health assessment contexts, for example, the assessment is typically requested or initiated by a third party (e.g., attorney, court). Unlike traditional therapy, the person being assessed may or may not be participating voluntarily in the evaluation and confidentiality is limited. Further, the goal of the evaluation is not to improve the well-being of the individual being evaluated, but to provide information to a third party (Otto, 2023). The first step in avoiding confusion surrounding multiple relationships is to appropriately label the individuals involved. Specifically, the person undergoing the evaluation should be viewed by the forensic mental health professional as an *examinee* rather than as a client. *The Principles of Medical Ethics with Annotations Especially Applicable to Psychiatry* does not describe the issue of role clarification with the retaining third party directly (American Psychiatric Association, 2013). However, Section 2 states that "psychiatric services, like all medical services, are dispensed in the context of a contractual arrangement between the patient and the treating physician. The provisions of the contractual agreement, which are binding on the physician as well as on the patient, should be explicitly established" (American Psychiatric Association, 2013, p. 3).

Although a psychologist still owes an examinee many duties, including respect, competence, and privacy, they are not the same duties that would be owed to a client in a typical therapist–client relationship. This concern about multiple relationships is reflected in EPPCC Standard 3.07:

> When psychologists agree to provide services to a person or entity at the request of a third party, psychologists attempt to clarify at the outset of the service the nature of the relationship with all individuals or organizations involved. This clarification includes the role of the psychologist (e.g., therapist, consultant, diagnostician, or expert witness), an identification of who is the client, the probable uses of the services provided or the information obtained, and the fact that there may be limits to confidentiality. (American Psychological Association, 2017, p. 6)

The SGFP also recommend that psychologists clarify their role and the nature and extent of services (American Psychological Association, 2013). Specifically, Guideline 6 states that "forensic practitioners strive to inform service recipients about the nature and parameters of the services to be provided" (American Psychological Association, 2013, p. 12).

Multiple Roles

In addition to the importance of clarifying roles at the outset of a professional relationship, forensic mental health professionals should seek to avoid mixing the roles of treatment provider and forensic examiner (Heilbrun, 2001). This role conflict may arise for multiple reasons, including a belief that the treating provider knows the individual best and would therefore be best suited to act as the evaluator, money-saving efforts, or lack of access to forensic mental health professions in the geographic area (Pirelli et al., 2017).

The Principles of Medical Ethics with Annotations Especially Applicable to Psychiatry does not address the difference between the role of a treating psychiatrist and a psychiatrist performing a forensic evaluation (American Psychiatric Association, 2013). However, the AAPL *Ethics Guidelines for the Practice of Forensic Psychiatry* explicitly states: "Psychiatrists who take on a forensic role for patients they are treating may adversely affect the therapeutic relationship with them. . . . Treating psychiatrists should therefore generally avoid acting as an expert witness for their patients or performing evaluations of their patients for legal purposes" (AAPL, 2005, p. 3).

For psychologists, Guideline 4.02.01 of the SGFP states that "providing forensic and therapeutic psychological services to the same individual or closely related individuals involves multiple relationships that may impair objectivity and/or cause exploitation or other harm" (American Psychological Association,

2013, p. 11). Additionally, although the EPPCC does not define multiple relationships as they apply in forensic contexts, Standard 3.05 prohibits multiple relationships that "could reasonably be expected to impair the psychologist's objectivity, competence, or effectiveness in performing his or her functions as a psychologist, or otherwise risks exploitation or harm to the person with whom the professional relationship exists" (American Psychological Association, 2017, p. 6).

Another matter involving multiple roles includes mixing the roles of forensic examiner and consultant. In the role of a forensic examiner, the fact finder expects that an expert witness will provide accurate, balanced, and unbiased testimony (Heilbrun, 2001). In the role of a consultant, the retaining third party is often asking for the consultant to assist solely in strengthening the case of the retaining party and attempting to weaken the case of the adversarial party. Because the responsibilities that accompany each role are so divergent, taking on both roles risks harming others by impairing the mental health professional's efficacy and/or objectivity (Otto, 2023).

Further, if the evaluator/consultant is called as an expert witness to testify, the blending of roles may present credibility issues on cross-examination (Heilbrun, 2001). Although the evaluator/consultant dual role is not expressly prohibited by any of the ethics codes or specialty guidelines for forensic psychiatrists and psychologists, forensic mental health professionals should use caution when assuming potentially dual roles and, at minimum, communicate the dual roles to the fact finder (Otto, 2023). This could include disclosure to the retaining attorney about the concern of conflicting roles being raised on cross-examination prior to agreeing to the role change. Further, if a forensic mental health professional assumes a dual role or switches from one role to another, it is better to go from an objective role (evaluator) to a subjective role (consultant) rather than the other way around.

Confidentiality

Forensic mental health professionals who engage in clinical forensic practice will likely be faced with dilemmas associated with limits to confidentiality in forensic contexts. [16] The bedrock of the therapeutic relationship is confidentiality between patient and clinician, and therefore many forensic examinees may have inaccurate expectations about the confidentiality of information they disclose during an evaluation (Trestman, 2014). Further, court-ordered forensic evaluations can become part of public record after submission to the court and may therefore be considered "public" to an examinee. When forensic mental health professionals are called to testify on a report they have provided, this may also constitute an unexpected "public" disclosure for forensic examinees who have a limited understanding of the limits of confidentiality.

The Principles of Medical Ethics with Annotations Especially Applicable to Psychiatry directly address the issue of limits to confidentiality in forensic contexts. Specifically, the code states: "Psychiatrists are often asked to examine individuals for security purposes, to determine suitability for various jobs, and to determine legal competence. The psychiatrist must fully describe the nature and purpose and lack of confidentiality of the examination to the examinee at the beginning of the examination" (American Psychiatric Association, 2013, p. 7). The AAPL *Ethics Guidelines* (2005) also have an entire subsection dedicated to confidentiality, stating in relevant part that "a forensic evaluation requires notice to the evaluee and to collateral sources of reasonably anticipated limitations on confidentiality" (AAPL, 2005, p. 2).

The EPPCC states in Standard 4.01: "Psychologists have a primary obligation and take reasonable precautions to protect confidential information obtained through or stored in any medium, recognizing that the extent and limits of confidentiality may be regulated by law or established by institutional rules or professional or scientific relationship" (American Psychological Association, 2017, p. 7). For forensic mental health professionals who engage in treatment in forensic settings, maintaining confidentiality can pose a challenge. In both state hospitals and correctional facilities, locating spaces where private, confidential communications can occur may be challenging. To the extent possible, forensic mental health professionals should strive to secure a private room for conducting both assessment and treatment and avoid "cell-side" conversations when motivated by convenience to the correctional institution or the professional (DeMatteo et al., 2023; Trestman, 2014).

The baseline requirement of confidentiality is further complicated by language in EPPCC Standard 4.01 stating that limits to confidentiality may be established by institutional rules or the nature of the professional relationship. Specifically, when forensic mental health professionals are working within a correctional (or even quasi-correctional) setting, institutional rules often require staff members to balance the confidentiality of the inmate with the security needs of the institution (DeMatteo et al., 2023). For example, many correctional facilities will require staff psychologists to report when an inmate discloses violations of institutional rules (Pinta, 2009).

Furthermore, there are necessary limits of confidentiality when a forensic mental health professional is retained by a third party to provide a forensic mental health assessment. The nature of the forensic evaluator's relationship with the third party as their client suggests that the forensic evaluator does not owe a full duty of confidentiality to an examinee. This subject is directly address by EPPCC Standard 3.07: “When psychologists agree to provide services to a person or entity at the request of a third party, psychologists attempt to clarify at the outset of the service the nature of the relationship with all individuals or organizations involved. This clarification includes the role of the psychologist, an identification of who is the client, the probable uses of the services provided or the information obtained, and the fact that there may be limits to confidentiality” (American Psychological Association, 2017, p. 6) (see more information regarding informed consent in the following section). The EPPCC also requires that psychologists inform individuals with whom they have a professional relationship of the “relevant limits of confidentiality and the foreseeable uses of the information generated through their psychological activities” at the outset of the relationship (American Psychological Association, 2017, p. 7). All sources of ethics guidance, both enforceable and aspirational, highlight the importance of early and affirmative disclosure of the limits of confidentiality that accompany any professional relationship with an individual in forensic settings.

Objectivity

Given the nature of the adversarial legal system, forensic mental health professionals are often retained by one of the two parties to the litigation when providing forensic evaluation services (e.g., defense or prosecution in criminal cases; plaintiff or defense in civil cases). Often, when a party is seeking a forensic mental health professional, that party is hoping the professional will reach a certain conclusion as part of the evaluation. When working with attorneys who are advocating strongly for their client and paying the forensic mental health professional for services rendered, the “pull” to reach conclusions favorable to the retaining party can be significant. Multiple studies have suggested the presence of affiliation or allegiance effects among forensic evaluators (e.g., Murrie & Boccaccini, 2015; Otto, 1989).

Despite this affiliation or relationship with the retaining party, forensic mental health professionals are obligated to work independently and obtain and offer opinions that are objective and unbiased (Otto, 2023). The AAPL *Ethics Guidelines for the Practice of Forensic Psychiatry* (2005) make special note of concerns of adversarial allegiance by forensic psychiatrists. Specifically, Principle 4 states:

> When psychiatrists function as experts within the legal process, they should adhere to the principle of honesty and should strive for objectivity. Although

> they may be retained by one party to a civil or criminal matter, psychiatrists should adhere to these principles when conducting evaluations, applying clinical data to legal criteria, and expressing opinions. (AAPL, 2005, p. 4)

The commentary to this principle goes on to state:

> The adversarial nature of most legal processes presents special hazards for the practice of forensic psychiatry. Being retained by one side in a civil or criminal matter exposes psychiatrists to the potential for unintended bias and the danger of distortion of their opinion. It is the responsibility of psychiatrists to minimize such hazards by acting in an honest manner and striving to reach an objective opinion. (AAPL, 2005, p. 4)

These aspirational principles are similar to those discussed in the psychology ethics code. Specifically, Principle C of the EPPCC states: "Psychologists seek to promote accuracy, honesty, and truthfulness in the science, teaching, and practice of psychology. In these activities, psychologists do not steal, cheat or engage in fraud, subterfuge, or intentional misrepresentation of fact" (American Psychological Association, 2017, pp. 3–4). Further, Guideline 11.01 of the SGFP states:

> When providing reports and other sworn statements or testimony in any form, forensic practitioners strive to present their conclusions, evidence, opinions, or other professional products in a fair manner. Forensic practitioners do not, by either commission or omission, participate in misrepresentation of their evidence, nor do they participate in partisan attempts to avoid, deny or subvert the presentation of evidence contrary to their own position or opinion (EPPCC Standard 5.01). This does not preclude forensic practitioners from forcefully presenting the data and reasoning upon which a conclusion or professional product is based. (American Psychological Association, 2013, p. 16)

Forensic mental health professionals should seek to practice in a way that minimizes threats to objectivity, impartiality, and fairness. These could include diversifying referral sources and ensuring that they are not accepting referrals only from sources with a particular adversarial allegiance (i.e., only defense or only prosecution) (Heilbrun, 2001), blinding the evaluator to the referral source (Robertson, 2010; Roberston & Yokum, 2012), or increasing the number of court-ordered referrals. Training and consultation on reducing adversarial allegiance can also be beneficial, although research has shown that knowledge of potential bias alone is not sufficient to eliminate bias (Murrie & Boccaccini, 2015; Neal et al., 2022).

Informed Consent

Informed consent is a core principle of ethical practice. However, it is also one that can pose challenges in a forensic setting. These challenges, and how they may apply in clinical and research settings, are briefly addressed below.

Clinical

Forensic mental health professionals must obtain appropriate authorization before commencing with a forensic mental health assessment. In some cases, initial authorization is provided via court order, or authorization is obtained by the attorney requesting the evaluation (Heilbrun, 2001). Interestingly, *The Principles of Medical Ethics with Annotations Especially Applicable to Psychiatry* does not address the nature of the authorization to be obtained prior to a forensic evaluation (American Psychiatric Association, 2013). The AAPL *Ethics Guidelines for the Practice of Forensic Psychiatry* (2005) state in Section 3: "The informed consent of the person undergoing the forensic evaluation should be obtained when necessary and feasible. If the evaluee is not competent to give consent, the evaluator should follow the appropriate laws of the jurisdiction" (p. 3). The commentary states further: "It is important to appreciate that in particular situations, such as court-ordered evaluations for competency to stand trial or involuntary commitment, neither assent nor informed consent is required" (AAPL, 2005, p. 3). The commentary goes on to state that impressions related to capacity or explicit refusal should be noted in the report and in testimony (AAPL, 2005).

The SGFP discuss the issue of authorization for forensic mental health assessments in detail and specify in Guideline 4 that authorization may be obtained via a contract with the legal representative of the party seeking services (American Psychological Association, 2013). Further, Guideline 6.03.03 provides guidance for obtaining informed consent from individuals lacking capacity:

> For examinees adjudicated or presumed by law to lack the capacity to provide informed consent for the anticipated forensic service, the forensic practitioner nevertheless provides an appropriate explanation, seeks the examinee's assent, and obtains appropriate permission from a legally authorized person, as permitted or required by law (EPPCC Standards 3.10, 9.03). For examinees whom the forensic practitioner has concluded lack capacity to provide informed consent to a proposed, non-court-order service, but who have not been adjudicated as lacking such capacity, the forensic practitioner strives to take reasonable steps to protect their rights and welfare (EPPCC Standard 3.10). (American Psychological Association, 2013, p. 13)

The guidance provided by the SGFP on this topic illustrates how the broader EPPCC standards can be applied specifically to forensic practice. Specifically, the EPPCC's guidance merely states the psychologist should "obtain appropriate permission from a legally authorized person" (American Psychological Association, 2017, p. 7). The SGFP applies this provision to forensic practice by explaining that the party retaining the forensic practitioner's services may serve as the "legally authorized person" described in the EPPCC.

Forensic mental health professionals can ensure they are following best practices of informed consent by educating themselves on when informed consent is required and the categories of individuals who can or cannot consent to evaluations. If an examinee falls into one of those categories, the mental health professional should determine whether the court (or another individual, such as a guardian) can consent on the individual's behalf. Lastly, it can be beneficial for forensic evaluators to create a "cheat sheet" of topics to address when obtaining informed consent, including the purpose and focus of the evaluation, legal issue being addressed, limits to confidentiality, creation of a report and who will receive it, and the possibility of testimony.

Research

Informed consent also presents ethical dilemmas to forensic mental health professionals conducting research with vulnerable populations. Guidelines outlining the process of obtaining informed consent to research participation are described in Standards 8.02 through 8.05 of the EPPCC (American Psychological Association, 2017). In summary, researchers must inform potential participants as to the purpose of the research, anticipated time commitment and procedures, their right to decline to participate and withdraw at any time, any foreseeable consequences of declining or withdrawing from the study, anticipated risks and benefits of participation, limits to confidentiality, incentives, and contact information for research and IRB personnel (American Psychological Association, 2017).

In contexts in which potential research participants are incapable of providing informed consent (e.g., due to intellectual disability, severe mental illness, or minor status), a surrogate decision-maker whose decisions are intended to reflect the wishes of the potential participant may be assigned (Chen et al., 2011; Pirelli et al., 2017). In addition to consent from a surrogate decision-maker, assent should be obtained from the potential participant (Pirelli et al., 2017). Potential research participants who are vulnerable due to age, psychological functioning, or incarceration status could benefit from a positive ethics approach to informed consent in which researchers attempt to enhance the decisional capacity of potential participants rather than aim to identify minimal competency to consent (Moser et al., 2004; Pirelli et al., 2017). This can include memory and visual aids and repeat-back strategies or more formal decisional capacity models that utilize semistructured interviews during the informed consent process (Hamilton et al., 2020).

Expert Immunity

The importance of expert witnesses in the modern legal system cannot be overstated (see DeMatteo et al., 2019). Expert witnesses often explain issues of complex subject matter to fact finders, and forensic mental health professionals may find themselves called as an expert witness on topic areas that sit at the intersection of psychology and law in both the criminal and civil justice systems. Traditionally, courts have provided blanket immunity to expert witnesses to prevent them from being sued for their performance, but this protection has been slowly eroded over time. Forensic mental health professionals who serve in an expert witness capacity should be aware of the case law and regulations surrounding expert witness immunity in their jurisdiction so they can decrease the likelihood of liability. After a brief review of the history of expert immunity, we discuss how expert immunity has been rescinded in various contexts, including perjury, spoliation, and negligence. Lastly, we discuss sanctions other than lawsuits for negligent practice.

History of Expert Immunity

The doctrine of witness immunity protects witnesses who testify at a legal proceeding from lawsuits arising from their testimony (Binder, 2002). This doctrine originated in the English common law for a variety of public policy reasons, one of which was to encourage open and honest testimony without fear of subsequent lawsuits (*Cutler v. Dixon*, 1585; *Henderson v. Broomhead*, 1859). The United States justice system maintained this doctrine and affirmed that it applied to expert witnesses who may have been negligent (see *Clark v. Grigson*, 1978). In *Grigson* (1978), a Texas Appeals Court stated that "no civil liability exists on the part of an expert witness who forms an opinion and states that opinion in the course of his testimony in a judicial proceeding, even though he may have been negligent in the process" (p. 263).[17]

The Supreme Court of the United States acknowledged the importance of blanket witness immunity in *Briscoe v. LaHue* (1983) when two police officers were sued civilly after giving perjured testimony, although the police officers were not testifying as expert witnesses at the time of the perjury. However, the

Supreme Court's reasoning reaffirmed the public policy rationale supporting common law blanket witness immunity, namely avoidance of intimidation and self-censorship for testifying witnesses (*Briscoe v. LaHue*, 1983). The *Briscoe* holding was largely adopted throughout various state court jurisdictions.

A few years later, in *Bruce v. Byrne-Stevens & Associates Engineers* (1989), the Supreme Court of Washington held that witness immunity prevented the plaintiff from suing his engineering expert. The court reasoned that retained experts are entitled to the same immunity as every other witness, and it stated that "the mere fact that the expert is retained or compensated by a party does not change the fact that, as a witness, he is a participant in a judicial proceeding. It is that state on which judicial immunity rests" (*Bruce v. Byrne-Stevens & Associates Engineers, Inc.*, 1989, p. 669). Similarly, in *Gootee v. Lightner* (1990), a California Appeals Court held that witness immunity applied to a psychologist who was jointly retained by divorcing parents to perform an evaluation for a custody dispute.

Critics of the witness immunity doctrine highlight the proliferation of expert witnesses in the modern era (Binder, 2002; Jensen, 1993). With increased use comes the increased potential for abuse, and some argue that cross-examination and potential prosecution for perjury do not adequately protect the court system from inaccurate or misleading expert testimony (McDowell, 1997). Criticism of the immunity doctrine also points to the similarities between consulting expert witnesses and lawyers, and namely the ability for lawyers to be sued for malpractice if they "failed to exercise the skill and knowledge ordinarily possessed by attorneys under similar circumstances" (Masterson, 1998, p. 394; *Mattco Forge Inc. v. Arthur Young & Co.*, 1997; *Murphy v. A.A. Mathews*, 1992). Some argue that expert witnesses should be judged by the same standard for malpractice (Jensen, 1993).

Exceptions to Expert Witness Immunity

Although courts have largely maintained the concept of immunity for expert witnesses, in the past 30 years, some courts have begun to allow for expert witnesses to be sued civilly in certain circumstances. These include when the expert witness has engaged in spoilation, perjury, or negligence. The nuances of each of these circumstances are discussed next. It is important to note that while the case law that will be reviewed is jurisdiction-specific, the issue of expert witness immunity is in flux in many jurisdictions, and forensic mental health professionals should be aware of the exceptions to expert witness immunity even if their own jurisdiction has not yet decided the issue.

Spoilation and Perjury

In 1999, the United States Court of Appeals for the Second Circuit defined spoilation as "the destruction or significant alteration of evidence or the failure to preserve property for another use as evidence in pending or reasonably foreseeable litigation" (*West v. Goodyear Tire & Rubber Co.*, 1999, p. 779). Rule 37(b)(2)(A) of the Federal Rules of Civil Procedure allows courts to impose sanctions on parties for failing to comply with discovery orders. Depending on the forensic mental health professionals' role in the case in question, they may be deemed to be "a party" in the litigation (Crumbley & Seago, 2021).[18] Forensic mental health professionals who are retained either as a forensic evaluator or a consultant on a case should carefully maintain documents relevant to the litigation. Even if the documentation is ultimately deemed to be subject to the work-product rule barring discovery,[19] this is an instance where the adage "better safe than sorry" would apply. In addition to spoilation, all witnesses that provide sworn testimony are subject to perjury charges if they lie while under oath (Crumbley & Seago, 2021). In 2003, a Secret Service ink expert was charged with perjury after testifying under oath about testing documents in Martha Stewart's obstruction of justice trial. Interestingly, the expert was acquitted of the perjury charges after a jury found that he lacked the specific intent and made the statement mistakenly (Moynihan, 2004).

Negligence

As of 2021, eight states permit expert witnesses to be sued for negligence: California, Connecticut, Louisiana, Massachusetts, Missouri, Pennsylvania, New Jersey, and West Virginia (Crumbley & Seago, 2021). The first case that permitted an expert witness to be sued for negligence was in California in 1992 (*Mattco Forge Inc. v. Arthur Young & Co.*, 1997). In *Mattco*, a forensic accountant was sued for professional negligence, fraudulent misrepresentation, and fraudulent concealment after it was alleged that he mixed his own work product with source documents and presented the collective documents as if they were all authentic source documents (*Mattco Forge Inc. v. Arthur Young & Co.*, 1997). The California trial court found that the forensic accountant could be held liable for professional negligence, and it established criteria for evaluating expert witness negligence (*Mattco Forge Inc. v. Arthur Young & Co.*, 1997). The professional must first be found to be negligent in the handling of the prior lawsuit, and then the court must find that the professional's negligence was a "substantial factor" in the plaintiff's loss of the prior lawsuit (*Mattco Forge Inc. v. Arthur Young & Co.*, 1997, p. 844). Lastly, the court must conclude that "the proper handling of the prior lawsuit by the professional would have resulted in a collectible judgment in the plaintiff's favor" (*Mattco Forge Inc. v. Arthur Young & Co.*, 1997, p. 844).

The next case to roll back immunity protections against expert witnesses occurred in Pennsylvania. In *LLMD of Michigan, Inc. v. Jackson-Cross Co.* (1999), the Supreme Court of Pennsylvania held that the plaintiff's expert witness was liable for professional malpractice. The expert witness was hired to calculate the damages the plaintiff accrued from a failed business deal. After the plaintiff settled the case based on the expert witness's damages appraisal, the plaintiff determined that the expert witness had made a mathematical error that resulted in a drastic miscalculation of lost profits (*LLMD of Michigan, Inc. v. Jackson-Cross Co.*, 1999). In its opinion, the court distinguished this case from a prior case in which immunity was upheld when an expert witness was sued when the retaining party was dissatisfied with the substance of the opinion rendered (*Panitz v. Behrend*, 1993).

Courts continued to expand the range of expert witnesses subject to liability when the expert's work product significantly impacted the outcome of an underlying case. In *Pollock v. Panjabi* (2000), a Yale University biomechanics expert was hired to serve as an expert witness in a personal injury action against a police officer accused of using excessive force. The expert witness was retained to perform experiments to prove that the officer caused the plaintiff's spinal injuries. At trial in the personal injury case, the judge held that the expert witness's reports were not admissible because the experiments were incorrectly performed. The Connecticut Superior Court held that the expert was liable for his negligence in incorrectly performing the experiments that were deemed inadmissible at trial (*Pollock v. Panjabi*, 2000).

In 2002, the Louisiana Supreme Court ended expert witness immunity when the expert witness was retained by the party who is now suing them, or the "friendly" expert witness (*Marrogi v. Howard*, 2002). In *Marrogi*, the expert witness was retained in the underlying suit to review medical billing reports in preparation of the plaintiff's impending litigation. The expert witness made errors in performing these services that were revealed on cross-examination. The Louisiana Supreme Court held that the expert witness could be held liable under tort law for negligent performance in providing litigation services (*Marrogi v. Howard*, 2002).[20] A Massachusetts Superior Court similarly limited expert witness immunity in holding that an expert witness hired to provide litigation services support could be sued for negligence, breach of contract, and malpractice (*Boyes-Bogie v. Horvitz and Associates*, 2001). The Supreme Court of Missouri also held that witness immunity does not bar a lawsuit if a professional is negligent in providing an agreed-upon service, even if that agreed-upon service involves preparation for litigation (*Murphy v. A.A. Mathews*, 1992).

In 1984, the New Jersey Supreme Court ruled that a court-appointed expert witness was not protected by the witness immunity doctrine (*Levine v. Wiss and Co.*, 1984). This represents a striking change from the previously described cases, all of which involved "friendly" experts, or experts were sued by the party who retained them. Because the Supreme Court of the United States has never explicitly protected absolute immunity for expert witnesses as a class, this permitted New Jersey (and other states) to make their own decisions on both "friendly" and court-appointed/neutral experts. The New Jersey Supreme Court reasoned that the court-appointed expert witness's role was comparable to that of any expert hired by a party to a contract to resolve a dispute (*Levine v. Wiss and Co.*, 1984). The court also reasoned that immunity "should not be available to shield from liability for negligence appraisers or other experts performing limited functions in the context of judicial proceedings" (*Levine v. Wiss and Co.*, 1984, p. 251).[21] In a more recent case (with an unpublished opinion), *Reilly, Supple & Wischusen, LLP v. Malcolm Blum* (2011), the New Jersey Superior Court held that an attorney did not have the right to sue the opposing party's expert. The court reasoned that the opposing expert witness did not owe any duty to the attorney and therefore could not be sued under tort law (*Reilly, Supple & Wischusen, LLP v. Malcolm Blum*, 2011).

As of 2024, the only state that allows for expert witnesses to be sued by the opposing party is West Virginia. In *Davis v. Wallace* (2002), a woman who had been convicted of murder in the underlying case sued numerous opposing medical expert witnesses who testified at her trial for the state. She alleged that the doctors "had negligently performed tests, negligently prepared for testimony, negligently testified, and otherwise failed to meet the standards of science and medicine as it existed at that time" (*Davis v. Wallace*, 2002, p. 386). The West Virginia Supreme Court reversed and remanded the expert witness's motion to dismiss and reasoned that a lawsuit against expert witnesses is not frivolous or done in bad faith because multiple states are undecided on the issue of expert witness immunity.

Professional Sanctions

In addition to civil lawsuits, forensic mental health professionals who are negligent in their duties as an expert witness may be subject to sanctions from both professional associations and state licensing boards. In 2001, the United States Court of Appeals for the Seventh Circuit held that a professional society could discipline a member who provided improper testimony (*Austin v. American Association of Neurological Surgeons*, 2001). The court reasoned that the neurosurgeon expert witness's improper testimony was "irresponsible and violated the ethical code of the association to provide the court with accurate and documentable opinions on the matters at hand" (*Austin v. American Association of Neurological Surgeons*, 2001, p. 967).

Similarly, state courts have upheld disciplinary proceedings on the basis of the violation of ethical standards in expert testimony. In 1997, the Washington Supreme Court held that disciplinary proceedings by the state Board of

Psychology were permitted against a psychologist who failed to meet professional ethical standards in work that formed the basis of expert testimony in several child custody cases (*Deatherage v. State of Washington Examining Board of Psychology*, 1997). Physician expert witnesses, including psychiatrists, may also be sanctioned by their medical licensing boards. The AMA passed a resolution in the late 1990s explicitly stating that expert testimony constitutes the practice of medicine and is therefore subject to peer review. If a psychiatrist's medical testimony is found to be negligent by the AMA, the psychiatrist may be reported to the state medical board and subject to discipline (Binder, 2002). It is interesting to note, however, that the primary governing organization for psychologists (APA) no longer conducts investigations regarding unethical conduct and instead refers those matters to state licensing boards.

Conclusion

A working understanding of the legal and ethical requirements for forensic practice is essential. Whether from a practical (e.g., knowing the applicable legal standard), professional (e.g., awareness of codes and best practice), or protective (e.g., appreciation for what falls in or out of the bounds of standard practice) perspective, familiarity with the requirements, considerations, and suggestions in this chapter can bolster the forensic mental health professional's practice and limit the likelihood of liability. This study of legal and ethical requirements may begin during graduate education, but it certainly does not end there. Given ever-changing demands on mental health professionals (e.g., the mass shift to telehealth practice [see Chapter 9] and evaluations during the COVID-19 pandemic) and constantly evolving laws, regulations, and professional codes and guidelines, most states specifically require professionals to enhance their understanding of ethics through continuing education coursework. This chapter is not the sole guide for ethical decision-making. Rather, we aimed to provide a framework for understanding relevant ethical and legal authorities in the context of discussing steps that can be taken to assess and improve forensic practice.

Chapter 9
Emerging Areas of Forensic Practice Regulation

Technological advances have led to fundamental changes to the way forensic mental professionals can and do offer their services to the public and the legal system (Batastini et al., 2023). This transformation in mental health practice was further accelerated during the COVID-19 pandemic in which even more forensic services were provided remotely, and the regulatory requirements in many states regarding telepsychology and temporary interjurisdictional practice were suspended due to the United States government's declared state of emergency (Clay, 2021).[1] A number of important benefits for forensic mental health practice clearly occurred from these changes, including but not limited to (1) clients/examinees in remote locations were more able to receive psychological and forensic services; (2) forensic mental health professionals were more able to provide their services across jurisdictional boundaries; (3) clients in clinical contexts received greater continuity in care when they moved between jurisdictions; and (4) travel for both clients/examinees and forensic mental health professionals was more limited, making consultation, assessment, treatment, and expert testimony oftentimes more efficient.

Two related areas of forensic mental health practice saw the most regulatory and practical developments in the last several years—temporary in-person interjurisdictional practice and telepsychology practice. While telepsychology, at least across jurisdictional boundaries, can be seen as a special case of temporary interjurisdictional practice, it is discussed separately to highlight some of its most important aspects and to highlight recent developments in both regulatory rules and professional guidelines created to specifically address its use.

Unfortunately, interjurisdictional practice, whether via telepsychology or in-person, is constrained by a confusing mixture of constitutional, state, administrative, and regulatory laws and rules. Further complicating the picture, the legal landscape has been affected by the profession's (i.e., Association of State & Provincial Psychology Boards [ASPPB]) recent attempts (e.g., development and implementation of Psychology Interjurisdictional Compact [PSYPACT]; https://psypact.site-ym.com/) to address many of these issues and advance the ability of mental health practitioners to provide telepsychology and temporary

Forensic Mental Health Practice and the Law. David DeMatteo, Daniel A. Krauss, Sarah Fishel, and Kellie Wiltsie, Oxford University Press. © Oxford University Press (2025). DOI: 10.1093/9780197686591.003.0009

in-person services across jurisdictional boundaries (Taube et al., 2023; Younggren et al., 2022).

This chapter will briefly outline (1) the history of legal authorities that govern telepsychology and interjurisdictional practice; (2) the profession's attempts to directly affect this complex regulatory scheme; (3) recent professional guidelines relevant to telepsychology practices; and (4) some recommendations for forensic mental health professionals faced with navigating this legally complex arena, and some legal and policy recommendations that might create a more effective and efficient regulatory scheme.

State Licensure and the Regulation of the "Practice of Psychology"

In the United States, individual states and their legislative and administrative bodies are largely responsible for the regulation of the psychology profession. The Tenth Amendment to the United States Constitution states: "[T]he powers not delegated to the United States by the Constitution, nor prohibited to it by the States, are reserved to the States respectively, or to the people." This amendment has been interpreted such that regulatory legal authority not expressly mentioned in the United States Constitution as part of the powers of the federal government is specifically delegated to the states to administer. In *Dent v. West Virginia* (1889), the Supreme Court of the United States expressly recognized this state power with regard to physicians and West Virginia's medical licensure statute:

> The power of the state to provide for the general welfare of its people authorizes it to prescribe all such regulations as in its judgement, will secure or tend to secure them against the consequences of ignorance and incapacity as well as of deception and fraud... The nature and the extent of the qualifications required must depend primarily upon the judgment of the state as to their necessity. (*Dent*, 129 U.S. 114, p. 122)

As a result, states have both the ability and right to oversee the licensure of psychologists and other forensic mental health professionals and to shape the scope of their practice covered by this licensure (see Table 9.1 for state definitions of the practice of psychology). There are good reasons for this—states have a vested interest in protecting their citizens from unqualified practitioners and protecting their citizens' health and welfare. Further, states already have implemented such measures across a wide variety of professions that interact with their citizenry. For example, there are separate state licensing boards for other professionals that have direct contact with the public, including medical doctors, counselors, attorneys, and many others. Additionally, when these laws and associated stated boards originated, there was limited communication between states, making local oversight more practical and efficient.

Significantly, with regard to psychologists, this has resulted in 65 different regulatory or licensure boards with differing legal provisions across the United States and Canada.[2] The first psychology licensure board was created by the State of Connecticut in 1945, and each state or jurisdiction has its own licensure laws, requirements, and examination process (DeMers et al., 2014). The unlicensed practice of psychology is subject to potential civil and/or criminal penalties, along with state psychology board disciplinary actions (e.g., suspension of licensure in the practitioner's home state if they practice in another) (Simon & Shuman, 1999; Tucillo et al., 2002). In a specific jurisdiction, the unlicensed practice of psychology is subject to sanction by the state's disciplinary board, oftentimes regardless of whether a particular court has recognized a forensic mental health professional as an expert and explicitly allowed them to participate in legal or forensic proceedings in that locale (Kane et al., 2023).

However, not all psychologists or forensic mental health professionals are required to be licensed by their state to deliver certain kinds of services—it is largely reserved for clinical psychologists who directly assess and treat clients/patients. In fact, licensure is mandated only for the "practice of psychology," which is defined somewhat differently by every jurisdiction. For example, California's rather expansive psychology licensure law reads:

(a) No person may engage in the practice of psychology, or represent himself or herself to be a psychologist, without a license granted under this chapter, except as otherwise provided in this chapter. The practice of psychology is defined as rendering or offering to render to individuals, groups, organizations, or the public any psychological service involving the application of psychological principles, methods, and procedures of understanding, predicting, and influencing behavior, such as the principles pertaining to learning, perception, motivation, emotions, and interpersonal relationships; and the methods and procedures of interviewing, counseling, psychotherapy, behavior modification, and hypnosis; and of constructing, administering, and interpreting tests of mental abilities, aptitudes, interests, attitudes, personality characteristics, emotions, and motivations.

(b) The application of these principles and methods includes, but is not restricted to: assessment, diagnosis, prevention, treatment, and intervention to increase effective functioning of individuals, groups, and organizations.

Table 9.1 Statutory Definitions of "Practice of Psychology" by State

State	Statute Citation	Relevant Excerpt
Alabama	Ala. Code § 34–26-1	"(1) A person practices as a "psychologist" within the meaning of this chapter when he or she holds himself or herself out to be a psychologist or renders to individuals or to the public for remuneration any service involving the application of recognized principles, methods, and procedures of the science and profession of psychology, such as interviewing or administering and interpreting tests of mental abilities, aptitudes, interests, and personality characteristics for such purposes as psychological evaluation or for such purposes as overall personality appraisal or classification, or treatment. The practice of psychologists specifically includes the use of projective assessment techniques, the diagnosis of mental disorders, and psychotherapy. (2) Nothing in this definition shall be construed as permitting the use of those forms of psychotherapy which involve the administration or prescription of drugs or electro-shock or in any way infringing upon the practice of medicine as defined in the laws of this state. A psychologist shall not attempt to diagnose, prescribe for, treat, or advise a client with reference to problems or complaints falling outside the boundaries of psychological practice. (3) Nothing in this definition shall be construed as preventing qualified school counselors, vocational guidance counselors, vocational rehabilitation counselors, speech and hearing therapists, speech pathologists and audiologists, reading therapists, or teachers of exceptional children from rendering to the public for remuneration services for which they are qualified by training and experience involving the techniques of interviewing, administering, and interpreting tests of mental abilities, achievement, interests, and aptitudes for such purposes as evaluation or for educational or vocational guidance, selection, or placement. Nothing in this definition shall be construed as preventing technical and support staff from providing functions associated with psychological assessments under the supervision of a licensed psychologist."

Continued

Table 9.1 *Continued*

State	Statute Citation	Relevant Excerpt
Alaska	Alaska Stat. § 08.86.180	"(a) Unless licensed under this chapter, a person may not practice psychology or hold out publicly as a psychologist or as practicing psychology. A person holds out as a psychologist by using a title or description of services incorporating the words 'psychology,' 'psychological,' 'psychologist,' 'psychometry,' 'psychotherapy,' 'psychotherapeutic,' 'psychotherapist,' 'psychoanalysis,' or 'psychoanalyst' or when holding out publicly to be trained, experienced, or qualified to render services in the field of psychology. (b) This section does not apply to (1) a person employed as a school psychologist, if the school district maintains appropriate supervision of psychological activities and professional conduct, and if the person is performing the psychological activities as part of the duties for which the person was employed, is performing the activities solely within the facilities of the school district in which the person is employed or under the supervision of the school district, and does not render or offer to render psychological services to the public for compensation in addition to the salary the person receives from the school district; (2) an officer or employee of the United States government practicing psychology while in the discharge of the officer's or employee's official duties; (3) a student, intern, or resident in psychology pursuing a course of study approved by the board as qualifying training and experience for a psychologist, if that person's activities constitute a part of that person's supervised course of study and that person is designated by titles such as 'psychology intern' or 'psychology trainee'; (4) a qualified member of another profession, in doing work of a psychological nature consistent with that person's training and consistent with the code of ethics of that person's profession, if the person does not hold out to the public by a title or description of services incorporating the words 'psychology,' 'psychological,' 'psychologist,' 'psychometry,' 'psychotherapy,' 'psychotherapeutic,' 'psychotherapist,' 'psychoanalysis,' or 'psychoanalyst' or represent to be trained, experienced, or qualified to render services in the field of psychology; or (5) a physician engaged in the normal practice of medicine for which the physician is licensed under AS 08.64. (c) Nothing in this chapter authorizes a person licensed as a psychologist to engage in the practice of medicine, as defined by the laws of the state. (d) Nothing in this section prohibits a licensed clinical social worker, a licensed marital and family therapist, or a licensed professional counselor from holding out to the public by a title or description of services incorporating the words 'psychoanalysis,' 'psychoanalyst,' 'psychotherapy,' 'psychotherapist,' or 'psychotherapeutic.'"

Arizona	Ariz. Rev. Stat. § 32–2061; Ariz. Rev. Stat. § 32–2076	Ariz. Rev. Stat. § 32–2061 states, "Practice of psychology" means the psychological assessment, diagnosis, treatment or correction of mental, emotional, behavioral or psychological abilities, illnesses or disorders or purporting or attempting to do this consistent with section 32–2076. Ariz. Rev. Stat. § 32–2076 states, "This chapter does not authorize a person to engage in any manner in the practice of medicine pursuant to chapter 13, 17 or 29 of this title, except that a person licensed as provided in this chapter may diagnose, treat and correct human conditions ordinarily within the scope of the practice of a psychologist."
Arkansas	Ark. Code Ann. § 17–97-102	"'Practice of psychology' means the observation, description, evaluation, interpretation, or modification of human behavior by a person who holds an advanced graduate degree in psychology and is trained in the application of psychological principles, methods, or procedures for one (1) or more of the following purposes: (i) Preventing or eliminating symptomatic, maladaptive, or undesired behavior; (ii) Enhancing interpersonal relationships, work and life adjustment, personal effectiveness, and behavioral and mental health; and (iii) Consulting, teaching, and research. (B) 'Practice of psychology' includes without limitation: (i) Testing and measuring, that consist of the administration and interpretation of tests measuring personal characteristics, such as intelligence, personality, abilities, interests, aptitudes, achievements, motives, personality dynamics, psychoeducational processes, neuropsychological brain functioning, and other psychological attributes of individuals or groups; (ii) (a) Diagnosis and treatment of mental and emotional disorders, that consist of the appropriate diagnosis of mental disorders, behavior disorders, and brain dysfunctions, according to standards of the profession and the ordering or providing of treatments according to need. (b) Treatment includes without limitation providing: (1) Counseling; (2) Psychotherapy; (3) Marital and family therapy; (4) Group therapy;

Continued

Table 9.1 *Continued*

State	Statute Citation	Relevant Excerpt
		(5) Behavior therapy; (6) Psychoanalysis; (7) Hypnosis; (8) Biofeedback; (9) Other psychological interventions that aim to modify and adjust perceptions, habits, or conduct; and (10) The psychological aspects of physical illness, pain, injury, or disability; and (iii) Psychological consulting, which consists of: (a) Interpreting or reporting on scientific theory or research in psychology; (b) Rendering expert psychological opinion or clinical psychological opinion; (c) Evaluating and engaging in applied psychological research; (d) Program or organizational development; and (e) Administration, supervision, and evaluation of psychological services. (C) The practice of psychology may be rendered: (i) To individuals, families, groups, organizations, institutions, and the public; and (ii) Whether or not payment is received for services rendered."
California	Cal. Bus. & Prof. Code § 2903	"(a) No person may engage in the practice of psychology, or represent himself or herself to be a psychologist, without a license granted under this chapter, except as otherwise provided in this chapter. The practice of psychology is defined as rendering or offering to render to individuals, groups, organizations, or the public any psychological service involving the application of psychological principles, methods, and procedures of understanding, predicting, and influencing behavior, such as the principles pertaining to learning, perception, motivation, emotions, and interpersonal relationships; and the methods and procedures of interviewing, counseling, psychotherapy, behavior modification, and hypnosis; and of constructing, administering, and interpreting tests of mental abilities, aptitudes, interests, attitudes, personality characteristics, emotions, and motivations. (b) The application of these principles and methods includes, but is not restricted to: assessment, diagnosis, prevention, treatment, and intervention to increase effective functioning of individuals, groups, and organizations. (c) Psychotherapy within the meaning of this chapter means the use of psychological methods in a professional relationship to assist a person or persons to acquire greater human effectiveness or to modify feelings, conditions, attitudes, and behaviors that are emotionally, intellectually, or socially ineffectual or maladaptive."

Colorado	Colo. Rev. Stat. § 12–245-303	"(1) For the purposes of this part 3, the 'practice of psychology' means the observation, description, evaluation, interpretation, or modification of human behavior by the application of psychological principles, methods, or procedures, for the purpose of: (a) Preventing, eliminating, evaluating, assessing, or predicting symptomatic, maladaptive, or undesired behavior; (b) Evaluating, assessing, or facilitating the enhancement of individual, group, or organizational effectiveness, including personal effectiveness, adaptive behavior, interpersonal relationships, work and life adjustment, health, and individual, group, or organizational performance; or (c) Providing clinical information to be utilized in legal proceedings. (2) The practice of psychology includes: (a) Psychological testing and the evaluation or assessment of personal characteristics such as intelligence; personality; cognitive, physical, or emotional abilities; skills; interests; aptitudes; and neuropsychological functioning; (b) Counseling, psychoanalysis, psychotherapy, hypnosis, biofeedback, and behavior analysis and therapy; (c) Diagnosis, treatment, and management of behavioral, mental, or emotional health disorders or disabilities; substance use disorders; and disorders of habit or conduct, as well as of the psychological aspects of physical illness, accident, injury, or disability; (d) Psychoeducational evaluation, therapy, and remediation; (e) Consultation with physicians, other health-care professionals, and patients regarding all available treatment options with respect to provision of care for a specific patient or client; (f) The provision of direct services to individuals or groups for the purpose of enhancing individual and thereby organizational effectiveness, using psychological principles, methods, or procedures to assess and evaluate individuals on personal characteristics for individual development or behavior change or for making decisions about the individual, such as selection; and (g) The supervision of any of the practices described in this subsection (2). (3) Psychological services may be rendered to individuals, families, groups, organizations, institutions, the public, and the courts. (4) The practice of psychology shall be construed within the meaning of this definition without regard to whether payment is received for services rendered."

Continued

Table 9.1 *Continued*

State	Statute Citation	Relevant Excerpt
Connecticut	Conn. Gen. Stat. § 20–187a	"No person shall practice psychology unless he has obtained a license as provided in section 20–188. The practice of psychology means the rendering of professional services under any title or description of services incorporating the words psychologist, psychological or psychology, to the public or to any public or private organization for a fee or other remuneration. Professional psychological services means the application, by persons trained in psychology, of established principles of learning, motivation, perception, thinking and emotional relationships to the assessment, diagnosis, prevention, treatment and amelioration of psychological problems or emotional or mental disorders of individuals or groups, including but not limited to counseling, guidance, psychotherapy, behavior modification and personnel evaluation, with persons or groups in the areas of work, family, school, marriage and personal relationships; measuring and testing of personality, intelligence, aptitudes, emotions, public opinion, attitudes and skills; and research relating to human behavior."
Delaware	Del. Code Ann. tit. 24, § 3502	"(5) 'Practice of psychology' shall mean the observation, description, evaluation, interpretation and modification of human behavior by the application of psychological principles, methods, and/or procedures, for the purpose of preventing or eliminating symptomatic, maladaptive or undesired behavior, and of enhancing interpersonal relationships, work and life adjustment, personal effectiveness, behavioral health and mental health. The practice of psychology includes psychological testing and the evaluation or assessment of personal characteristics, such as intelligence, personality, abilities, interests, aptitudes and neuropsychological function; counseling, psychoanalysis, psychotherapy, hypnosis, biofeedback, and behavior analysis and therapy; diagnosis and treatment of mental and emotional disorder or disability, alcoholism and substance abuse, disorders of habit or conduct, as well as the psychological aspects of physical illness, accident, injury or disability; and psychoeducational evaluation, therapy, remediation, and consultation. Psychological services may be rendered to individuals, families, groups, organizations, institutions and the public. The practice of psychology shall be construed within the meaning of this definition without regard to whether or not payment is received for services rendered. a. 'Psychological testing' shall mean, but not be limited to: Administration and interpretation of standardized intelligence and neuropsychological tests which yield an intelligence quotient and/or are the basis for a diagnosis of organic brain syndromes for the purposes of classification and/or disability determination; and b. The administration and interpretation of psychological tests which are the basis of a diagnosis of mental or emotional disorder."

District of Columbia	D.C. Code § 3–1201.02	"'Practice of psychology' means the development and application, with or without compensation, of scientific concepts, theories, methods, techniques, procedures, and principles of psychology to aid in the understanding, measuring, explaining, predicting, preventing, fostering, and treating of abilities, disabilities, attributes, or behaviors that are: (I) Principally cognitive, such as aptitudes, perceptions, attitudes, or intelligence; (II) Affective, such as happiness, anger, or depression; or (III) Behavioral, such as physical abuse. (ii) The term 'practice of psychology' includes: (I) Coaching, consulting, counseling, and various types of therapy, such as behavior therapy, group therapy, hypnotherapy, psychotherapy, and marriage, couples, and family therapy; (II) Intellectual, personality, behavioral, educational, neuropsychological, and psycho-physiological testing; and (III) Professional activities, such as research, teaching, training, interviewing, assessment, evaluation, pharmacology, and biofeedback. (B) Nothing in this paragraph shall be construed as preventing or restricting the practice, services, or activities of: (i) An individual bearing the title of psychologist in the employ of an academic institution, research organization, or laboratory, if the psychology-based activities or services offered are within the scope of employment, are consistent with his or her professional training and experience, and provided within the confines of employment; or (ii) A school psychologist employed by District of Columbia Public Schools or a public charter school and working in accordance with regulations issued by the Office of the State Superintendent of Education."
Florida	Fla. Stat. Ann. § 490.003	"(4) 'Practice of psychology' means the observations, description, evaluation, interpretation, and modification of human behavior, by the use of scientific and applied psychological principles, methods, and procedures, for the purpose of describing, preventing, alleviating, or eliminating symptomatic, maladaptive, or undesired behavior and of enhancing interpersonal behavioral health and mental or psychological health. The ethical practice of psychology includes, but is not limited to, psychological testing and the evaluation or assessment of personal characteristics such as intelligence, personality, abilities, interests, aptitudes, and neuropsychological functioning, including evaluation of mental competency to manage one's affairs and to participate in legal proceedings; counseling, psychoanalysis, all forms of psychotherapy, sex therapy, hypnosis, biofeedback, and behavioral analysis and therapy; psychoeducational evaluation, therapy, remediation, and consultation; and use of psychological methods to diagnose and treat mental, nervous, psychological, marital, or emotional disorders, illness, or disability, alcoholism and substance abuse, and disorders of habit or conduct, as well as the psychological aspects of physical illness, accident, injury, or disability, including neuropsychological evaluation, diagnosis, prognosis, etiology, and treatment.

Continued

Table 9.1 *Continued*

State	Statute Citation	Relevant Excerpt
		(a) Psychological services may be rendered to individuals, couples, families, groups, and the public without regard to place of service. (b) The use of specific modalities within the practice of psychology is restricted to psychologists appropriately trained in the use of such modalities. (c) The practice of psychology shall be construed within the meaning of this definition without regard to whether payment is requested or received for services rendered."
Georgia	Ga. Code Ann. § 43–39-1	"(7) 'To practice psychology' or 'practice of psychology' means to render or offer to render to individuals, groups, organizations, or the public for a fee or any remuneration, monetary or otherwise, any service involving the application of recognized principles, methods, and procedures of the science and profession of psychology, including, but not limited to, diagnosing and treating mental and nervous disorders and illnesses; rendering opinions concerning diagnoses of mental disorders, including, but not limited to, organic brain disorders and brain damage; engaging in neuropsychology; engaging in psychotherapy; interviewing, administering, and interpreting tests of mental abilities, aptitudes, interests, and personality characteristics, including, but not limited to, psychological testing, for such purposes as psychological classification or evaluation or for educational or vocational placement, or for such purposes as psychological counseling, guidance, or readjustment. When engaged in the practice of psychology, licensed psychologists may describe or label any testing, assessment, or evaluation they conduct within the scope of practice described in this Code section as 'psychological' in nature; provided, however, that any such description or labeling shall not be construed to alter the meaning of psychological testing as defined in paragraph (6) of this Code section and in paragraph (9) of Code Section 43–39-7. Nothing in this paragraph shall be construed as permitting the administration or prescription of drugs or in any way infringing upon or restricting the practice of medicine as defined in the laws of this state."

Hawaii	Haw. Rev. Stat. Ann. § 465–1	"'Practice of psychology' means the observation, description, evaluation, interpretation, or modification of human behavior by the application of psychological principles, methods, or procedures, for the purpose of preventing or eliminating symptomatic, maladaptive, or undesired behavior and of enhancing interpersonal relationships, work and life adjustment, personal effectiveness, behavioral health, and mental health. The practice of psychology includes, but is not limited to, psychological testing and the evaluation or assessment of personal characteristics, such as intelligence, personality, abilities, interests, aptitudes, and neuropsychological functioning; counseling, psychoanalysis, psychotherapy, hypnosis, biofeedback, and behavior analysis and therapy; diagnosis and treatment of mental and emotional disorder or disability, alcoholism and substance abuse, and disorders of habit or conduct, as well as of the psychological aspects of physical illness, accident, injury, or disability; and psychoeducational evaluation, therapy, remediation, and consultation. Psychological services may be rendered to individuals, families, groups, organizations, institutions, and the public. The practice of psychology shall be construed within the meaning of this definition without regard to whether payment is received for services rendered."
Idaho	Idaho Code § 54–2302	"(7) 'Practice of psychology' means the application of established principles of learning, motivation, perception, thinking, and emotional relationships to problems of personnel evaluation, group relations, and behavior adjustment. The application of said principles includes, but is not restricted to, counseling and the use of psychotherapeutic measures with persons or groups to eliminate symptomatic, maladaptive or undesired behavior so as to enhance interpersonal relationships in the areas of work, family, school, and personal relationships; measuring and testing of personality, intelligence, aptitudes, emotions, public opinion, attitudes, and skills; diagnosing and treating mental and emotional disorders or disabilities; and doing research on problems relating to human behavior. (8) A person represents himself to be a psychologist when he holds himself out to the public by any title or description incorporating the words 'psychological,' 'psychologist' or 'psychology' or offers to render or renders psychological services for remuneration."
Illinois	225 Ill. Comp. Stat. Ann. 15/2	"(5) 'Clinical psychology' means the independent evaluation, classification, diagnosis, and treatment of mental, emotional, behavioral or nervous disorders or conditions, developmental disabilities, alcoholism and substance abuse, disorders of habit or conduct, and the psychological aspects of physical illness. The practice of clinical psychology includes psychoeducational evaluation, therapy, remediation and consultation, the use of psychological and neuropsychological testing, assessment, psychotherapy, psychoanalysis, hypnosis, biofeedback, and behavioral modification when any of these are used for the purpose of preventing or eliminating psychopathology, or for the amelioration of psychological disorders of individuals or groups. 'Clinical psychology' does not include the use of hypnosis by unlicensed persons pursuant to Section 3 [225 ILCS 15/3].

Continued

Table 9.1 *Continued*

State	Statute Citation	Relevant Excerpt
		(6) A person represents himself to be a 'clinical psychologist' or 'psychologist' within the meaning of this Act when he or she holds himself out to the public by any title or description of services incorporating the words 'psychological,' 'psychologic,' 'psychologist,' 'psychology,' or 'clinical psychologist' or under such title or description offers to render or renders clinical psychological services as defined in paragraph (7) of this Section to individuals or the public for remuneration. (7) 'Clinical psychological services' refers to any services under paragraph (5) of this Section if the words 'psychological,' 'psychologic,' 'psychologist,' 'psychology' or 'clinical psychologist' are used to describe such services by the person or organization offering to render or rendering them."
Indiana	Ind. Code Ann. § 25–33-1-2	"'Practice of psychology' includes the following: (1) Construction, administration, and interpretation of tests of intellectual and cognitive abilities, aptitudes, skills, interests, attitudes, personality characteristics, perception, emotion, motivation, and opinion. (2) Diagnosis and treatment of mental and behavioral disorders by a health service provider in psychology. (3) Educational and vocational planning and guidance. (4) Personnel selection and management. (5) Arrangement of effective work and learning situations. (6) Resolution of interpersonal and social conflicts. (7) Techniques used in interviewing, counseling, psychotherapy, and behavior modification of individuals or groups. (8) Supervision of psychological services. (9) Teaching of any of the practices listed in this subsection. (10) The planning and conduct of research on human behavior. 'Psychological services' means acts or behaviors coming within the purview of the practice of psychology (as defined in this article). 'Psychologist' means a person who is licensed under this chapter to engage in the practice of psychology."

Iowa	Iowa Code § 154B.1	"6. 'Practice of psychology' means the application of established principles of learning, motivation, perception, thinking, and emotional relations to problems of behavior adjustment, group relations, and behavior modification, by persons trained in psychology for compensation or other personal gain. The application of principles includes but is not limited to counseling and the use of psychological remedial measures with persons, in groups or individually, with adjustment or emotional problems in the areas of work, family, school, and personal relationships; measuring and testing personality, intelligence, aptitudes, public opinion, attitudes, and skills; and the teaching of such subject matter, and the conducting of research on the problems relating to human behavior."
Kansas	Kan. Stat. Ann. § 74–5302	"(f) 'Practice of psychology' means the application of established principles of learning, motivation, perception, thinking and emotional relationships to problems of behavior adjustment, group relations and behavior modification, by persons trained in psychology. The application of such principles includes, but is not restricted to, counseling and the use of psychological remedial measures with persons, in groups or individually, having adjustment or emotional problems in the areas of work, family, school and personal relationships; measuring and testing personality, intelligence, aptitudes, public opinion, attitudes and skills; the teaching of such subject matter; and the conducting of research on problems relating to human behavior, except that in all cases involving the care of the sick and ill as defined by the laws of this state, the primary responsibility devolves upon those licensed under the Kansas healing arts act. The practice of psychology includes the diagnosis and treatment of mental disorders specified in the edition of the diagnostic and statistical manual of mental disorders of the American psychiatric association designated by the board by rules and regulations. If a licensed psychologist cannot make an independent diagnosis of a mental disorder, such psychologist shall consult with the client's primary care physician or psychiatrist to determine if there may be a medical condition or medication that may be causing or contributing to the client's symptoms of a mental disorder. A client may request in writing that such consultation be waived and such request shall be made a part of the client's record. A licensed psychologist may continue to evaluate and treat the client until such time that the medical consultation is obtained or waived. (g) 'Represents oneself to be a psychologist' means that a person engages in the practice of psychology for a fee, monetary or otherwise, or holds oneself out to the public by any title or description of services incorporating the word 'psychologic,' 'psychological,' 'psychologist' or 'psychology' and under such title or description offers to render or renders services to individuals, corporations or the public for a fee, monetary or otherwise."

Continued

Table 9.1 *Continued*

State	Statute Citation	Relevant Excerpt
Kentucky	Ky. Rev. Stat. § 319.010	"(7) 'Practice of psychology' means rendering to individuals, groups, organizations, or the public any psychological service involving the application of principles, methods, and procedures of understanding, predicting, and influencing behavior, such as the principles pertaining to learning, perception, motivation, thinking, emotions, and interpersonal relationships; the methods and procedures of interviewing, counseling, and psychotherapy; and psychological testing in constructing, administering, and interpreting tests of mental abilities, aptitudes, interests, attitudes, personality characteristics, emotion, and motivation. The application of said principles in testing, evaluation, treatment, use of psychotherapeutic techniques, and other methods includes, but is not limited to: diagnosis, prevention, and amelioration of adjustment problems and emotional, mental, nervous, and addictive disorders and mental health conditions of individuals and groups; educational and vocational counseling; the evaluation and planning for effective work and learning situations; and the resolution of interpersonal and social conflicts"
Louisiana	La. Rev. Stat. Ann. § 37:2352	"(7) 'Practice of psychology' is defined as the observation, description, evaluation, interpretation, and modification of human behavior, by the application of psychological principles, methods, and procedures, for the purpose of eliminating symptomatic, maladaptive, or undesired behavior, and of improving interpersonal relationships, work and life adjustment, personal effectiveness, behavioral health, and mental health. The practice of psychology includes but is not limited to psychological testing and evaluation or assessment of personal characteristics such as intelligence, personality, abilities, interests, aptitudes, and neuropsychological functioning; counseling, psychoanalysis, psychotherapy, hypnosis, stress management, biofeedback, behavior analysis and therapy; diagnosis and treatment of mental and emotional disorder or disability, alcoholism and substance abuse, and of the psychological aspects of physical illness, accident, injury, or disability; psycho educational evaluation, therapy, remediation, and consultation. Psychological services may be rendered to individuals, families, groups, institutions, organizations, and the public. The practice of psychology shall be construed within the meaning of this definition without regard to whether payment is received for services rendered."

Maine	Me. Rev. Stat. tit. 32, § 3811	"Two levels of psychological practice are defined for the purpose of this chapter. Such levels shall be known and referred to as 'psychological examiner' and 'psychologist.' 1. Psychological examiner. A person practices as a 'psychological examiner' within the meaning of this chapter when he holds himself out to be a psychological examiner, or renders to individuals or to the public for remuneration services involving the application of recognized principles, methods and procedures of the science and profession of psychology, but limited to interviewing or administering and interpreting tests of mental abilities, aptitudes, interests and personality characteristics, for such purposes as psychological evaluation or for educational or vocational selection, guidance or placement. A psychological examiner may provide intervention, such as consultation, behavior management or social skills training under the supervision of a licensed psychologist or as otherwise provided in law or rules issued in accordance with this chapter. A psychological examiner may not provide psychotherapy services under any circumstances. The State Board of Examiners of Psychologists shall establish rules for supervision of psychological examiners for intervention services. 2. Psychologist. A person practices as a 'psychologist' within the meaning of this chapter when he holds himself out to be a psychologist, or renders to individuals or to the public for remuneration any service involving the application of recognized principles, methods and procedures of the science and profession of psychology. Services which may be provided by psychologists include diagnosing, assessing and treating mental, emotional and psychological illness, disorders, problems and concerns and evaluation and treatment of vocational, social, educational, behavioral, intellectual and learning and cognitive disorders. These functions are performed through recognized psychological techniques such as, but not limited to, psychological testing, psychological interviews, psychological assessments, psychotherapy, personality counseling, behavior modification, cognitive therapies, learning therapies, biofeedback, hypnotherapy and psychological consultation to individuals and organizations. 3. Limitation. Nothing in this chapter shall be construed as permitting the practice of medicine as defined in section 3270 by psychological examiners or psychologists."
Maryland	Md. Code Ann., Health Occ. § 18–101	"(1) 'Practice psychology' means to provide to any person: (i) Any service for compensation involving the application of psychological principles, psychological methods, or psychological procedures for understanding, predicting, or influencing behavior, including the principles that relate to learning, perception, motivation, emotions, organizational relationships, and interpersonal relationships; (ii) Any service for compensation involving the application of psychological methods or psychological procedures for interviewing, counseling, psychotherapy, behavior modification, or hypnosis; or

Continued

Table 9.1 *Continued*

State	Statute Citation	Relevant Excerpt
		(iii) Any service for compensation involving the application of psychological methods or psychological procedures for constructing, administering, or interpreting tests of mental abilities, neuropsychological functioning, aptitudes, interests, attitudes, personality characteristics, emotions, or motivations. (2) 'Practice psychology' includes: (i) The application of psychological principles and psychological methods in the diagnosis, prevention, treatment, and amelioration of psychological problems, emotional conditions, or mental conditions of individuals or groups; (ii) The use of psychological methods to assist an individual in acquiring greater human effectiveness or to modify feelings, conditions, attitudes, or behavior that is emotionally, intellectually, or socially ineffectual or maladjusted; and (iii) The use of biofeedback instruments that do not pierce or cut the skin to measure physical and mental functioning. (3) In this subsection, 'psychological methods,' 'psychological principles,' and 'psychological procedures' include the body of information that can be derived from a graduate program in psychology, and other education or training recognized by the Board as prerequisites for a license under this title, and that does not amount to the practice of medicine."
Massachusetts	Mass. Ann. Laws ch. 112, § 118	"'The practice of psychology,' rendering or offering to render professional service for any fee, monetary or otherwise, to individuals, groups of individuals, organizations or members of the public which includes the observation, description, evaluation, interpretation, and modification of human behavior, by the application of psychological principles, methods and procedures, for the purpose of assessing or effecting changes in symptomatic, maladaptive or undesired behavior and issues pertaining to interpersonal relationships, work and life adjustment, personal effectiveness and mental health. The practice of psychology includes, but is not limited to, psychological testing, assessment and evaluation of intelligence, personality, abilities, attitudes, motivation, interests and aptitudes; counseling, psychotherapy, hypnosis, biofeedback training and behavior therapy; diagnosis and treatment of mental and emotional disorder or disability, alcoholism and substance abuse, and the psychological aspects of physical illness or disability; psychoeducational evaluation, therapy, remediation and consultation. Psychological services may be rendered to individuals, families, groups, and the public. For purposes of this definition, the practice of psychology does not include the teaching of psychology, the conduct of psychological research, or the provision of psychological consultation to organizations, unless such teaching research or consultation involves the delivery or supervision of the types of direct services described above, to individuals or groups of individuals."

Michigan	Mich. Comp. Laws Serv. § 333.18201	"(b) 'Practice of psychology' means the rendering to individuals, groups, organizations, or the public of services involving the application of principles, methods, and procedures of understanding, predicting, and influencing behavior for the purposes of the diagnosis, assessment related to diagnosis, prevention, amelioration, or treatment of mental or emotional disorders, disabilities or behavioral adjustment problems by means of psychotherapy, counseling, behavior modification, hypnosis, biofeedback techniques, psychological tests, or other verbal or behavioral means. The practice of psychology does not include the practice of medicine such as prescribing drugs, performing surgery, or administering electro-convulsive therapy."
Minnesota	Minn. Stat. Ann. § 148.89	"'Practice of psychology' means the observation, description, evaluation, interpretation, prediction, or modification of human behavior by the application of psychological principles, methods, or procedures for the purpose of preventing, eliminating, evaluating, assessing, or predicting symptomatic, maladaptive, or undesired behavior; applying psychological principles in legal settings; and enhancing interpersonal relationships, work, life and developmental adjustment, personal and organizational effectiveness, behavioral health, and mental health. The practice of psychology includes, but is not limited to, the following services, regardless of whether the provider receives payment for the services: (1) psychological research and teaching of psychology subject to the exemptions in section 148.9075; (2) psychological testing and the evaluation or assessment of personal characteristics, such as intelligence, personality, cognitive, physical and emotional abilities, skills, interests, aptitudes, and neuropsychological functioning; (3) counseling, psychoanalysis, psychotherapy, hypnosis, biofeedback, and behavior analysis and therapy; (4) diagnosis, treatment, and management of mental or emotional disorders or disabilities, substance use disorders, disorders of habit or conduct, and the psychological aspects of physical illness, accident, injury, or disability; (5) psychoeducational evaluation, therapy, and remediation; (6) consultation with physicians, other health care professionals, and clients regarding available treatment options, including medication, with respect to the provision of care for a specific client; (7) provision of direct services to individuals or groups for the purpose of enhancing individual and organizational effectiveness, using psychological principles, methods, and procedures to assess and evaluate individuals on personal characteristics for individual development or behavior change or for making decisions about the individual; and (8) supervision and consultation related to any of the services described in this subdivision."

Continued

Table 9.1 *Continued*

State	Statute Citation	Relevant Excerpt
Mississippi	Miss. Code Ann. § 73–31-3	"(i) 'Practice of psychology' means the observation, description, evaluation, interpretation, prediction and modification of human behavior through the application of psychological principles, methods and procedures, for the purposes of: 1. Preventing, eliminating, evaluating, assessing, or predicting symptomatic, maladaptive, or undesirable behavior; 2. Evaluating, assessing and/or facilitating the enhancement of individual, group and/or organizational effectiveness including personal effectiveness, adaptive behavior, interpersonal relationships, work and life adjustment, health, and individual, group and/or organizational performance; or 3. Assisting in legal decision-making. (ii) The practice of psychology includes, but is not limited to: 1. Psychological testing and the evaluation or assessment of personal characteristics, such as intelligence; personality; cognitive, behavioral, physical and/or emotional abilities; skills; interests; aptitudes; and neuropsychological functioning; 2. Counseling, psychoanalysis, psychotherapy, hypnosis, biofeedback, and behavior analysis and therapy; 3. Diagnosis, treatment, and management of mental and emotional disorder or disability, alcoholism and substance abuse, disorders of habit or conduct, as well as of the psychological aspects of physical illness, accident, injury, or disability; 4. Psychoeducational evaluation, therapy and remediation; 5. Consultation with physicians, other health care professionals and patients regarding all available treatment options, as well as consultation with attorneys, judges, business, and industry; 6. Provision of direct services to individuals and/or groups for the purpose of enhancing individual and thereby organizational effectiveness, using principles, methods and/or procedures to assess and evaluate individuals on personal characteristics for individual development and/or behavior change or for making decisions about the individual, such as selection; and 7. The supervision of any of the above. (iii) Psychological services are provided to individuals, families, groups, systems, organizations, and the public. The practice of psychology shall be construed within the meaning of this definition without regard to whether payment is received for services rendered and without regard to the means of service provision (e.g., face-to-face, telephone, Internet, or telehealth)."

Missouri	Mo. Rev. Stat. § 337.015	"3. The 'practice of psychology' within the meaning of this chapter is defined as the observation, description, evaluation, interpretation, treatment, and modification of human behavior by the application of psychological principles, methods, and procedures, for the purpose of preventing, treating, or eliminating symptomatic, maladaptive, or undesired behavior and of enhancing interpersonal relationships, work and life adjustment, personal effectiveness, behavioral health, and mental health. The practice of psychology includes, but is not limited to, psychometric or psychological testing and the evaluation or assessment of personal characteristics, such as intelligence, personality, abilities, interests, aptitudes, and neuropsychological functioning; counseling, psychoanalysis, psychotherapy, hypnosis, biofeedback, and behavior analysis and therapy; diagnosis and treatment of mental and emotional disorder or disability in both inpatient and outpatient settings, alcoholism and substance abuse, disorders of habit or conduct, as well as the psychological aspects of physical illness, accident, injury, or disability; psychoeducational evaluation, therapy, remediation, and consultation; and teaching and training of psychological competence. Psychological services may be rendered to individuals, families, groups, and the public. The practice of psychology shall be construed within the meaning of this definition without regard to whether payment is received for services rendered."
Montana	Mont. Code Ann. § 37–17-102	"(a) 'Practice of psychology' means the observation, description, interpretation, and modification of human behavior by the application of psychological principles, methods, and procedures for the purpose of eliminating symptomatic, maladaptive, or undesired behavior and improving interpersonal relations, work and life adjustment, personal effectiveness, and mental health. (b) The practice of psychology includes but is not limited to psychological testing and evaluation or assessment of personal characteristics such as intelligence, personality, abilities, interests, aptitudes, and neuropsychological functioning; counseling, psychoanalysis, psychotherapy, hypnosis, biofeedback, and behavior analysis and therapy; diagnosis and treatment of mental and emotional disorders or disabilities, chemical dependency, substance abuse, and the psychological aspects of physical illness, accident, injury, or disability; and psychoeducational evaluation, therapy, remediation, and consultation."

Continued

Table 9.1 *Continued*

State	Statute Citation	Relevant Excerpt
Nebraska	Neb. Rev. Stat. Ann § 38–3108	"(1) Practice of psychology means the observation, description, evaluation, interpretation, or modification of human behavior by the application of psychological principles, methods, or procedures for the purpose of preventing or eliminating symptomatic, maladaptive, or undesired behavior and of enhancing interpersonal relationships, work and life adjustment, personal effectiveness, behavioral health, and mental health. (2) The practice of psychology includes, but is not limited to, psychological testing and the evaluation or assessment of personal characteristics such as intelligence, personality, abilities, interests, aptitudes, and psychophysiological and neuropsychological functioning; counseling, psychoanalysis, psychotherapy, hypnosis, biofeedback, and behavior analysis and therapy; diagnosis and treatment of mental and emotional disorders, alcoholism and substance abuse, disorders of habit or conduct, and the psychological aspects of physical illness, accident, injury, or disability; psychoeducational evaluation, therapy, remediation, and consultation; and supervision of qualified individuals performing services specified in this section. (3) Psychological services may be rendered to individuals, families, groups, organizations, institutions, and the public. The practice of psychology shall be construed within the meaning of this definition without regard to whether payment is received for services rendered."
Nevada	Nev. Rev. Stat. Ann. § 641.025	"'Practice of psychology' means the observation, description, evaluation, interpretation or modification of human behavior by the application of psychological principles, methods or procedures to prevent or eliminate problematic, unhealthy or undesired behavior and to enhance personal relationships and behavioral and mental health. The term includes, without limitation, such specialized areas of competence as: 1. Psychological testing and the evaluation of personal characteristics, including, without limitation, intelligence, personality, abilities, interests, aptitudes and neuropsychological functioning; 2. Counseling; 3. Psychoanalysis; 4. Psychotherapy; 5. Hypnosis; 6. Biofeedback; 7. Analysis and therapy relating to behavior; 8. Diagnosis and treatment of mental or emotional disorders and alcohol and other substance use disorders, including, without limitation, disorders of habit or conduct; 9. Psychological aspects of physical injury, illness, accident or disability; and 10. Evaluation, therapy, remediation and consultation relating to the academic performance of the patient."

New Hampshire	N.H. Rev. Stat. Ann. § 329-B:2	"VII. 'Psychology practice by a licensed psychologist' means: (a) The observation, description, evaluation, interpretation, prediction, and modification of human behavior by the application of psychological principles, methods, and procedures, for the purposes of: (1) Preventing, eliminating, evaluating, assessing, or predicting symptomatic, maladaptive, or undesired behavior; (2) Evaluating, assessing, or facilitating the enhancement of individual, group, or organizational effectiveness, including personal effectiveness, adaptive behavior, interpersonal relationships, work and life adjustment, health, and individual, group, or organizational performance; or (3) Assisting in legal decision-making. (b) Psychological testing and the evaluation or assessment of personal characteristics, such as intelligence; personality; cognitive, physical, and emotional abilities; skills; interests; aptitudes; and neuropsychological functioning; (c) Counseling, consultation, psychoanalysis, psychotherapy, hypnosis, biofeedback, and behavior analysis and therapy; (d) Diagnosis, treatment, and management of mental and emotional disorder or disability, alcoholism and substance abuse, disorders of habit or conduct, and the psychological and behavioral aspects of medical/physical illness, accident, injury, or disability; (e) Psycho-educational evaluation, therapy, and remediation; (f) Consultation and coordination with other psychologists, physicians, other health care professionals, and patients regarding all available treatment options, including medication, with respect to provision of care for a specific client or patient or group; (g) Provision of direct services to individuals or groups for the purpose of enhancing individual and organizational effectiveness, or using psychological principles, methods, or procedures to assess and evaluate individuals on personal characteristics for individual development or behavior change, or for making decisions about the individual, such as selection; (h) Provision of any of these services or activities by any means, including electronic or telephonic; and (i) The supervision, ordering, referring, and prescribing of any of these services or activities; The practice of psychology shall be construed within the meaning of this definition without regard to whether payment is received for services rendered.

Continued

Table 9.1 *Continued*

State	Statute Citation	Relevant Excerpt
		VIII. 'Psychology services by a licensed psychologist' means the observation, description, evaluation, interpretation, diagnosis, and modification of human behavior by the application of psychological and systems principles, methods, and procedures for the purpose of preventing or eliminating symptomatic, maladapted, or undesirable behavior and of enhancing interpersonal relationships, work and life adjustments, personal effectiveness, behavioral health, and mental health, as well as the diagnosis and treatment of the psychological and social aspects of physical illness, accident, injury, or disability. Psychology services may include, but shall not be limited to, those services based on diagnosis and treatment of mental and emotional disorders and psycho-educational or consultative techniques integral to the treatment of such disorders when diagnosis is specified in the most current edition of the Diagnostic and Statistical Manual of Mental Disorders, published by the American Psychiatric Association, The International Classification of Disease Manual (ICD), or an equivalent of such manual as determined by the board. Psychological services may be rendered to individuals, families, groups, systems, or organizations."
New Jersey	N.J. Stat. § 45:14B-2	"(b) The 'practice of psychology' means the rendering of professional psychological services to individuals, singly or in groups, whether in the general public or in organizations, either public or private, for a fee, monetary or otherwise. 'Professional psychological services' means the application of psychological principles and procedures in the assessment, counseling or psychotherapy of individuals for the purposes of promoting the optimal development of their potential or ameliorating their personality disturbances and maladjustments as manifested in personal and interpersonal situations. Within the meaning of this act, professional psychological services does not include the application for a fee, monetary or otherwise, of psychological principles and procedures for purposes other than those described in this section."
New Mexico	N.M. Stat. Ann. § 61-9-3	"I. 'practice of psychology' means the observation, description, evaluation, interpretation and modification of human behavior by the application of psychological principles, methods and procedures for the purpose of preventing or eliminating symptomatic, maladaptive or undesired behavior and of enhancing interpersonal relationships, work and life adjustment, personal effectiveness, behavioral health and mental health, and further means the rendering of such psychological services to individuals, families or groups regardless of whether payment is received for services rendered. The practice of psychology includes psychological testing or neuropsychological testing and the evaluation or assessment of personal characteristics such as intelligence, personality, abilities, interests, aptitudes and neuropsychological functioning; counseling, psychoanalysis, psychotherapy, hypnosis, biofeedback, behavior analysis and therapy; diagnosis and treatment of a mental and emotional disorder or disability, alcoholism and substance abuse, disorders of habit or conduct and the psychological aspects of physical illness, accident, injury and disability; and psychoeducational evaluation, therapy, remediation and consultation."

New York	N.Y. Educ. Law § 7601-a	"1. The practice of psychology is the observation, description, evaluation, interpretation, and modification of behavior for the purpose of preventing or eliminating symptomatic, maladaptive or undesired behavior; enhancing interpersonal relationships, personal, group or organizational effectiveness and work and/or life adjustment; and improving behavioral health and/or mental health. The practice includes, but is not limited to psychological (including neuropsychological) testing and counseling; psychoanalysis; psychotherapy; the diagnosis and treatment of mental, nervous, emotional, cognitive or behavioral disorders, disabilities, ailments or illnesses, alcoholism, substance abuse, disorders of habit or conduct, the psychological aspects of physical illness, accident, injury or disability, psychological aspects of learning (including learning disorders); and the use of accepted classification systems."
North Carolina	N.C. Gen. Stat. § 90–270.136	"(8) Practice of psychology.—The observation, description, evaluation, interpretation, or modification of human behavior by the application of psychological principles, methods, and procedures for the purpose of preventing or eliminating symptomatic, maladaptive, or undesired behavior or of enhancing interpersonal relationships, work and life adjustment, personal effectiveness, behavioral health, or mental health. The practice of psychology includes, but is not limited to: psychological testing and the evaluation or assessment of personal characteristics such as intelligence, personality, abilities, interests, aptitudes, and neuropsychological functioning; counseling, psychoanalysis, psychotherapy, hypnosis, biofeedback, and behavior analysis and therapy; diagnosis, including etiology and prognosis, and treatment of mental and emotional disorder or disability, alcoholism and substance abuse, disorders of habit or conduct, as well as of the psychological and neuropsychological aspects of physical illness, accident, injury, or disability; and psychoeducational evaluation, therapy, remediation, and consultation. Psychological services may be rendered to individuals, families, groups, and the public. The practice of psychology shall be construed within the meaning of this definition without regard to whether payment is received for services rendered."

Continued

Table 9.1 *Continued*

State	Statute Citation	Relevant Excerpt
North Dakota	N.D. Cent. Code § 43–32-01	"6. 'Practice of psychology' means the observation, description, evaluation, interpretation, or modification of human behavior by the application of psychological principles, methods, and procedures for the purpose of preventing or eliminating symptomatic, maladaptive, or undesired behavior and enhancing interpersonal relationships, work and life adjustment, personal effectiveness, behavioral health, and mental health. The term includes psychological testing and the evaluation or assessment of personal characteristics, such as intelligence, personality, abilities, interests, aptitudes, and neuropsychological functioning; counseling, psychotherapy, biofeedback, behavior analysis and therapy, clinical applications of hypnosis, and other therapeutic techniques based on psychological principles; diagnosis and treatment of mental and emotional disorder or disability, compulsive disorders, disorders of habit or conduct as well as of the psychological aspects of physical illness, accident, injury, or disability; and psychoeducational evaluation, therapy, remediation, and consultation. The term includes providing psychological services to individuals, families, groups, organizations, institutions, and the public regardless of whether payment is received for services rendered. The term includes supervising others who are engaged in the practice of psychology."
Ohio	Ohio Rev. Code Ann. § 4732.01	"(B) 'The practice of psychology' means rendering or offering to render to individuals, groups, organizations, or the public any service involving the application of psychological procedures to assessment, diagnosis, prevention, treatment, or amelioration of psychological problems or emotional or mental disorders of individuals or groups; or to the assessment or improvement of psychological adjustment or functioning of individuals or groups, whether or not there is a diagnosable pre-existing psychological problem. Practice of psychology includes the practice of independent school psychology and the practice of school psychology. For purposes of this chapter, teaching or research shall not be regarded as the practice of psychology, even when dealing with psychological subject matter, provided it does not otherwise involve the professional practice of psychology in which an individual's welfare is directly affected by the application of psychological procedures. (C) 'Psychological procedures' include but are not restricted to application of principles, methods, or procedures of understanding, predicting, or influencing behavior, such as the principles pertaining to learning, conditioning, perception, motivation, thinking, emotions, or interpersonal relationships; the methods or procedures of verbal interaction, interviewing, counseling, behavior modification, environmental manipulation, group process, psychological psychotherapy, or hypnosis; and the methods or procedures of administering or interpreting tests of mental abilities, aptitudes, interests, attitudes, personality characteristics, emotions, or motivation."

Oklahoma	Okla. Stat. tit. 59, § 1352	"3. 'Practice of psychology' means the observation, description, evaluation, interpretation, and modification of human behavior by the application of psychological principles, methods, and procedures, for the purpose of preventing or eliminating symptomatic, maladaptive, or undesired behavior and of enhancing interpersonal relationships, work and life adjustment, personal effectiveness, behavioral health, and mental health. The practice of psychology, a branch of the healing arts, includes, but is not limited to, psychological testing and the evaluation or assessment of personal characteristics, such as intelligence, personality, abilities, interests, aptitudes, and neuropsychological functioning; counseling, psychoanalysis, psychotherapy, hypnosis, biofeedback, and behavior analysis and therapy; diagnosis and treatment of mental and emotional disorder or disability, alcoholism and substance abuse, disorders of habit or conduct, as well as of the psychological aspects of physical illness, accident, injury, or disability; and psychoeducational evaluation, therapy, remediation, and consultation. Psychological services may be rendered to individuals, families, groups, and the public. The practice of psychology shall be construed within the meaning of this definition without regard to whether payment is received for services rendered."
Oregon	Or. Rev. Stat. Ann. § 675.010	"(4) 'Practice of psychology' means rendering or offering to render supervision, consultation, evaluation or therapy services to individuals, groups or organizations for the purpose of diagnosing or treating behavioral, emotional or mental disorders. 'Practice of psychology' also includes delegating the administration and scoring of tests to technicians qualified by and under the direct supervision of a licensed psychologist."
Pennsylvania	63 Pa. Stat. Ann. § 1202	"'Practice of psychology' means offering to render or rendering to individuals, corporations, institutions, governmental agencies, or the public for remuneration any service involving the following: (i) The application of established principles of learning, motivation, perception, thinking, and emotional relationships to problems of personality evaluation, group relations, and behavior adjustment. The application of said principles includes, but is not restricted to, counseling and the use of psychological methods with persons or groups with adjustment problems in the areas of work, family, school, and personal relationships; measuring and testing of personality, intelligence, aptitudes, and emotions, and offering services as a psychological consultant. Psychologists with appropriate education, training and experience may diagnose and use psychological methods in the treatment of a mental, emotional or nervous illness or disability; alcoholism and other substance abuse; disorders of habit or conduct; psychological aspects of physical illness, accident, injury or disability; and psychoeducational evaluation, therapy, remediation and consultation.

Continued

Table 9.1 *Continued*

State	Statute Citation	Relevant Excerpt
		(ii) (a) 'Measuring and testing,' consisting of the psychological assessment and evaluation of abilities, attitudes, aptitudes, achievements, adjustments, motives, personality dynamics and/or other psychological attributes of individuals, or groups of individuals by means of standardized measurements or other methods, techniques or procedures recognized by the science and profession of psychology, (b) 'psychological methods,' consisting of the application of principles of learning and motivation in an interpersonal situation with the objectives of modification of perception and adjustment, and requiring highly developed skills in the disciplines, techniques, and methods of altering through learning processes, attitudes, feelings, values, self-concept, personal goals and adaptive patterns, (c) 'psychological consulting,' consisting of interpreting or reporting upon scientific fact or theory in psychology, rendering expert psychological opinion, psychological evaluation, or engaging in applied psychological research."
Rhode Island	R.I. Gen. Laws Section 5–44-1	"(7) 'Practice of psychology' means the rendering of professional psychological services to individuals, groups, families, or any public or private organization for remuneration. Professional psychological services means applying established psychological principles, methods, or procedures for the purpose of preventing or eliminating symptomatic, maladaptive, or undesired behavior and of enhancing interpersonal relationships, work and life adjustment, personal effectiveness, and mental health. The practice of psychology includes, but is not limited to: (i) Diagnoses and treatment of emotional, mental, or behavioral dysfunction, disorder, or disability, alcoholism and substance-abuse disorders of habit or conduct, as well as of the psychological aspects of physical illness, accident, injury, or disability; (ii) Psychological testing and evaluation of intelligence, personality, abilities, interests, aptitudes, and neuropsychological functioning; (iii) Psychoeducation evaluation, therapy, remediation, and consultation; and (iv) Counseling, psychotherapy, psychoanalysis, hypnotherapy, biofeedback, and behavior analysis and therapy."

South Carolina	S.C. Code Ann. § 40–55-50	"(A) A person practices as a psychologist within the meaning of this chapter when that person holds himself or herself out as a psychologist or applies the principles, methods, or procedures of psychology in the conduct of any of the following activities: (1) Assessment of individual, family, or group behavioral, emotional, and/or intellectual functioning for the purpose of one or more of the following: (a) diagnosing mental disorders; (b) identifying psychological or neuropsychological aspects of other dysfunctions, diseases, or disabilities; (c) evaluating mental or emotional status including intelligence and aptitude; (d) identifying personality characteristics; (e) identifying psychological factors influencing well-being; (f) selecting, placing, or referring into treatments, programs, or settings; (g) evaluating the effectiveness of treatments, programs, or settings; (h) preventing mental disorders or maladaptive behavior related to other dysfunction, disease, or disability. For purposes of this section, 'assessment' refers to, but is not limited to, one or more of the following practices insofar as they involve the application of psychological principles, methods, or procedures: observation, description, testing, appraisal, evaluation, screening, test interpretation, interviewing, diagnosis of mental disorders, neuropsychological testing, psychological testing or evaluation or psycho-educational testing or evaluation, or a combination of any of these for any of the purposes identified in this item. (2) Engaging in a therapeutic relationship with an individual, family, or group for the purpose of one or more of the following: (a) improving the quality of mental health or social adjustment, or both; (b) reducing, preventing, modifying, or eliminating maladaptive or undesired behaviors, cognitions, emotions, or psychological or physical characteristics; (c) treating diagnosed mental disorders, whether treatment is focused on behavioral manifestations of the disorder, the environmental context of the disorder, or underlying causal processes; (d) improving individual performance; (e) modifying cognitions, emotions, or behaviors, or a combination of these, in order to influence psychological well-being;

Continued

Table 9.1 *Continued*

State	Statute Citation	Relevant Excerpt
		(f) psychological research; or (g) any combination of subitems (a) through (f). (3) Engaging in a psychological consulting relationship with an individual organization, group or community, or a combination of these, for the purpose of: (a) designing or delivering psychological programs or services, or both; (b) evaluating psychological programs or services. (B) A person not otherwise exempt from this chapter is engaged in the practice of psychology when performing any of the activities enumerated in subsection (A), regardless of whether or not payment is received for the services. Specifically excluded from psychological practice within the meaning of this chapter are the physical, chemical, and nonbehavioral aspects of Chapter 47. Nothing in this chapter shall prohibit or limit a licensed physician in the practice of his profession as provided by law. (C) A person is deemed to be practicing as a psychologist within the meaning of this chapter if the person engages in any of the activities enumerated in subsection (A) electronically within this State including, but not limited to, by means of the internet, phone lines, and personal computer modems."
South Dakota	S.D. Codified Laws § 36–27A-1	"5) 'The practice of psychology,' the observation, description, evaluation, interpretation, and modification of human behavior by the application of psychological principles, methods, and procedures for the purpose of preventing or eliminating symptomatic, maladaptive, or undesired behavior and of enhancing interpersonal relationships, work and life adjustment, personal effectiveness, behavioral health, and mental health. The term includes psychological testing and the evaluation or assessment of personal characteristics, such as intelligence, personality, abilities, interests, aptitudes, and neuropsychological functioning; individual, marital, family, or group counseling; psychotherapy and other therapeutic techniques based on psychological principles; diagnosis and treatment of mental and emotional disorders or disabilities, compulsive disorders, disorders of habit or conduct as well as of the psychological aspects of physical illness, accident, injury, or disability; and psychoeducational evaluation, therapy, remediation, and consultation. The practice of psychology is the rendering of psychological services to individuals, families, groups, and the public and is without regard to whether payment is received for services rendered."

Tennessee	Tenn. Code Ann. § 63–11-203	"(1) 'Practice of psychologist' means the observation, description, evaluation, interpretation and modification of human behavior by the application of psychological principles, methods and procedures for the purpose of assessing, preventing or eliminating symptomatic, maladaptive or undesired behavior and of enhancing interpersonal relationships, work and life adjustment, personal effectiveness, behavioral health and mental health. (2) (A) 'Practice of psychologist' includes, but is not limited to: (i) Psychological testing and the evaluation or assessment of personal characteristics, such as intelligence, personality, abilities, interests, aptitudes and neuropsychological functioning; (ii) Counseling, psychoanalysis, psychotherapy, hypnosis, biofeedback and behavior analysis and therapy; (iii) Psychological diagnosis and treatment of mental, emotional and nervous disorders or disabilities, alcoholism and substance abuse, disorders of habit or conduct, as well as of the psychological aspects of physical illness, accident, injury or disability; (iv) Case management and utilization review of psychological services; (v) Psychoeducational evaluation, therapy, remediation and consultation; (vi) Forensic evaluation; provided, that a person licensed under this chapter performing forensic evaluation is considered to be acting within their lawful scope of practice and the practice of forensic evaluation is not exclusive to individuals licensed under this chapter; (vii) Parent coordination; provided, that a person licensed under this chapter performing parent coordination is considered to be acting within their lawful scope of practice and the practice of parent coordination is not exclusive to individuals licensed under this chapter; and (viii) Telepsychology, which means the practice of psychology via electronic communications technology by persons licensed under this chapter. (B) Psychological services may be rendered to individuals, families, groups and the public. (3) 'Practice of psychologist' is construed within the meaning of this definition without regard to whether payment is received for services rendered. (b) A person represents that person to be a psychologist if that person uses any title or description of services incorporating the words 'psychology,' 'psychological' or 'psychologist,' if such person possesses expert qualification in any area of psychology or if that person offers to the public or renders to individuals or to groups of individuals services defined as the practice of psychology in this chapter."

Continued

Table 9.1 *Continued*

State	Statute Citation	Relevant Excerpt
Texas	Tex. Occ. Code § 501.003	"(1) 'Practice of psychology' means: (A) the observation, description, diagnosis, evaluation, assessment, interpretation, or treatment of and intervention in human behavior by applying education, training, methods, and procedures for the purpose of: (i) preventing, predicting, treating, remediating, or eliminating: (a) symptomatic, maladaptive, or undesired behavior; (b) emotional, interpersonal, learning, substance use, neuropsychological, cognitive, or behavioral disorders or disabilities, including those that accompany medical problems; or (c) mental illness; (ii) evaluating, assessing, or facilitating, by a license holder or a person who represents the person to the public by a title or description of services that includes the word 'psychological,' 'psychologist,' or 'psychology,' the enhancement of individual, group, or organizational effectiveness, including evaluating, assessing, or facilitating: (a) personal effectiveness; (b) adaptive behavior; (c) interpersonal relationships; (d) academic, vocational, and life adjustment; (e) health; or (f) individual, group, or organizational performance; (iii) providing psychological, neuropsychological, and psychoeducational evaluation, therapy, and remediation as well as counseling, psychoanalysis, psychotherapy, hypnosis, and biofeedback; or (iv) consulting with others, including other mental health professionals, physicians, school personnel, or organizations within the scope of the provider's competency and training with respect to services provided for a specific individual; or

(B) the supervision of an activity or service described by Paragraph (A).

(2) 'Psychological services' means acts or behaviors that are included within the purview of the practice of psychology.

(b) A person is engaged in the practice of psychology if the person:

(1) when providing or offering to provide psychological services to another in a professional relationship, represents the person to the public by a title or description of services that includes the word 'psychological,' 'psychologist,' or 'psychology';

(2) provides or offers to provide psychological services to individuals, groups, organizations, or the public in a professional relationship;

(3) is a psychologist or psychological associate employed as described by Section 501.004(a)(1) who offers or provides psychological services, other than lecture services, to the public for consideration separate from the salary that person receives for performing the person's regular duties; or

(4) is employed as a psychologist or psychological associate by an organization that sells psychological services, other than lecture services, to the public for consideration.

(c) A person is not engaged in the practice of psychology based solely on the person offering, regardless of whether the person is solicited, advice, counsel, or guidance addressing or affecting the mental, emotional, or behavioral health of another, if the person does not represent that the person is licensed under this chapter or engaged in the delivery of psychological services and does not represent that the advice, counsel, or guidance is psychological in nature, and:

(1) the advice, counsel, or guidance is not offered in the context of a professional relationship;

(2) if the person is offering the advice, counsel, or guidance in connection with the person's occupation, the primary focus of the occupation is not the delivery of mental, emotional, or behavioral health care services; or

(3) the advice, counsel, or guidance is offered through an organized or structured program or peer support service that is designed to support or assist a person with a self-identified goal of changing or improving certain aspects of the person's mental, emotional, or behavioral health."

Continued

Table 9.1 *Continued*

State	Statute Citation	Relevant Excerpt
Utah	Utah Code Ann. § 58–61-102	"(a) 'Practice of psychology' includes: (i) the practice of mental health therapy by means of observation, description, evaluation, interpretation, intervention, and treatment to effect modification of human behavior by the application of generally recognized professional psychological principles, methods, and procedures for the purpose of preventing, treating, or eliminating mental or emotional illness or dysfunction, the symptoms of any of these, or maladaptive behavior; (ii) the observation, description, evaluation, interpretation, or modification of human behavior by the application of generally recognized professional principles, methods, or procedures requiring the education, training, and clinical experience of a psychologist, for the purpose of assessing, diagnosing, preventing, or eliminating symptomatic, maladaptive, or undesired behavior and of enhancing interpersonal relationships, work and life adjustment, personal effectiveness, behavioral health, and mental health; (iii) psychological testing and the evaluation or assessment of personal characteristics such as intelligence, personality, abilities, interests, aptitudes, and neuropsychological functioning; (iv) counseling, marriage and family therapy, psychoanalysis, psychotherapy, hypnosis, and behavior analysis and therapy; (v) diagnosis and treatment of mental and emotional disorders of disability, alcoholism and substance abuse, disorders of habit or conduct, and the psychological aspects of physical illness, accident, injury, or disability; and (vi) psychoeducational evaluation, therapy, remediation, and consultation. (b) An individual practicing psychology may provide services to individuals, couples, families, groups of individuals, members of the public, and individuals or groups within organizations or institutions."
Vermont	Vt. Stat. Ann. tit. 26, § 3001	"(1) 'Practice of psychology' means rendering or offering to render to individuals, groups, or organizations, for a consideration, any service involving the application of principles, methods, and procedures of understanding, predicting, and influencing behavior that are primarily drawn from the science of psychology. The science of psychology includes assessment, diagnosis, prevention, and amelioration of adjustment problems and emotional and mental disorders of individuals and groups."

Virginia	Va. Code Ann. § 54.1–3600	"'Practice of psychology' means the practice of applied psychology, clinical psychology, or school psychology. 'Practice of applied psychology' means application of the principles and methods of psychology to improvement of organizational function, personnel selection and evaluation, program planning and implementation, individual motivation, development and behavioral adjustment, as well as consultation on teaching and research. 'Practice of clinical psychology' includes, but is not limited to: 1. 'Testing and measuring' that consists of the psychological evaluation or assessment of personal characteristics such as intelligence, abilities, interests, aptitudes, achievements, motives, personality dynamics, psychoeducational processes, neuropsychological functioning, or other psychological attributes of individuals or groups. 2. 'Diagnosis and treatment of mental and emotional disorders' that consists of the appropriate diagnosis of mental disorders according to standards of the profession and the ordering or providing of treatments according to need. Treatment includes providing counseling, psychotherapy, marital/family therapy, group therapy, behavior therapy, psychoanalysis, hypnosis, biofeedback, and other psychological interventions with the objective of modification of perception, adjustment, attitudes, feelings, values, self-concept, personality, or personal goals, the treatment of alcoholism and substance abuse, the treatment of disorders of habit or conduct, as well as of the psychological aspects of physical illness, pain, injury, or disability. 3. 'Psychological consulting' that consists of interpreting or reporting on scientific theory or research in psychology, rendering expert psychological or clinical psychological opinion or evaluation, or engaging in applied psychological research, program or organizational development, or administration, supervision, or evaluation of psychological services. The 'practice of school psychology' means: 1. 'Testing and measuring' that consists of psychological assessment, evaluation, and diagnosis relative to the assessment of intellectual ability, aptitudes, achievement, adjustment, motivation, personality, or any other psychological attribute of persons as individuals or in groups that directly relates to learning or behavioral problems that impact education. 2. 'Counseling' that consists of professional advisement and interpretive services with children or adults for amelioration or prevention of problems that impact education. Counseling services relative to the practice of school psychology include but are not limited to the procedures of verbal interaction, interviewing, behavior modification, environmental manipulation, and group processes. 3. 'Consultation' that consists of educational or vocational consultation or direct educational services to schools, agencies, organizations, or individuals. Psychological consulting relative to the practice of school psychology is directly related to learning problems and related adjustments. 4. Development of programs such as designing more efficient and psychologically sound classroom situations and acting as a catalyst for teacher involvement in adaptations and innovations."

Continued

Table 9.1 *Continued*

State	Statute Citation	Relevant Excerpt
Washington	Wash. Rev. Code Ann. § 18.83.010	"(1) The 'practice of psychology' means the observation, evaluation, interpretation, and modification of human behavior by the application of psychological principles, methods, and procedures for the purposes of preventing or eliminating symptomatic or maladaptive behavior and promoting mental and behavioral health. It includes, but is not limited to, providing the following services to individuals, families, groups, organizations, and the public, whether or not payment is received for services rendered: (a) Psychological measurement, assessment, and evaluation by means of psychological, neuropsychological, and psychoeducational testing; (b) Diagnosis and treatment of mental, emotional, and behavioral disorders, and psychological aspects of illness, injury, and disability; and (c) Counseling and guidance, psychotherapeutic techniques, remediation, health promotion, and consultation within the context of established psychological principles and theories. This definition does not include the teaching of principles of psychology for accredited educational institutions, or the conduct of research in problems of human or animal behavior. Nothing in this definition shall be construed as permitting the administration or prescribing of drugs or in any way infringing upon the practice of medicine and surgery as defined in chapter 18.71 RCW."
West Virginia	W. Va. Code § 30–21-2	"(e) 'Practice of psychology' means the rendering or offering to render for a fee, salary or other compensation, monetary or otherwise, any psychological service involving: (i) The application of the principles, methods and procedures of understanding, predicting and influencing behavior; (ii) the application of the principles pertaining to learning, perception, motivation, thinking, emotions and interpersonal relationships; (iii) the application of the methods and procedures of interviewing and counseling; (iv) the application of the methods and procedures of psychotherapy, meaning the use of learning, conditioning methods and emotional reactions, in a professional relationship, to assist a person or persons to modify feelings, attitudes and behavior, which are intellectually, socially or emotionally maladjustive or ineffectual; (v) the constructing, administering and interpreting of tests of intelligence, special abilities, aptitudes, interests, attitudes, personality characteristics, emotions and motivation; (vi) the psychological evaluation, prevention and improvement of adjustment problems of individuals and groups; and (vii) the resolution of interpersonal and social conflicts.

		However, for the purpose of this article, the term 'practice of psychology' shall not include: (1) Teaching, lecturing or engaging in research in psychology as part of salaried employment at an institution of higher learning; (2) The official duties of a person employed as a psychologist by the State of West Virginia or any of its departments, agencies, divisions or bureaus, or local governments, except for the West Virginia Department of Education, a county board of education, or a regional education agency, which duties are performed under the direct and regular supervision of a licensee; (3) The official duties of a person employed as a psychologist by any department, agency, division or bureau of the United States of America; (4) The official duties of a person working under the direct and regular supervision of a licensee for the purpose of gaining the experience required for a license hereunder by the provisions of subdivision (4), subsection (a), section seven [§ 30–21-7] of this article, which experience is of a type approved by the board; (5) The use, in good faith, of certain psychological techniques, procedures, methods and principles as an incident to engaging in a recognized occupation or profession, other than the practice of psychology, including, but not limited to, the occupation or profession of a physician, lawyer, dentist, social worker, sociologist, political scientist, economist, probation or parole officer, rehabilitation or marriage counselor, clergyman, audiologist, speech pathologist, teacher, educational or guidance counselor and a placement or personnel director; (6) The activities of a student of psychology, psychological intern or psychological resident, which activities are a part of and are engaged in pursuant to a course of study at an institution of higher learning; or (7) The activities of an assistant or technician which are performed under the direct and regular supervision of a licensee."
Wisconsin	Wis. Stat. Ann. § 455.01	"(a) 'Practice of psychology' means the observation, description, evaluation, interpretation, prediction, or modification of human behavior by the application of psychological principles, methods, or procedures for any of the following purposes, in exchange for a fee: 1. Preventing, eliminating, evaluating, assessing, or predicting symptomatic, maladaptive, or undesired behavior and promoting adaptive health maintaining behavior or psychological functioning. 2. Assisting in legal decision-making. (b) 'Practice of psychology' includes all of the following if done in exchange for a fee: 1. Psychological testing and the evaluation or assessment of a person's characteristics, including intelligence; personality; cognitive, physical, or emotional abilities; skills; interests; aptitudes; or neuropsychological functioning. 2. Counseling, consultation, psychoanalysis, psychotherapy, hypnosis, biofeedback, behavior therapy, and applied behavior analysis.

Continued

Table 9.1 *Continued*

State	Statute Citation	Relevant Excerpt
		3. The diagnosis, treatment, or management of mental and emotional disorders or disabilities, substance use disorders, disorders of habit or conduct, and the psychological aspects of physical illnesses, accidents, injuries, or disabilities. 4. Psychoeducational evaluation, therapy, or remediation. 5. Consultation with other psychologists, physicians, or other health care professionals and with a patient regarding all available treatment options with respect to the provision of care for a specific patient or client. 6. The supervision of anything specified in subds. 1. to 5."
Wyoming	Wyo. Stat. Ann. § 33–27-113	"(iii) 'Practice of psychology' means the observation, description, evaluation, interpretation and modification of human behavior by the application of psychological principles, methods and procedures, for the purpose of any one (1) or any combination of the following: (A) Preventing, eliminating, evaluating or assessing symptomatic, maladaptive or undesired behavior; (B) Enhancing interpersonal relationships, work and life adjustment, personal effectiveness, behavioral health and mental health; (C) Consulting in legal decision making; (D) Psychological testing and the evaluation or assessment of personal characteristics such as intelligence, personality, abilities, interests, aptitudes and neuropsychological functioning; (E) Psychoanalysis, psychotherapy, hypnosis, biofeedback and behavior analysis and therapy; (F) Diagnosis and treatment of mental and emotional disorder or disability, alcoholism and substance abuse, disorders of habit or conduct, as well as of psychological aspects of physical illness, accident, injury or disability; (G) Psychoeducational evaluation, therapy, remediation and consultation."

(c) Psychotherapy within the meaning of this chapter means the use of psychological methods in a professional relationship to assist a person or persons to acquire greater human effectiveness or to modify feelings, conditions, attitudes, and behaviors that are emotionally, intellectually, or socially ineffectual or maladaptive. (California Business and Professional Code § 2903, 2023)

Several aspects of this definition of the "practice of psychology" are notable. California does not limit licensure to (1) a particular type of psychologist (e.g., clinical psychologists); (2) only those individuals who refer to themselves as "psychologists"; (3) only those who work with individual or groups; or (4) only to the diagnosis and treatment of individuals or groups. One could imagine many industrial and organizational psychologists working with or consulting with corporations potentially falling under this standard as well as many other mental health activities commonly performed by other types of psychologists or even other groups of mental health professionals meeting this definition. Not every jurisdiction has adopted a broad definition of psychological practice, but all jurisdictions include psychological diagnosis and treatment as part of their legal standards (Kane et al., 2023).

Most forensic mental health assessments and treatment would fall under the purview of licensure laws. However, what is less clear across different "practice of psychology" definitions is whether jury consultation, more general consultation with attorneys about forensic issues not related to diagnosis and treatment (i.e., child abuse evaluations), expert testimony without a forensic evaluation (i.e., review of another's expert report), or legal case consultation unrelated to diagnosis and treatment would fall under these definitions. For example, is a testifying expert that reviews the quality of the report of another psychological expert in a personal injury case, but does not perform their own evaluation, considered to be practicing psychology in the jurisdiction in which they testify? Does it matter if their expert testimony is specifically related to the diagnosis and treatment of a legally involved individual? Forensic mental health practice is only problematic and/or subject to legal or disciplinary sanction if the jurisdiction where the event is taking place defines the action (evaluation, testimony, consultation, etc.) as the "practice of psychology." Given all this, it is incumbent on the practitioner to be aware of the scope of the "practice of psychology" in the jurisdiction where they are providing psychological services. If the practitioner's services fall under such practice laws and regulations, the next question is what is required by that jurisdiction to meet the requirements of licensure or recognized temporary practice for those actions.[3]

To be recognized as a licensed psychologist in a particular jurisdiction, certain educational, practice, supervision, and examination requirements must be met. While many of them are consistent across different jurisdictions, there are important variations in aspects of these requirements, including but not limited to (1) whether the practitioner's graduate program needs to be accredited by the American Psychological Association/Canadian Psychological Association or another recognized professional body (i.e., ASPPB/National Register Joint Designation Committee); (2) the required number of supervised hours; (3) the training and years of licensure necessary for the supervisor of the practitioner; (4) the required number of hours that must be accrued predoctoral versus post-doctoral; (5) the required number of hours that involve direct contact with clients/patients; and (6) additional examination(s) (e.g., specific state examination in addition to the more general Examination of Professional Practice in Psychology [EPPP]) and continuing education courses that must be successfully completed to be eligible for licensure (Herman & Sharer, 2013; see Chapter 8 for more discussion about the qualifications for becoming a licensed psychologist). One noteworthy attempt to create a compendium of these licensure requirements across all U.S. jurisdictions became untenable because there was contradictory information available, information that was available was incomplete, or available information was not frequently updated (Herman & Sharer, 2013; Younggren et al., 2022).

Temporary In-Person Interjurisdiction Practice and Telepsychology Practice

These detailed and divergent psychology licensing requirements make it challenging to obtain licenses in multiple jurisdictions.[4] Additionally, there are separate fees and continuing education requirements for renewal that can make maintaining multiple state licenses confusing, expensive, and time-consuming. Nonetheless, forensic mental health professionals may need or want to temporarily practice across jurisdictional boundaries for a variety of reasons. For example, a defendant subject to a competency to stand trial evaluation in State A, where the practitioner is licensed, might be incarcerated in State B while awaiting trial for a different legal proceeding; a licensed practitioner in State A who is performing a child custody evaluation for the court in State A may want to evaluate a parent who has moved to State B; an expert in guardianship evaluations licensed in State A may be called by an attorney in State B to perform a forensic evaluation of that individual in State B; a defendant may have partially completed court-mandated treatment in State A, but moves to State B and wishes to fully complete their therapy through telepsychology with their initial psychologist in State A. There are clearly myriad reasons for mental health professionals, particularly forensic mental health professionals, to practice in multiple jurisdictions.

However, telepsychology and temporary in-person interjurisdictional practice, which might allow the mental health professional from State A to provide these services in State B, are also governed by an even more confusing array of state licensure requirements and regulations (Tucillo et al., 2002). Almost all states allow the temporary practice of a licensed psychologist from another jurisdiction to practice in their state (in-person or otherwise) for a set period of time not to exceed a certain limit (e.g., 30 days, but there are wide discrepancies in lengths). Yet these rules vary in terms of whether the licensed out-of-state practitioner must (1) contact the in-state licensing board (e.g., Alaska); (2) pay a fee and obtain a temporary license from the licensing board (e.g., Nebraska); (3) live in a state that shares a border with the state where the psychological services will be provided (e.g., Michigan); and (4) be supervised by an in-state licensed professional (e.g., Massachusetts); some states combine these requirements and/or have additional requirements (see Table 9.2 for list of state temporary practice laws) (Kane et al., 2023).[5] Further, state licensing boards have only recently begun contemplating interjurisdictional telepsychology-related issues and treating these requirements differently or similarly to in-person interjurisdictional restrictions (American Psychological Association, 2013; Batastini et al., 2023). In sum, there is a complex and almost impenetrable legal landscape for mental health professionals who wish to provide forensic services across jurisdictional boundaries through telepsychology or temporary in-person practice.

One additional legal caveat should be noted with regard to interjurisdictional practice complexity. If the practitioners' services, even if they would normally meet a jurisdiction's definition of the "practice of psychology," occur on federal land or in a "federal enclave,"[6] the forensic mental health professional may only need to be licensed in any state and not in the state where the facility is located and services are provided. This is why psychologists who practice in federal prisons, military courts, Veteran Administration hospitals, or on tribal land need only to be licensed in (at least) one state, but not necessarily in the state in which they work and provide psychological services (see 10 U.S. Code § 1094; Department of Justice, 2014; 25 U.S. Code § 1621t). However, even if a forensic evaluation, treatment, or service is performed for a federal court, if the services occur outside federal land or enclave and the actions meet that jurisdiction's definition of the "practice of psychology," then that practitioner may be subject to that jurisdiction's temporary licensure requirements. For example, if a Bureau of Prison's psychologist evaluates a criminal defendant for competency to stand trial while the defendant is housed in a state facility and the psychologist is not licensed in the state where the state facility is located, then the psychologist is likely engaged in the unlawful temporary practice of psychology in that jurisdiction unless other conditions are met.

Table 9.2 Temporary Psychological Practice in the United States

State	National Register accepted?	CPQ Accepted?	PSYPACT State?	Temporary Practice Permitted Outside PSYPACT?	Statute
Alabama	No	Yes	Yes	Yes, up to 60 days each calendar year in response to declared disaster or state of emergency, or up to 30 days per calendar year under normal conditions	Code of Ala. Section 34–26-41(d)(3)(f) + (g)
Alaska	No	No	No	Yes, up to 30 days in 1 year, once in a person's lifetime	12 Alaska Admin. Code 60.035(a)
Arizona	Yes	Yes	Yes	Yes, "if the activities and services conducted in this state are within the psychologist's customary area of practice, do not exceed 20 days per year and are not otherwise in violation of this chapter and the client or patient, the public or the consumer is informed of the limited nature of these activities and services and that the psychologist is not licensed in this state. A person may exceed the 20-day limit of this paragraph to assist in the public service that is related to a disaster as acknowledged by the board."	A.R.S. Section 32–2075
Arkansas	Yes	Yes	Yes	Yes, the provision of expert testimony is exempted from licensure requirements.	A.C.A. Section 17–97-103
California	Yes	Yes	No	Yes, may offer psychological services in this state for a period not to exceed 30 days in any calendar year	Cal Bus & Prof Code Section 2912

Colorado	Yes	Yes	Yes	Yes, may practice up to 20 days per year if they inform the relevant party that they are not licensed in Colorado	C.R.S. 12–245-217
Connecticut	No	Yes	Yes	No, does not offer temporary practice outside of the PSYPACT, but does offer licensure by endorsement, which is a form of reciprocity	Conn. Gen. Stat. Section 20–190
Delaware	Yes	Yes	Yes	Yes, up to 6 days of professional services as a psychologist per calendar year	24 Del. C. Section 3510
District of Columbia	Yes	Yes	Yes	Yes, it is permitted if the psychologist is providing care for a visit not exceeding 30 days, or if the individual is providing consultation services, or if the individual is retained to assess or evaluate a subject and to testify as an expert witness.	D.C. Code Section 3–1205.02
Florida	In Process—Board voted to approve	No	Yes	Yes, if such services are performed for no more than 5 days in any month and no more than 15 days in any calendar year and the psychologist is licensed in a state where the licensing requirements are equivalent to or higher than Florida's licensure requirements	Fla. Stat. Section 490.014
Georgia	No	Yes	Yes	Yes, permits temporary practice for up to 30 days within a calendar year so long as the requirements for a license in the other jurisdiction are equal to or exceed the requirements for licensure in Georgia	O.C.G.A. Section 43–39-7
Hawaii	Yes	Yes	No	Yes, may petition the Board for a temporary permit to engage in the practice of psychology for a period not to exceed 90 days within a calendar year	HRS Section 465–9

Continued

Table 9.2 *Continued*

State	National Register accepted?	CPQ Accepted?	PSYPACT State?	Temporary Practice Permitted Outside PSYPACT?	Statute
Idaho	Yes	Yes	Yes	Yes, permits temporary practice for up to 30 days within a calendar year so long as they hold a license in another state, have had no disciplinary action, and pay the required fee	Idaho Code Section 54–2321
Illinois	Yes	Yes	Yes	Yes, may be issued a temporary permit for up to 10 calendar days per year, consecutively or in the aggregate. Any portion of a calendar day in which the psychologist provides services in this state is considered one working day. Time devoted to providing testimony in court or in deposition shall not be counted in the 10 calendar days.	225 ILCS 15/11.5
Indiana	In Process—Board voted to approve	No	Yes	Yes, may be issued a temporary permit for a nonrenewable period not to exceed 30 days every 2 years	Burns Ind. Code Ann. Section 25–33-1-4.5
Iowa	Yes	Yes	No	Yes, must submit application for an exemption from licensure and once approved, the exemption will be valid for 10 consecutive business days or not to exceed 15 business days in any 90-day period	I.A.C. 645–240.8(154B)
Kansas	No	No	Yes	Yes, an individual may engage in independent practice of psychology for not more than 30 days per year. Any psychology services rendered within any 24-hour period shall count as one entire day of psychology services.	K.S.A. Section 74–5316a
Kentucky	Yes	Yes	Yes	Yes, an individual may render psychological services for not more than 30 days every 2 years.	KRS Section 319.015

Louisiana	No	Yes	No	Yes, may practice for a period not to exceed 30 days in any 1 calendar year	LAC 46: LXIII.1001
Maine	Yes	Yes	Yes	Yes, "the use of occasional services of qualified consultant psychologists from another state or jurisdiction or the use of the services of organizations from another state or jurisdiction employing qualified psychologists does not constitute the unlawful practice of psychology." Also states that a consultant must notify the board when consulting in Maine, and may ordinarily consult in Maine for no more than 10 days or parts thereof in a calendar year. M.A.C. 02–415	32 M.R.S. Section 3812
Maryland	Yes	Yes	Yes	Yes, the Board may authorize an unlicensed individual to practice psychology if the Board finds that the circumstances warrant and the individual is not a resident of this state and meets the qualifications for a license, other than residence and examination.	Md. Health Occupations Code Ann. Section 18–301
Massachusetts	Yes	Yes	No	Yes, may provide consultative services for a fee no more than 1 day a month. Also states that the board may grant temporary license for a period not to exceed 1 year to an out-of-state psychologist who practices either in consultation with or under the supervision of a licensed psychologist OR possesses qualifications acceptable to the board.	ALM GL ch. 112, Section 123 and 124
Michigan	No	Yes	Yes	Yes, if "in an exceptional circumstance, is called in for consultation or treatment by a health professional in this state" or "an individual who resides adjacent to the land border between this state and an adjoining state and whose practice may extend into this state, but who does not maintain an office or designate a place to meet patients or receive calls in this state."	MCLS Section 333.16171

Continued

Table 9.2 *Continued*

State	National Register accepted?	CPQ Accepted?	PSYPACT State?	Temporary Practice Permitted Outside PSYPACT?	Statute
Minnesota	Yes	Yes	Yes	Yes, a nonresident shall apply to the board for guest licensure if the psychologist intends to practice in Minnesota for more than 30 days. The practice in Minnesota is limited to no more than 9 consecutive months per calendar year. This subsection does not apply to psychologists serving in a consultant role.	Minn. Stat. Section 148.916
Mississippi	No	Yes	Yes	Yes, applicants may obtain a temporary practice certificate. The practice of psychology must be limited in scope and duration, not exceeding 30 days during a consecutive 12-month period.	Miss. Code Ann. Section 73–31-14
Missouri	Yes	Yes	Yes	Yes, the temporary period shall not exceed 10 consecutive business days in any period of 90 days, nor in the aggregate exceed 15 business days in any 9-month period. The provision of expert testimony is also exempt from licensure requirements.	Missouri Annotated Statutes Section 337.045
Montana	No	Yes	No	Yes, an individual may render consulting psychological services in this state when these services are rendered for a period which does not exceed in the aggregate, 60 days during a calendar year or 45 consecutive calendar days if the person is authorized under their resident state to perform these activities and services. Must report to the department if the services are to exceed 10 days in a calendar year.	M.C.A. 37–17-104

Nebraska	Yes	Yes	Yes	Yes, allows for temporary practice of psychology for 30 days within a 1-year period	Nebraska Admin. Code Title 172, Ch. 155.008
Nevada	Yes	Yes	Yes	Yes, if the psychologist is licensed in a state with equivalent licensure requirements, then the individual may practice psychology up to 30 days within a calendar year. May also practice if invited as a consultant by a psychologist licensed in Nevada.	N.R.S. Ann. Section 641.0295
New Hampshire	Yes	Yes	Yes	Yes, under multiple different circumstances. First, an individual may practice psychology if the practice is limited to no more than 30 days per year, the psychologist is not the subject of a past or pending disciplinary action in another jurisdiction, and the psychologist holds either a CPQ, IPC, ABPP, or National Register certification. Second, an individual seeking to perform an evaluation under a court order may be allowed a temporary license for no more than 30 days which may be nonconsecutive during a 12-month period. Third, an individual may provide services in response to a declared disaster for no more than 60 days per year without applying for a state license. Lastly, the board may issue a temporary license to practice for not more than 90 days in a 12-month period provided that the psychologist's licensing jurisdiction's requirements are equal to or exceed the requirements to be licensed in NH, the applying psychologists meets the requirements for admission to the examination process, and the psychologist is not the subject of a past or pending disciplinary action in another jurisdiction.	NH R.S.A. 329-B:20

Continued

Table 9.2 *Continued*

State	National Register accepted?	CPQ Accepted?	PSYPACT State?	Temporary Practice Permitted Outside PSYPACT?	Statute
New Jersey	Yes	Yes	Yes	Yes, if the practice of psychology does not exceed 10 consecutive business days or 15 business days in any 90-day period. The psychologist must give the board a summary of their qualifications and a minimum of 10 days written notice of intent to practice in NJ. The psychologist's resident state's licensing requirements must be equivalent of the requirements for licensing in NJ. The board may also issue a temporary permit for a period not exceeding 1 year for an individual who has applied for licensure in NJ.	N.J. Stat. Section 45:14B-6
New Mexico	Yes	Yes	No	Yes, a temporary 6-month license may be issued if the psychologist is licensed in good standing in another jurisdiction and completes the required form including the reason for seeking a temporary license.	N.M.A.C. 16.22.5.13
New York	No	No	No	Yes, exempt practice must be approved by the department, and practice under this one-time exemption shall not exceed 10 consecutive business days or a total of 15 business days in a 90-day period.	New York Codes, Rules and Regulations, Title 8, Section 72.5
North Carolina	Yes	Yes	Yes	Yes, may engage in the practice of psychology for up to 5 days in any calendar year. Requires notification in writing of the intent to practice in North Carolina	

North Dakota	No	Yes	Yes	Yes, may practice if licensed in good standing in another jurisdiction and the practice does not exceed 30 full or partial days per calendar year. Must submit an application to the board	N.D. Admin. Code 66–02-01-16
Ohio	Yes	Yes	Yes	Yes, may not exceed 30 days a year, and must be approved by the board	O.R.C. Ann. 4732.22
Oklahoma	No	Yes	Yes	Yes, temporary practice is permitted if the individual is rendering consulting or other psychological services for a period which does not exceed in the aggregate more than 5 days during any year and if the nonresident is licensed in good standing in their resident state. Must notify the board prior to initiation of services. May also perform consulting or other psychological services if such activities and services are rendered in response to a national disaster and in coordination with the American Red Cross or APA	59 Okl. St. Section 1353
Oregon	Yes	Yes	No	Yes, may obtain a visitors permit that limits practice to no more than 30 days in a 12-month period	O.A.R. 858–010-0055
Pennsylvania	Yes	Yes	Yes	Yes, may practice on temporary assignment for up to 6 months if the psychologist has a current license in good standing and notifies the board. May also practice on temporary assignment without notification to the board if the practice of psychology does not exceed 14 days in the aggregate	49 Pa. Code Section 41.52

Continued

Table 9.2 *Continued*

State	National Register accepted?	CPQ Accepted?	PSYPACT State?	Temporary Practice Permitted Outside PSYPACT?	Statute
Rhode Island	Yes	Yes	Yes	Yes, may perform psychological services without obtaining a license for up to 10 calendar days per calendar year with no more than 5 days of this activity occurring consecutively. This calendar-day limit shall not apply to service as an expert witness in a legal proceeding.	R.I. Gen. Laws Section 5–44-23
South Carolina	Yes	Yes	Yes	Yes, must petition the board for a temporary permit and may practice for a period not to exceed 60 days within a calendar year. The psychologist's licensing state must have licensing requirements deemed equivalent to the licensing requirements of SC.	S.C. Code Ann. Section 40–55-110
South Dakota	Yes	No	Yes	Yes, may render psychological services for a period which does not exceed an aggregate of more than 20 days during any 1 year, as long as the provider has not established offices in this state and is a nonresident. If a provider exceeds 10 consecutive days of practice in any calendar year, the provider shall report the activities in writing to the board.	S.D. Codified Laws Section 36–27A-2
Tennessee	Yes	Yes	Yes	Yes, may practice for a period not to exceed 12 days within a 1-year period. Must submit written request to the board and have a valid license in good standing	Tenn. Comp. R. & Regs. R. 1180–02-.05

Texas	No	Yes	Yes	Yes, must have a license in good standing, be supervised/sponsored by a psychologist licensed in Texas, and provide documentation of passing the EPPP at the Texas cut off (may submit CPQ documentation for this). The sponsorship by a licensed psychologist in Texas shall consist of the psychologist being available for consultation. Temporary licensure shall be granted for delivery of psychological services totaling no more than 30 days in one calendar year. A psychologist must wait 1 year after the issuance of their previous temporary license to apply for another temporary license.	22 TAC Section 463.12
Utah	Yes	Yes	Yes	Yes, if the individual is called in for a consultation by an individual licensed in this state, and the services provided are limited to that consultation. An individual offering expert testimony is also exempt from licensure requirements.	Utah Code Ann. Section 58-1-307 and 58–61-307
Vermont	Yes	No	Yes	Yes, states that individuals practicing psychology in an official evaluation for court purposes are exempt from licensure requirements.	26 V.S.A. Ch. 55, Subch. 1, Section 3005
Virginia	Yes	Yes	Yes	Yes, if the psychologist is licensed in another state and is consulting with licensed psychologists in VA. Also permitted if the licensed psychologist is testifying as a treating psychologist or who is employed as an expert for the purpose of possible testifying as an expert witness. It is also permitted for continuity of care purposes if a client moves from the psychologist's licensing state to VA.	Va. Code Ann. Section 54.1–3601

Continued

Table 9.2 *Continued*

State	National Register accepted?	CPQ Accepted?	PSYPACT State?	Temporary Practice Permitted Outside PSYPACT?	Statute
Washington	Yes	Yes	Yes	Yes, for a period not to exceed 90 days within a calendar year. The individual must petition the board and be licensed by a state with equivalent licensing requirements to WA or hold a certificate that suggests they meet standards equivalent to WA licensure.	Rev. Code Wash. (ARCW) Section 18.83.082
West Virginia	Yes	Yes	Yes	Yes, if the individual holds a license or certificate to engage in the practice of psychology issues by a state with licensing or certification requirements determined by the board to be at least as great as those of WV, does not have a regular place of practice in WV, and the practice of psychology does not exceed more than 10 days in any calendar year.	W. Va. Code Section 30–21-3
Wisconsin	In Process—Under Consideration by Board	No	Yes	Yes, may provide psychological services on not more than 60 days in any year, provided the individual is licensed in a state with requirements equivalent to or higher than the requirements for licensure in WI. Must report to the examining board the nature of the services if practicing more than 20 days within a year	Wis. Stat. Section 455.03
Wyoming	Yes	Yes	Yes	Yes, a temporary license may be issued to a psychologist who is licensed by a state with requirements whose standards are equal to or exceed the requirements for licensure in WY. A temporary license allows the psychologist to offer services for not more than 30 working days in any year without holding a permanent license. The temporary licensee shall report to the board the nature of the activities if that practice exceeds 20 working days in any calendar year.	Wyo. Stat. Section 33–27-117

The Profession's Attempt to Affect Telepsychology and Temporary Interjurisdictional Practice Regulation

Given the difficulty and complexity of cross-jurisdictional psychology practice, it is not surprising that professional psychological organizations have attempted to influence, simplify, and improve existing legal regulations. The Association of State and Provincial Psychology Boards (ASPPB) is a conglomeration "of state, territorial, and provincial agencies responsible for the licensure and certification of psychologists throughout the United States and Canada" with the goal "of advancing public protection" (ASPPB, 2020, p. 1). In total, there are 65 jurisdictions that ASPPB represents, including all 50 states, the District of Columbia, four U.S. territories (Guam, Puerto Rico, the Commonwealth of the Northern Mariana Islands, and U.S. Virgin Islands), and all 10 provinces of Canada. Although ASPPB was originally created to develop a standardized examination for psychological licensure, one of its primary continuing goals is to increase the mobility of licensed psychologists.

Since the 1990s, ASPPB has spearheaded several mobility programs intended to increase the mobility of licensed psychologists (ASPPB, 2020). In 1992, the Agreement of Reciprocity (AOR) program was initiated by ASPPB to allow practitioners who were licensed in one jurisdiction to practice in another jurisdiction regardless of the licensure requirements in the latter. Yet only 12 jurisdictions eventually approved this program and, as a result, it was largely unsuccessful (Herman & Sharer, 2013; Younggren et al., 2022). Initiated in 1998, ASPPB's subsequent Certificate of Professional Qualifications in Psychology (CPQ) program requires a practitioner to possess specific doctoral education, supervised experience, professional work experience, and sufficient examination scores on the EPPP and/or a board certification in a specialty recognized by ABPP to be granted a CPQ certificate (ASPPB, 2020). The certificate connotes that the psychologist has ample training experience to be recognized as a competent practitioner in another jurisdiction, and it is intended to serve as evidence that a license without further requirements is warranted in the new jurisdiction.

Along with the CPQ, ASPPB initiated the Credentials Bank (CB), which is a repository for practitioners' education information, professional work experience, and examination scores that may be relevant for later licensure in a different jurisdiction or for evidence of meeting requirements for one of ASPPB's mobility programs. In 2007, the Inter-Jurisdictional Practice Certificate (IPC) was created by ASPPB with the purpose of allowing the temporary in-person interjurisdictional practice (i.e., 30 days) of licensed psychologists who met its educational and professional work experience requirements to offer psychological services in a different jurisdiction without meeting that jurisdiction's existing temporary practice requirements (ASPPB, 2020). ASPBB also subsequently developed the E.Passport in 2015 that was intended to promote "standardization in the criteria of interjurisdictional telepsychology practice and facilitates the process for licensed psychologists to provide telepsychological services across jurisdictional lines" (ASPPB, 2020 p. 14). While all these programs were well-intentioned, none of them achieved the cross-jurisdictional success of ASPPB's initial development of a standardized licensure examination (i.e., EPPP), which was eventually adopted by 62 of the 65 jurisdictions across the United States, U.S. territories, and Canada (Younggren et al., 2022).

Most recently, in 2015, ASPPB established the Psychology Interjurisdictional Compact (PSYPACT), which involves several of their other mobility programs and "is an agreement between member states designed to facilitate the practice of telepsychology and the temporary in-person, face-to-face practice of psychology across state boundaries without having to become licensed in additional member states" (ASPPB, 2023, p. 1). ASPPB also created a Commission to oversee its implementation. Interstate compacts like PSYPACT are legally binding agreements between states for a common purpose; of note, interstate compacts are explicitly mentioned in the United States Constitution (Compact Clause; Art. I, § 10, Clause 3; see, e.g., *Virginia v. Tennessee*, 1893). States adopt compact agreements with other states with regard to numerous state-regulated activities (e.g., driver's licenses). Compacts allow licenses from one state to be recognized as compliant with the laws regulating those actions in another state (National Center for Interstate Compacts). PSYPACT has separate tracks, certification procedures, and fee structures for temporary in-person and telepsychology interjurisdictional practice. According to the PSYPACT webpage:

> In order to *practice telepsychology* in PSYPACT states, psychologists licensed in PSYPACT states only can apply to the PSYPACT Commission for an Authority to Practice Interjurisdictional Telepsychology (APIT™). One required component of this authority granted from the PSYPACT Commission is that psychologists must obtain an E.Passport Certificate from ASPPB.
>
> In order to conduct *temporary practice* in PSYPACT states, psychologists licensed in PSYPACT states only can apply to the PSYPACT Commission for a Temporary Authorization to Practice (TAP™). One required component of this authorization granted from the PSYPACT Commission is that psychologists must apply for and obtain an Interjurisdictional Practice Certificate (IPC) from ASPPB.[7] (PSYPACT, n.d., p.1, emphasis added)

For a state to join PSYPACT, the state must adopt ASBPP's model legislation and submit to the rules and regulation created by PSYPACT's Commission to continue the compact's performance (ASPPB, 2023). By July of 2024, 40 states, the District of Columbia, and one territory had adopted PSYPACT legislation with two additional states currently considering its enactment (ASPPB, n.d.).

Although ASPPB's creation of the PSYPACT Compact and its regulatory Commission was clearly well-intentioned and has seemingly improved in-person temporary interjurisdictional and telepsychology practice for some mental health professionals, it also added another layer of complexity to an already complicated legal landscape. As one group of scholars aptly states: "In ASPBB's attempts to ease interjurisdictional practice restrictions with the creation of PSYPACT, ASPPB unfortunately has added a significant additional level of confusion to interstate regulation of professional practice" (Younggren et al., 2022, p. 336). Perhaps the gravest problem with PSYPACT is that it is unlikely to be adopted across all U.S. jurisdictions, thereby limiting the ability of PSYPACT member practitioners to engage in temporary in-person or telepsychology services without additional steps in those nonadopting states.

Why is the nonuniform adoption of the PSYPACT compact so problematic? Imagine not being able to drive in 10 states with your out-of-state driver's license because those states had not joined the Driver's License Compact. The driver would need to know exactly which states were members of the compact, how the regulations in nonmember states differed from their own state, and what additional procedures need to be followed if they temporarily entered those states while driving. Additionally, a practitioner in a non-PSYPACT state will need to know the rules and regulations governing the "practice of psychology," telepsychology, and temporary in-person interjurisdictional practice in all states in which the practitioner wants to provide services.

For example, after considering joining PSYPACT, California failed to enact the necessary legislation for several reasons (California Board of Psychology, 2018). Among the problems noted are that the education requirements for PSYPACT's telepsychology and temporary in-person certification are different from those that are required for licensure as a psychologist in California and some other states. To be eligible for PSYPACT's twin programs, the practitioner needs to have graduated from an APA/CPA approved program, one recognized by the ASPPB National Register Designation Project, or deemed to be equivalent by a recognized foreign credential service. California has a more expansive definition of psychology doctoral programs that can lead to licensure (see California Business and Professions Code § 2914, 2022). As a result, a duly licensed psychology practitioner in California may not be eligible to become a member of either track of PSYPACT's Compact while other licensed California psychologists would be able to become PSYPACT members and practice out of state, thereby creating a two-tier system of licensed practitioners in the state (Younggren et al., 2022).

Additionally, a state joining PSYPACT delegates considerable rule-making authority to the Commission, which is a nongovernmental body.[8] Conversely,

California imposes additional continuing education requirements on practitioners for psychology licensure that PSYPACT does not require, and the California Board was concerned that outside PSYPACT practitioners could jeopardize the health and safety of their citizens without this additional experience (California Board of Psychology, 2018). Although each state is represented on the Commission, PSYPACT states and their practitioners must abide by majority decisions of PSYPACT member states.

Yet, even if all U.S. states were to join PSYPACT, there are continuing legal complexities with its use, particularly for forensic mental health professionals. PSYPACT practitioners are still required to know and abide by the scope of the "practice of psychology" in any state in which they offer services by telepsychology or in-person. It is daunting to understand the parameters of psychological practice in every other U.S. state, and whether practitioners would be required to notify PSYPACT because they were engaged in psychological practice in any of its member states. For example, the provision of expert testimony without an evaluation might not fall under the "practice of psychology" in their home state where they are licensed, but it may require notification of PSYPACT authorities if that practitioner engages in that activity by telepsychology or in-person in another PSYPACT state.

Relatedly, but even more daunting for practitioners, are conflicts of laws between PSYPACT member states. Different jurisdictions have different and potentially conflicting requirements with regard to duty to warn or protect, child abuse reporting, elder abuse reporting, and other professional duties (Younggren et al., 2022). Generally, mental health professionals are governed by the state law in which their client/patient resides when their services are rendered (e.g., Harris & Younggren, 2011; *Prince v. Urban*, 1996). Yet an interpretation of PSYPACT regulations by PSYPACT's attorney appears to require that a PSYPACT practitioner abide by both the state laws where the practitioner is located and the state where the practitioner is providing temporary in-person or telepsychology services if the law is related to the public health and safety of its citizens:

> [T]he appropriate interpretation is that both the psychologist who is practicing under a Temporary Authorization to Practice and a psychologist who is practicing under the Authority to Practice Interjurisdictional Telepsychology are subject to the Receiving or Distant State's applicable law to protect the health and safety of that state's citizens. Yet, to also give effect to the language exclusively applicable to a psychologist who is practicing under a Temporary Authorization to Practice requires that such language be construed to also subject psychologist to other laws of the state that apply to a psychologist who physically practices in that state—not just those that protect the public's health and safety. (Wolfberg, 2021, pp. 3–4)

This interpretation suggests that PSYPACT practitioners must (1) know the state laws of all jurisdictions (currently 42 different PSYPACT jurisdictions) their client/patient may be located in (regardless of whether the contact is telepsychology or in-person) and their home state's laws, and (2) be able to determine whether the laws are related to public health and/or safety.[9] Furthermore, it is still not clear what the practitioner should do if the law relates to public health and safety, and the state law requirements in which the practitioner is duly licensed conflict with those of the state where the client/patient is located. For example, with regard to a duty to protect or warn, there are numerous jurisdictional differences regarding (1) what constitutes dangerous behavior; (2) whether the law requires mandatory or permissive breaching of confidentiality and reporting; (3) the behavior that triggers the reporting requirement (i.e., serious threat against a reasonably identifiable victim versus third parties whose circumstances place them within the reasonably foreseeable area of danger where the violent conduct of the patient is a threat); and (4) the legal duties that reporting requires (i.e., warning the intended victim vs. protecting the victim) (Schopp, 1991; Wiltsie et al., 2021). Which laws should the mental health professional follow if the two states laws on these reporting requirements conflict?

Furthermore, the PSYPACT telepsychology guidelines appear to restrict normal telepsychology practice within the practitioners' home state (i.e., where they commonly reside and which they have designated as their home state in their PSYPACT telepsychology credentialing process)[10] when they leave their home PSYPACT state. If PSYPACT practitioners leave their home state due to any sort of travel, it is not clear that they can engage in a telepsychology interaction with clients/patients in another PSYPACT state even if the state to which they travel is another PSYPACT state and/or even one in which they are duly licensed (PSYPACT Art VI (A)(1), 2016). Even more strangely, it appears that PSYPACT practitioners cannot legally engage in telepsychology interactions with clients who reside in their home PSYPACT state once they leave their home state and travel to another PSYPACT or other state (Younggren et al., 2022).

A full discussion of the problems with the PSYPACT Compact and its legal regulations and implications is beyond the scope of this chapter. It should be apparent, however, from even this limited discussion, that PSYPACT's adoption may have further confused rather than made easier the temporary interjurisdictional in-person and telepsychology practice. The layers of complexity that PSYPACT has added to an already highly problematic legal regulatory scheme and made understanding forensic mental health professionals' legal obligations even more difficult. Some recommendations for how this legal context can be successfully navigated and improved will be offered in the final section of this chapter, but we now briefly turn to some relevant foundational guidance relating to general telepsychology practice.

Guidelines Relevant to Telepsychology Practice

Regardless of whether psychological services occur across or within a jurisdiction's borders, the use of technology to effectuate client and patient interactions has greatly expanded in recent years and will likely grow as technological advances continue. Such developments have been instrumental in providing more efficient and affordable psychological care to underserved individuals and groups as well as individuals in rural and/or remote locations (Batastini et al., 2023). Further, preliminary meta-analytic research suggests that telepsychology treatment results in similar outcomes to in-person interactions across a wide range of disorders (e.g., Abrams, 2020), although the validation of most assessment instruments in this context, forensic or otherwise, is in its infancy (Batastini et al., 2023).

Telepsychology services, however, necessarily raise a host of important legal considerations for the forensic mental health professionals who use them. To aid in this endeavor, the profession has created several useful sources of information to help practitioners facing the unique challenges and considerations of telepsychology practice more generally, such as *Guidelines for the Practice of Telepsychology* ("Telepsychology Guidelines") (American Psychological Association, 2013), and recommendations specific to forensic psychological practice, such as *Recommendations for the Use of Telepsychology in Psychology-Law Practice and Research: A Statement by American Psychology-Law Society (APA Division 41)* ("Telepsychology Recommendations") (Batastini et al., 2023). A brief discussion of aspects of these documents is warranted because they highlight important legal issues for telepsychology practice, and they also highlight important considerations about whether adherence to these guidelines and recommendations is required.

As previously mentioned throughout this book, APA guidelines, like the Telepsychology Guidelines, are aspirational in nature and should not dictate specific legal practice. Such guidelines are "created to educate and to inform the practice of psychologists," and they "are also intended to stimulate debate and research" (American Psychological Association, 2002, p. 1048). They "are not intended to be mandatory or exhaustive and may not be applicable to every professional or clinical situation," and they "are not definitive and they are not intended to take precedence over the judgment of psychologists" (American Psychological Association, 2002, p. 1050). However, at least one jurisdiction (i.e., Pennsylvania) has statutorily made all APA policies, including both standards and guidelines, mandatory and enforceable to all psychologists in the jurisdiction, regardless of APA membership status (see 49 Pa. Code § 41.61(3)(e)).[11] In contrast, the Telepsychology Recommendations are intended as additional guidance or "best practices" with respect to forensic mental health professional telepsychology services, and they are intended to augment the directives of the Telepsychology Guidelines. The Telepsychology Recommendations are not legally enforceable in any jurisdiction. Both documents define telepsychology in the following manner:

> [T]he provision of psychological services using telecommunication technologies. Telecommunications is the preparation, transmission, communication, or related processing of information by electrical, electromagnetic, electromechanical, electro-optical, or electronic means (Committee on National Security Systems, 2010). Telecommunication technologies include but are not limited to telephone, mobile devices, interactive videoconferencing, email, chat, text, and Internet (e.g., self-help websites, blogs, and social media). The information that is transmitted may be in writing, or include images, sounds or other data. These communications may be synchronous with multiple parties communicating in real time (e.g., interactive videoconferencing, telephone) or asynchronous (e.g., email, online bulletin boards, storing and forwarding information). Technologies may augment traditional in-person services (e.g., psychoeducational materials online after an in-person therapy session), or be used as stand-alone services (e.g., therapy or leadership development provided over videoconferencing). (American Psychological Association, 2013, p. 792)

This extremely expansive definition goes well beyond conducting psychological treatment over the telephone or videoconference, and it encompasses (among other things) aspects of remote evaluation, legal proceedings conducted by video conference, transmission of digital health records, storage and transmission of research data, remote instruction, Internet communication with clients/patients, and advertising. Unfortunately, almost all facets of telepsychology practice can involve additional legal considerations that have not yet been fully regulated. As a result, using privacy or confidentiality issues as an exemplar, this chapter will simply highlight several important considerations for forensic mental health professionals that are noted by both the Telepsychology Guidelines and Telepsychology Recommendations.

Before any telepsychology interaction occurs with a client/patient, privacy or confidentiality concerns are implicated in terms of whether this is the appropriate means to conduct the client/patient interaction. A practitioner should consider privacy or confidentiality constraints related but not limited to (1) the security of the technology being employed (e.g., is it Health Insurance Portability and Accountability Act [HIPAA] compliant?); (2) the space where the evaluation or treatment will occur (e.g., will there be third parties present or others in a position to overhear proceedings?); (3) recording (e.g., will the interaction be recorded and do additional procedures need to be implemented if it is?); (4) use of technology in the facility (e.g., will the jail or facility allow the client/patient access to the necessary technology and will it be monitored by outside parties?); (5) informed consent (e.g., how should the practitioner modify informed consent based on the technology being employed?); and (6) data storage and access (e.g., who will have access to data collected and where will it be stored?). These issues are particularly complex in a forensic context, and the forensic mental health professional should contemplate each consideration before determining whether telepsychology would be appropriate for the interaction. Importantly, the Telepsychology Recommendations discuss all these issues in more detail and provide a useful resource guide for modifying such elements as informed consent based upon a provided template by APA's Trust insurance organization (see https://parma.trustinsurance.com/Resource-Center/COVID-19-Resources).

Given the myriad legal issues raised, the use of telepsychology to provide services in a forensic context, although clearly useful and efficient, should not be taken lightly. Without a doubt, further legal regulation of various forensic areas is likely to occur in the near future, and forensic mental health professionals need to be knowledgeable of these changes as they occur. They should be especially aware of the risks and benefits associated with this practice as well as the changing legal landscape that regulates these services.

Navigating Telepsychology and Interjurisdiction Practice and Some Legal and Policy Recommendations Going Forward

Both telepsychology and temporary interjurisdictional in-person practice raise a large number of legal questions, many of which have yet to be fully resolved. This presents a serious dilemma for forensic mental health professionals desiring to engage in and employ these practices. At a minimum, practitioners need to be cognizant of the complexity of the legal regulatory scheme regarding these services. Further training through continuing education, specialty programs, self-study, and supervision should be considered before engaging in either of these specialty endeavors. Additionally, contacting necessary authorities (if appropriate and the practitioner is eligible for such services) for additional guidance is a reasonable step, including but not limited to attorneys and judges in a particular case, the boards of psychology in the various jurisdictions (see https://www.asppb.net/page/BdContactNewPG), PSYPACT (see https://psypact.org/page/LegislativeResources), the APA Ethics Office (see https://www.apa.org/ethics/education), and ABPP's ethical consultation (https://abpp.org/specialists/ethics-education-consultation/ethics-consultation-process/). However, it is also incumbent on forensic mental health professionals to conduct additional research on their own, as none of the resources offer true legal advice that will necessarily protect practitioners from legal sanctions for violating relevant law.

As mentioned earlier in the chapter, the profession has also directly and indirectly contributed to the problems in these areas. Although PSYPACT and its Commission are a well-intended endeavor for easing telepsychology and temporary in-person interjurisdictional practice, PSYPACT currently falls short of its lofty goal. Its distinction involving separate pathways for credentialing of telepsychology and in-person interjurisdictional practice is overly complicated. Further, its educational requirements for their credentials are greater than some states' existing licensure requirements, which makes it likely that not all states will join the Compact, or if they do, some forensic mental health professionals in these joining states will be ineligible for the credential and interjurisdictional practice exemption it allows. In addition, PSYPACT and its Commission's direction concerning which states' laws need to be followed is confusing and complicated, requires the practitioners to be knowledgeable about every jurisdiction's laws, and could potentially lead to an unresolvable conflict when there are differences in the laws of the state where the forensic mental health professional resides and where the client/patient is located.

PSYPACT or a future compact would benefit from a simpler structure in which there was (1) a common or consistent definition of the "practice of psychology" across jurisdictions; (2) one credential for telepsychology and temporary interjurisdictional practice; (3) a provision that a psychological license in any state, regardless of the educational requirements of that state, makes the practitioner eligible for the credential and limited cross-jurisdictional telepsychology and temporary in-person practice (e.g., for 30 days); (4) reliance on the state law where the client/patient is present to resolve all conflict of laws, or some other mechanism that is definitive in deciding what legal rules to follow when state laws conflict; and (5) a governmental body to oversee the Compact, adduce new rules and regulations, resolve conflicts, and provide legal advice to practitioners facing ethical or legal dilemmas. These last two points would be further aided by a frequently updated repository in easily searchable form of all state laws that relate to the practice of psychology.

It should be noted that the legal issues associated with temporary interjurisdictional practice are not new. Over 20 years ago, a collaboration of legal and forensic scholars suggested a model rule to allow the temporary in-person practice of forensic mental health professionals. It stated:

1. The evaluation, diagnosis, or expert testimony regarding the mental condition or characteristics of a person to assist a party or the court in assessing the validity of a claim or defense or to provide other assistance to the parties or the court (including, but not limited to, litigation or reasonably anticipated litigation involving personal injury, child custody,

bail, juvenile waiver, various competencies, mental state at time of offense, and sentencing determinations) constitutes the practice of psychology for which a valid and current license to practice in this state is required.

2. A psychologist who holds a valid and current license to practice psychology in another state may engage in the temporary practice of psychology in this state for up to 30 days (consecutive or dispersed) in that calendar year, as an expert consultant or witness to assist a party or the court in assessing the validity of a claim or defense, or provide other assistance to the parties or the court if within 10 days prior to entering the state to perform these services the psychologist provides the board with written notice of the intent to do so along with a statement of all states in which the psychologist is licensed and the payment of a once-per-annum fee of $100. (Shuman et al., 2003, pp. 236–237)

Unfortunately, no such model rule was ever uniformly adopted across jurisdictions, and PSYPACT's and other professional attempts have done little to untangle the confusing regulatory scheme that surrounds telepsychology and temporary in-person interjurisdictional practice. These problems are unlikely to be resolved in the near future. As such, practitioners will necessarily be forced to continuously update themselves on changes that occur and seek to understand how the changes should affect their practice.

Conclusion

The emerging areas of telepsychology and interjurisdiction practice have the potential to greatly increase client/patient access to necessary psychological services. However, a regulatory scheme created by a mix of constitutional, state, administrative, regulatory rules and laws has resulted in an overly complex legal landscape for forensic mental health professionals. These issues have been further complicated by the profession's attempts to ease these practices through the PSYPACT Compact and its Commission. Unfortunately, although PSYPACT's intentions were laudable, it has not been successful in achieving its aim of making delivery of these services easier. As a result, and for the near future, forensic mental health professionals will need to keep abreast of these developing areas of law and practice, with the hopes that the future will eventually bring less confusion.

Notes

Chapter 1

1. Some resources provide additional classifications of law, including juvenile law and administrative law, but the broadest classifications are criminal and civil. Most other classifications of law can be subsumed under the broad criminal and civil law classifications. Military law is a distinct category of law that will not be discussed in this book due to its complexity and notable differences from civilian law. There are some informative resources regarding the practice of forensic psychology in military contexts (e.g., Stein & Younggren, 2019).
2. There are three levels of proof for a party to prove its case at trial, but there are several other standards of proof that are used in other legal contexts. For example, probable cause is required for police to obtain a search warrant, and a "reasonable belief" is a required part of establishing probable cause (see McCauliff, 1982, for a discussion of various standards of proof).
3. Some authors have made attempts to quantify the various standards of proof in probabilistic terms. For example, McCauliff (1982) surveyed more than 150 federal judges to ascertain their quantification of the three standards of proof. She found that the judges quantified preponderance of the evidence as 55.33%, clear and convincing as 74.99%, and beyond a reasonable doubt as 90.28% (McCauliff, 1982). This may be an interesting and useful academic exercise, but such quantifications have not been explicitly endorsed by most courts, except perhaps for conceptualizing preponderance of the evidence as requiring 51% probability. Kaplow (2012) provides a detailed discussion of arguments for and against assigning probability estimates to the standard of beyond a reasonable doubt.
4. There are various tests for insanity in the jurisdictions that offer the insanity defense (see DeMatteo et al., 2022, for a review of insanity tests).
5. In *Estelle v. Gamble* (1976), the Supreme Court of the United States held that the Eighth Amendment to the United States Constitution requires the government to provide medical care for prison inmates. Subsequently, the United States Court of Appeals for the Fourth Circuit held that there was no distinction between the right to medical care and the right to mental health care (*Bowring v. Godwin*, 1977), and this decision has been adopted by most other jurisdictions (Gibson & Phillips, 2016; see DeMatteo et al., 2023).
6. This premise is attributed to William Blackstone (1765), in what has become known as the Blackstone Ratio, which states that it is better that 10 guilty people escape punishment than one innocent person suffers.
7. A mistrial is an invalid trial due to an error in the proceedings.
8. There is an important caveat to the constitutional double jeopardy protection afforded to criminal defendants. The prohibition against double jeopardy does not apply between the state government and federal government, so an unsuccessful prosecution of a criminal charge in a state court does not prohibit the federal government from prosecuting the defendant in federal court if the underlying act is also a violation of federal law.
9. Most states have even "lower" courts (e.g., magisterial district courts) that have jurisdiction over minor matters. In Pennsylvania, for example, magisterial districts courts have jurisdiction over criminal preliminary arraignments, criminal preliminary hearings, summary criminal offenses, traffic offenses, municipal code violations, landlord/tenant suits, and civil claims in which alleged damages do not exceed $12,000.
10. Federal district courts also sometimes have magistrate judges, who are appointed by a majority vote of the district court judges and serve for a term of 8 years (or 4 years if part-time).
11. In some legal contexts, an appeal may be granted by a circuit court before the district court reaches a final decision. Examples of these types of appeals are collateral order appeals (i.e., immediate appeal when a court has adjudicated a collateral matter but not the entire case) and interlocutory appeals (e.g., immediate appeal of a court's order regarding an injunction). The premise behind these exceptions to the final judgment rule is that some legal issues need

to be addressed before the court reaches a final judgment because the legal issue cannot be effectively remedied via the standard appeals process after the court enters a final judgment (see Kilbert, 2017).

12. The discussion of courts in this chapter was necessarily simplified because there are a wide variety of courts. Other types of courts include immigration, tax, chancery, probate, small claims, and landlord-tenant. Several problem-solving courts have also been developed over the past 40 years. These courts have specialized dockets and are designed to handle subsets of justice-involved individuals who present with special needs. Some of the more common problem-solving courts include drug courts, mental health courts, and veteran's courts (see DeMatteo et al., 2019, and Wiener & Brank, 2013, for reviews).
13. There is no binding authority on cases of first impression, which are cases that are presenting a legal issue to a court for the first time.
14. Although personal jurisdiction can be consented to, and thus the issue waived, subject matter jurisdiction can never be waived and must be established independently.
15. For an interesting court decision relating to personal jurisdiction, see *United States ex Rel. Gerald Mayo v. Satan & His Staff (W.D. Pa. 1971)*. In this case, an inmate in a Pennsylvania prison sued Satan in federal court, alleging that Satan, among other things, caused the inmate's downfall. The United States District Court for the Western District of Pennsylvania dismissed the case for several reasons, one of which was the court's lack of personal jurisdiction over Satan.
16. As a note for those conducting legal research and writing, unlike other court systems, the Supreme Court of the United States is always capitalized when using its full name (Supreme Court of the United States), abbreviated name (Supreme Court), or simply referring to it as the Court. Similarly, when discussing judicial opinions, the "Court" makes a decision, rather than any individual judge.
17. Astute readers may notice that Kansas's insanity defense is more akin to a diminished capacity (or *mens rea*) standard (see DeMatteo et al., 2022).
18. A key difference between APA7 and the Bluebook is that legal writing uses footnotes, not a References list.
19. The font used in various citations for the Bluebook, including the font for the journal name, also differs from that in APA7. The Bluebook requires this information to be expressed in small caps.
20. Some court opinions can be confusing because judges may concur with some parts of the opinion but not with others. For example, part of a court's opinion may have a majority because a majority of judges agree with the reasoning, but another part of the court's opinion may not have a majority if less than half of the judges agree with that section of the opinion. Careful reading of the opinion is necessary to avoid improper attribution of authority to a section of the opinion that should not be granted said authority.

Chapter 2

1. There may, of course, be external pressure from an insurance company that limits the number of sessions for which reimbursement is available.
2. In some situations, a retaining attorney may decide that no report should be written, particularly if the results of the FMHA are not in the party's favor.
3. Technically, federal inmates can earn "good time" for supervised release at the rate of 54 days per year for each year of their sentence, but it is not the same as parole.
4. Prosecution and adjudication are essentially the same thing, with the former term used in the criminal justice system and the latter term used in the juvenile court (or family court) system.
5. There is a distinction between forensic psychology and correctional psychology; the latter is narrower and involves the provision of psychological services (e.g., assessment, treatment) in correctional settings. For a valuable discussion of the differences between forensic psychology and correctional psychology, see Neal (2018).

Chapter 3

1. As of this writing, the *Specialty Guidelines for Forensic Psychology* are being revised.
2. As of this writing, the *Ethical Principles of Psychologists and Code of Conduct* are being revised.

Chapter 4

1. The term "alienist" is an antiquated term for a psychiatrist, particularly those who assess trial competence.
2. McAllister wrote the opinion, which is binding, but the court only agreed on the issue of whether the decision should be affirmed. McAllister, though writing the general opinion, was in the minority regarding his approach to psychological testimony.
3. Furthermore, and as an aside, the differing descriptions the judges use regarding the professor's qualifications should underscore the importance of the qualifying process when testifying in court, which is a topic discussed later in this chapter.
4. An *amicus curiae* brief, or "friend of the court" brief, is filed by a nonparty to the case who has information or expertise that may assist the court in reaching a decision.
5. The American Board of Examiners in Professional Psychology was renamed the American Board of Professional Psychology in 1968.
6. Indeed, perhaps in reference to the "magic" of mental health testimony, New Mexico State Senator Duncan Scott pushed through a 1995 amendment requiring that during testimony:

   > A psychologist or psychiatrist shall wear a cone-shaped hat that is no less than two feet tall. The surface of the hat shall be imprinted with stars and lightning bolts. Additionally, a psychologist or psychiatrist shall be required to don a white beard that is not less than 18 inches in length, and shall punctuate crucial elements of his testimony by stabbing the air with a wand. Whenever a psychologist or psychiatrist provides expert testimony regarding a defendant's competency, the bailiff shall contemporaneously dim the courtroom lights and administer two strikes to a Chinese gong. (S. Floor Amend 1 to SB 459, 1995).

   The amendment passed in the State Senate and was kept in a larger bill that also passed in the House, but it was vetoed by the governor in 1996 (Oswald, 1995; "Your Lawmakers at Work," 1996).
7. The justification behind allowing more evidence in certain proceedings is that the trial, where the rules are most stringent, often occurs in front of laypeople (i.e., the jury). The jury is considered more susceptible to the emotion behind evidence and less able to see through the emotion to the legal question at hand. Thus, evidence that is particularly prejudicial to the defendant is kept from the jury to reduce these biases. For hearings in front of a judge, the protections afforded by a strict approach to evidentiary admissibility have historically been seen as unnecessary.
8. Given these rules, all evidence must satisfy what is often referred to as the FRE 401/403 relevance/prejudice hurdle.
9. Of note, several amendments to the FRE, including FRE 702, took effect on December 1, 2023, so the current version of FRE 702 is relatively new. For comparison purposes, here is the version of FRE 702 that was in effect prior to December 1, 2023:

   > A witness who is qualified as an expert by knowledge, skill, experience, training, or education may testify in the form of an opinion or otherwise if: (a) the expert's scientific, technical, or other specialized knowledge will help the trier of fact to understand the evidence or to determine a fact in issue; (b) the testimony is based on sufficient facts or data; (c) the testimony is the product of reliable principles and methods; and (d) the expert has reliably applied the principles and methods to the facts of the case.

10. There are a few reasons a nonretaining attorney would stipulate to the expertise of the opposing party's proffered expert. For example, if the individual is, in fact, qualified, the lengthy process wherein those qualifications are highlighted for a jury may bolster the credibility of the witness's testimony. Stipulating would skip this step and downplay the expert's record. Another reason to stipulate to the opposing party's expert is expediency. If the proffered expert is clearly qualified or has been admitted as an expert many times before, the qualifying process can be an unnecessary use of time and other resources best spent elsewhere in the trial. This process typically happens through the submission of *motions in limine*, which are requests that certain testimony should be excluded; these motions are argued and ruled upon outside of the jury's presence.

11. A fairly recent amendment to the Federal Rules of Criminal Procedure now requires experts to furnish the court with a list of *all* publications from the previous 10 years and all cases in which the expert provided testimony (at trial or deposition) from the previous 4 years (Rule 16; 2022). Changes like this underscore the importance of keeping abreast of the legal requirements for expert testimony (and keeping your CV updated). A similar rule is used in the civil context (Fed. R. Civ. P., Rule 26(a)(2)(B)).
12. Some jurisdictions outside of the United States have adopted alternative methods of presenting expert testimony. For example, some Australian courts have adopted a model of concurrent testimony, colloquially known as "hot tubbing," wherein experts take the stand at the same time and discuss the relevant issues together. The idea is that this presentation limits the "battle of the experts" and, by facilitating a professional conversation, presents the information to the fact finder with less bias and less ultimate authority than in the traditional procedure. (For more discussion on this approach to testimony, see Krauss et al., 2018.)
13. In *General Electric Co. v. Joiner* (1997), a case in which the Supreme Court of the United States held that the standard on appeal for admissibility decisions regarding proffered experts is abuse of discretion, Justice Breyer (in a concurring opinion) emphasized the utility of 706 experts in helping judges to perform their gatekeeping functions under *Daubert v. Merrell Dow Pharmaceuticals* (1993).
14. The American Bar Association has published a handbook for litigators that discusses each of these issues and offers solutions for many (see Brennan et al., 2010). This is particularly important in light of *Ake v. Oklahoma* (1985), which held, in part, that an indigent defendant has the right to a defense expert.
15. The FRE also includes a "catchall" (Rule 807), which offers an avenue for hearsay to be admitted if: (1) the statement is supported by sufficient guarantees of trustworthiness and (2) it is more probative than any other reasonably available evidence. If a party intends to invoke this rule, they must provide written notice to the adverse party.

Chapter 5

1. Dr. Marston received his law degree and his doctorate in psychology from Harvard University, where he worked with Dr. Hugo Münsterberg, who wrote *On the Witness Stand* in 1908 (Weiss et al., 2014).
2. Of note, Dr. Marston later consulted for a publishing company that became DC Comics and invented the superhero character Wonder Woman. Readers who are familiar with Wonder Woman may recall that she uses her own "lie detector" called the Golden Lasso of Truth (see Weiss et al., 2014, for an interesting discussion).
3. Mr. Frye was paroled in 1939 after spending nearly 18 years in prison.
4. In *Laney v. United States* (1923), a case involving the admissibility of novel firearms identification, Judge Van Orsdel made no mention of the *Frye* test he had articulated earlier in the day.
5. Faigman et al. (2022) discussed the challenges courts face when defining the relevant field: "The more narrowly a court defines the pertinent field, the more agreement it is likely to find. The general acceptance test thus degenerates into a process of deciding whose noses to count" (p. 17).
6. As an example, Isaac Newton is generally regarded as one of the greatest thinkers in human history, but much of what he wrote was later found to be incorrect.
7. There has been some debate about the correct pronunciation of *Daubert*. According to Michael Gottesman, who represented the families of Jason Daubert and Eric Schuller, the correct pronunciation is Dow-burt (Gottesman, 1994).
8. A party who files a motion for summary judgment is asking the court to enter a judgment based on the merits without holding a trial because there is no reasonable dispute of fact and, as a matter of law, one side should therefore win the case.
9. A teratogen is an agent or factor that causes malformation of an embryo in utero.
10. Certiorari is a writ or order by which a higher court reviews the decision of a lower court.
11. The Federal Rules of Evidence were not enacted until 1975, which was more than 50 years after *Frye* was decided.
12. At the time *Daubert* was decided, FRE 702 looked different than it does today. It explicitly stated: "If scientific, technical, or other specialized knowledge will assist the trier of fact

to understand the evidence or to determine a fact in issue, a witness qualified as an expert by knowledge, skill, experience, training, or education, may testify thereto in the form of an opinion or otherwise."

13. In a footnote, the Supreme Court stated:

> We note that scientists typically distinguish between "validity" (does the principle support what it purports to show?) and "reliability" (does application of the principle produce consistent results?). [internal citation omitted] Although "the difference between accuracy, validity, and reliability may be such that each is distinct from the other by no more than a hen's kick" [internal citation omitted], our reference here is to *evidentiary* reliability—that is, trustworthiness. [internal citations omitted] In a case involving scientific evidence, *evidentiary reliability* will be based upon *scientific validity*. (Daubert, 1993, p. 590, fn9)

    This quote makes it clear that the Court had difficulty differentiating reliability from validity. Moreover, what the Court meant by evidentiary reliability is actually scientific validity.

14. When discussing the gatekeeping function of trial court judges faced with a proffer of expert scientific evidence, the Court stated: "We are confident that federal judges possess the capacity to undertake this review" (*Daubert*, 1993, p. 593). We will return to this important topic in Chapter 6.
15. The Supreme Court also recognized the flexible nature of the *Daubert* gatekeeping analysis in *Kumho Tire Co. v. Carmichael (1999)*: "But, as the Court stated in *Daubert*, the test of reliability is 'flexible,' and *Daubert*'s list of specific factors neither necessarily nor exclusively applies to all experts or in every case" (p. 141).
16. As noted in Chapter 4, FRE 702 was recently amended again, with the changes taking effect on December 1, 2023. See Chapter 4 and Chapter 6 for discussions of amended FRE 702.
17. Although there are varying estimates regarding the exact prevalence of expert witnesses in court cases, it is clear that "experts are a permanent and enormous part of modern litigation" (Jurs & DeVito, 2013, p. 678 fn11; see Jurs, 2016). When looking specifically at mental health professionals, Melton et al. (2018) estimate that psychiatrists, psychologists, and social workers testify in approximately 2 million cases per year.
18. It is important to note that although trial court determinations regarding the admissibility of proffered expert evidence are reviewed on appeal using the abuse of discretion standard, whether the trial court has properly fulfilled its gatekeeping responsibility (i.e., assessed the validity of the proffered expert evidence) is reviewed on appeal using the less deferential de novo standard (see Faigman et al., 2022, citing *Chapman v. Maytag Corp.*, 2002).
19. Before appealing the District Court's decision, the plaintiffs asked the District Court for reconsideration of the issue. Upon reconsideration, the District Court agreed with the plaintiffs that the *Daubert* criteria should be applied flexibly, but the District Court nevertheless affirmed its earlier order excluding Carlson's testimony and granting the defendant's motion for summary judgment (*Carmichael v. Samyang Tires, Inc.*, 1996b).
20. After holding that the *Daubert* admissibility standard applies to all expert testimony, the Supreme Court addressed the specific expert testimony at issue in *Kumho*. The Court had no concerns about Carlson's qualifications, but rather with Carlson's conclusion that a defect caused the tire blowout because he did not see evidence of other causes. The Court famously stated: "[N]othing in either *Daubert* or the Federal Rules of Evidence requires a district court to admit opinion evidence that is connected to existing data only by the *ipse dixit* of the expert" (*Kumho Tire Co.*, 1999, p. 158; quoting *General Electric Co. v. Joiner*, 1997, p. 146).
21. Federal Rule of Civil Procedure (FRCP) 50 provides the relevant rule for judgment as a matter of law in a jury trial. FRCP 50 provides that if a party has been fully heard on an issue during a jury trial and the court finds that a reasonable jury would not have a legally sufficient evidentiary basis to find for the party on that issue, the court may resolve the issue against the party and grant a motion for judgment as a matter of law against the party on a claim or defense that, under the controlling law, can be maintained or defeated only with a favorable finding on that issue.
22. Several other federal courts have discussed the differences between *Frye* and *Daubert* in terms of the judicial rigor applied to the admissibility determination. For example, in *United States v. Kwong* (1995), the United States Court of Appeals for the Second Circuit concluded that the FRE are more liberal than *Frye*. In another case, the Second Circuit stated that *Daubert*

loosens the strictures on scientific evidence set by *Frye* and, therefore, "reinforces the idea that there should be a presumption of admissibility" (*Borawick v. Shay*, 1995, p. 610).

23. A motion *in limine* is a request for the court to address (outside the presence of a jury) potentially prejudicial, irrelevant, or inadmissible information that could unduly influence a jury or hinder the fair administration of justice.

Chapter 6

1. It is worth repeating that *Daubert* applies to all proffered expert evidence, whereas *Frye* was limited to novel techniques, methods, or procedures.
2. As noted in Chapter 4, the first part of FRE 702 (i.e., expert attributes) is disjunctive, so a proffered expert does not need to have all of the FRE 702 attributes to be admitted as an expert, but the lettered requirements of FRE 702 are conjunctive, which means that the expert and the expert's testimony must satisfy (a) through (d) to be admitted
3. *Ipse dixit* is translated as "he himself said it," and it typically refers to assertions made by someone without any supporting evidence.
4. As noted in Chapter 5, the Supreme Court had difficulty differentiating reliability from validity. Specifically, what the Court meant by evidentiary reliability is actually scientific validity.
5. Several courts have discussed the use of the peer review and publication criterion in admissibility decisions. For example, in *United States v. Gissantaner* (2021), the United States Court of Appeals for the Sixth Circuit stated that subjecting "a new technology to 'peer review and publication' offers another measure of reliability" (p. 464). In *Gissantaner* (2021), the Sixth Circuit also stated:

    Peer review is not student review. It "conditions publication on a bona fide process" of review by other scientists and experts in the field. *Merrell Dow Pharms., Inc.*, 43 F.3d 1311, 1318 n.6 (9th Cir. 1995). The scientific community uses different conventions for publication from most journals published in the legal community. No offense to former, current, and future members of law journals everywhere: But it is one thing to convince lawyers in training to publish a piece; it is quite another to convince peers in a professional community to publish a piece. (p. 464)

6. Although the judges in the Gatowski et al. (2001) study believed in the usefulness of the error rate criterion in admissibility decisions, some research suggests that it is the least analyzed *Daubert* criterion (e.g., Haug & Baird, 2011).
7. There is mixed evidence regarding the value judges attribute to the peer review and publication criterion. As noted in the text, 92% of the judges in the Gatowski et al. (2001) study believed that peer review and publication was a useful criterion in determining the admissibility of proffered expert testimony. However, in a study that involved the manipulation of both the peer review status and internal validity of an expert's research, results revealed that 17% of the judges were willing to admit evidence regardless of its peer review status or internal validity (Kovera & McAuliff, 2000).
8. When reviewing the Gatowski et al. (2001) results regarding judges' understanding of general acceptance, DeMatteo et al. (2024) noted that nearly 20% of the judges did not have an adequate understanding of a relatively straightforward admissibility standard that has been around for more than 100 years.
9. Regarding the testing criterion, some judges understood that it focuses on whether a method, procedure, or technique can be tested and potentially proven false, while other judges mistakenly equated falsifiability with whether the evidence was falsified (Gatowski et al., 2001).
10. FRE 706 (Court-Appointed Expert Witnesses) states:

    (a) **Appointment Process.** On a party's motion or on its own, the court may order the parties to show cause why expert witnesses should not be appointed and may ask the parties to submit nominations. The court may appoint any expert that the parties agree on and any of its own choosing. But the court may only appoint someone who consents to act.

    (b) **Expert's Role.** The court must inform the expert of the expert's duties. The court may do so in writing and have a copy filed with the clerk or may do so orally at a conference in which the parties have an opportunity to participate. The expert:
    (1) must advise the parties of any findings the expert makes;
    (2) may be deposed by any party;
    (3) may be called to testify by the court or any party; and

(4) may be cross-examined by any party, including the party that called the expert.

(c) **Compensation.** The expert is entitled to a reasonable compensation, as set by the court. The compensation is payable as follows:

(1) in a criminal case or in a civil case involving just compensation under the Fifth Amendment, from any funds that are provided by law; and

(2) in any other civil case, by the parties in the proportion and at the time that the court directs—and the compensation is then charged like other costs.

(d) **Disclosing the Appointment to the Jury.** The court may authorize disclosure to the jury that the court appointed the expert.

(e) **Parties' Choice of Their Own Experts.** This rule does not limit a party in calling its own experts.

Chapter 7

1. For purposes of this chapter, we treat "reasonable degree of psychological certainty," "reasonable degree of medical certainty," "reasonable degree of scientific certainty," and various other formulations of these words equivalently unless otherwise noted in the text. It is possible for jurisdictions to view these different phrases divergently, but by and large they have been treated relatively similarly by the legal system.

Chapter 8

1. There are many resources that provide in-depth discussions and guidance on the topics of test security and third-party observers (e.g., American Psychological Association, 2017b; American Psychological Association Committee on Psychological Tests and Assessment, 2022; Bütz et al., 2023; Frederick et al., 2024; Marcopulos et al., 2024; Otto & Krauss, 2009; Sims et al., 2023).
2. Although a detailed description of licensure laws by state is beyond the scope of this chapter, there are multiple websites that provide concise summaries of licensing requirements for all 50 states. https://www.psychology-license.com/.
3. For example, Virginia law requires that clinicians conducting court-ordered forensic evaluations complete training recognized by the Commissioner of the Virginia Department of Behavioral Health and Developmental Services (DBHDS). The nature of the required training depends on the type of evaluation(s) the forensic evaluator plans to conduct (Virginia Code of Criminal Procedure, 2023).
4. Of note, Washington, D.C., and Georgia currently require individuals to pass the EPPP Part 2, which includes questions about applied, real-world situations that psychologists face in practice.
5. For example, in Pennsylvania, prospective psychologists must pass the Pennsylvania Psychology Law Exam after they pass the EPPP.
6. These jurisdictions include Florida, Georgia, Maryland, Mississippi, Montana, New Mexico, North Dakota, Pennsylvania, Rhode Island, Utah, and Washington, DC. A list of requirements for licensure catalogued by state can be found at http://psybook.asppb.org/.
7. Boards that require peer review and evaluation should not be confused with "vanity boards," which only require paying a fee to obtain a "certification" (DeAngelis, 2014).
8. The American Board of Professional Psychology was founded in 1947 as the American Board of Examiners in Professional Psychology. It was renamed the American Board of Professional Psychology in 1968.
9. The legal principle of *ignorantia juris non excusat* (translation: ignorance of the law excuses not, or ignorance of the law excuses no one) was derived from Roman law and cited by the Supreme Court of the United States in *Barlow v. United States* (1833).
10. See Chapter 1 for a detailed discussion of case law precedent, including conflicts of laws.
11. Forensic research is defined broadly as research that can be used to inform a legal decision (see Chapter 2).
12. As of this writing, the EPPCC is being revised.
13. A comprehensive list of APA's practice guidelines can be accessed at https://www.apa.org/about/policy/approved-guidelines.
14. As of this writing, the *Specialty Guidelines for Forensic Psychology* are being revised.
15. A comprehensive list of APA-approved standards and guidelines can be found at https://www.apa.org/research-practice/standards-guidelines.

16. There are important differences between confidentiality and privilege. For example, confidentiality is primarily an ethical requirement (although it could also be imposed as a legal requirement), but privilege is a legal requirement that sometimes overlaps and sometimes does not with confidentiality. Moreover, confidentiality is a duty owed by the professional, whereas privilege (against disclosure) belongs to the client.
17. This decision was partially overruled by the Supreme Court of Texas in *James v. Brown* (1982). In *James*, the plaintiff, after being released from involuntary commitment, filed an action for libel and medical malpractice against three psychiatrists who had submitted reports attesting to the plaintiff's mental incompetency with a probate court. The court reasoned that Texas's common law immunity does not shield physicians from malpractice liability for failure to exercise a reasonable standard of care in certifying the plaintiff's need for involuntary commitment. The court based their support for the cause of action on the statutory duty of care arising from Texas's Mental Health Code, rather than on a cause of action for negligence as to the experts' testimony, which is an important distinction that prevents this case from being a revocation of expert witness immunity.
18. See Chapter 3 for best practices in discovery.
19. See Chapter 3 for an in-depth discussion of the work-product rule.
20. A tort is a civil wrong other than a breach of contract for which the law provides a remedy, and it includes both negligence and malpractice. The four elements required to establish a tort are duty, breach, causation, and damages. Specifically, the accused owed a duty to the plaintiff, breached that duty, and the breach of that duty was the proximate cause of the plaintiff's damages.
21. Both the United States Court of Appeals for the Third Circuit and the United States Court of Appeals for the D.C. Circuit have upheld expert witness immunity for court appointed expert witnesses (*Hughes v. Long*, 2001; *Johnson v. United States*, 1976).

Chapter 9

1. The end of the federal "state of emergency" led to the return of existing pre-COVID-19 telepsychology and temporary interjurisdictional practice legal requirements in almost all jurisdictions (Younggren et al., 2022).
2. This includes all 50 states, the District of Columbia, the North Mariana Islands, Guam, Puerto Rico, the Virgin Islands, and the 10 Canadian provinces (see https://ASPPB.org).
3. Contacting the state's board of psychology for information concerning their licensure requirements and "practice of psychology" definition is often a good first step in determining the viability of providing certain services in that jurisdiction. Contact information for state boards of psychology can be found at https://www.asppb.net/page/BdContactNewPG.
4. Certain jurisdictions allow waiver of some of their normal licensure requirements for practitioners who are board-certified by ABPP (see ABPP.org) or who are registered with the National Registry of Health Service Psychologists (see https://www.nationalregister.org/tools-services/licensure-mobility/).
5. See Table 9.2 for temporary practice requirements taken from Kane et al. (2023).
6. A federal enclave refers to land ceded to the federal government by states for a specific federal governmental function, which includes military bases, federal courthouses, federal prisons, veteran's hospitals, national parks, and post offices (Miller, 2011).
7. PSYPACT allows temporary in-person interjurisdictional practice for 30 nonconsecutive days per year.
8. A nongovernmental body is not protected from liability for many of its actions, may not be able to successfully promulgate regulations on states and practitioners within those states, and/or may lack legal authority and ability to effectively sanction practitioners who fail to abide by the rules and regulations it creates (PSYPACT, 2016).
9. This is because PSYPACT makes a distinction between telepsychology and temporary in-person interjurisdictional practice with regard to state law. The PSYPACT regulations explicitly note that in-person interjurisdiction practice is governed by *all* the laws of both states (i.e., the client/patient and the practitioner is located), but telepsychology interjurisdictional practice is governed by the laws of both when those laws involve public health and safety, but the state laws of *only* where the practitioner is located for other requirements.

10. PSYPACT requires practitioners to pick one state as their "home" state and where they reside even if they are licensed in multiple PSYPACT states.
11. 49 Pa. Code § 41.61(3)(e) states: "As practitioners and researchers, psychologists act in accord with American Psychological Association standards and guidelines related to practice and to the conduct of research with human beings and animals."

References

Court Cases, Statutes, & Court Rules

10 U.S.C. § 1094. https://www.law.cornell.edu/uscode/text/10/1094
18 U.S.C. § 17.
18 U.S.C. § 4247.
18 U.S.C. § 4241-48.
25 U.S.C. § 1621t. https://www.law.cornell.edu/uscode/text/25/1621t
49 Pa. Code § 41.61(3)(e).
Addington v. Texas, 441 U.S. 418 (1979).
Ake v. Oklahoma, 470 U.S. 68 (1985).
Atkins v. Virginia, 536 U.S. 304 (2002).
Austin v. American Association of Neurological Surgeons, 253 F.3d 967 (7th Cir. 2001).
Barlow v. United States, 32 U.S. 404 (1833).
Beech Aircraft Corp. v. Rainey, 488 U.S. 153 (1988).
Borawick v. Shay, 68 F.3d 597 (2nd Cir. 1995).
Boucher v. Pennsylvania Hospital, 831 A.2d 623 (Pa. Sup. Ct. 2003).
Bowring v. Godwin, 551 F.2d 44 (4th Cir. 1977).
Boyes-Bogie v. Horvitz, 14 Mass. L. Rptr. 208 (2001).
Boykin v. Alabama, 395 U.S. 238 (1969).
Brady v. Maryland, 373 U.S. 83 (1963).
Briscoe v. LaHue, 460 U.S. 325 (1983).
Brown v. Board of Education, 347 U.S. 483 (1954).
Bruce v. Byrne-Stevens & Associates Engineers, Inc., 776 P.2d 666 (Wash. 1989).
California Business & Professional Code § 2903. https://codes.findlaw.com/ca/business-and-professions-code/bpc-sect-2903/#:~:text=(a)%20No%20person%20may%20engage,otherwise%20provided%20in%20this%20chapter
California Psychology Licensing Law, Business & Professional Code § 2914. (2022). https://law.justia.com/codes/california/2022/code-bpc/division-2/chapter-6-6/article-1/section-2914/
Carmichael v. Samyang Tires, Inc., 923 F. Supp. 1514 (S.D. Ala. 1996) (1996a).
Carmichael v. Samyang Tires, Inc., 1996 U.S. Dist. LEXIS 22431 (S.D. Ala. 1996) (1996b).
Carmichael v. Samyang Tires, Inc., 131 F.3d 1433 (11th Cir. 1997).
Carpenter v. Superior Court, 45 Cal. Rptr. 3d 821 (2006).
Chapman v. Maytag Corp., 297 F.3d 682 (7th Cir. 2002).
Clark v. Grigson, 579 S.W.2d 263 (Tex. 1978).
Collins v. TIAA-CREF, 2008 WL 3981462 (W.D. N.C. 2008).
Cutler v. Dixon, 76 Eng, Rep. 886 (Q.B. 1585).
Daubert v. Merrell Dow Pharmaceuticals, 727 F. Supp. 570 (S.D. Cal. 1989).
Daubert v. Merrell Dow Pharmaceuticals, 951 F.2d 1128 (9th Cir. 1991).
Daubert v. Merrell Dow Pharmaceuticals, 509 U.S. 579 (1993).
Daubert v. Merrell Dow Pharmaceuticals, 43 F.3d 1311 (9th Cir. 1995).
Davis v. Fuller, 12 Vt. 178 (1840).
Davis v. Wallace, 565 S.E.2d 386 (W. Va. 2002).
Deatherage v. State of Washington Examining Board of Psychology, 948 P.2d. 828 (Washington Sup. Ct. 1997).

Dent v. West Virginia, 129 U.S. 114 (1889).
Drope v. Missouri, 420 U.S. 162 (1975).
Dusky v. United States, 362 U.S. 402 (1960).
Estelle v. Gamble, 429 U.S. 97 (1976).
Ewing v. Goldstein, 15 Cal. Rptr. 3d 864 (Cal. Ct. App. 2004).
Federal Rules of Civil Procedure. (2022). Title I, Scope of Rules, Rule 1. https://www.uscourts.gov/file/64234
Federal Rules of Civil Procedure. (2022). Title V, Disclosures and Discovery, Rule 26, Rule 30, Rule, & Rule 37. https://www.uscourts.gov/file/64234
Federal Rules of Civil Procedure. (2022). Title VI, Trials, Rule 45. https://www.uscourts.gov/file/64234
Federal Rules of Criminal Procedure. (2020). Title IV, Arraignment and Preparation for Trial, Rule 16. https://www.uscourts.gov/sites/default/files/federal_rules_of_criminal_procedure_-_december_2020_0.pdf
Federal Rules of Evidence. (1975). Article VII, Rule 704.
Federal Rules of Evidence. (2021). Article VII, Rule 403. https://www.rulesofevidence.org/article-vii/rule-403/
Federal Rules of Evidence. (2021). Article VII, Rule 704(a) & 704(b). https://uscode.house.gov/view.xhtml?req=granuleid%3AUSC-1999-title28a-node246-article7&edition=1999#:~:text=Rule%20704.,by%20the%20trier%20of%20fact
Federal Rules of Evidence. (2021). Article VII, Rule 704(b), advisory committee notes. https://uscode.house.gov/view.xhtml?req=granuleid%3AUSC-1999-title28a-node246-article7&edition=1999#:~:text=Rule%20704.,by%20the%20trier%20of%20fact
Federal Rules of Evidence. (2023). Article VII, Rule 702, advisory committee notes. https://casetext.com/statute/united-states-code/title-28-appendix/federal-rules-of-evidence/article-vii-opinions-and-expert-testimony/rule-702-testimony-by-expert-witnesses
Federal Rules of Evidence. (2023). https://www.rulesofevidence.org/
Fellows-Kimbrough v. Chicago City Ry. Co. 111 N.E 499 (Ill. S.Ct. 1916).
Folkes v. Chadd, 99 Eng. Rep. 589 (1782).
Ford v. Wainwright, 477 U.S. 399 (1986).
Frye v. United States, 293 F. 1013 (D.C. Cir. 1923).
Gavin v. Hilton Worldwide, Inc., 291 F.R.D. 161 (N.D. Cal. 2013).
General Electric Co. v. Joiner, 522 U.S. 136 (1997).
Godinez v. Moran, 509 U.S. 389 (1993).
Gootee v. Lightner, 274 Cal. Rptr. 697 (1990).
Herbst v. Levy, 279 Ill. App. 353 (1935).
Henderson v. Broomhead, 157 Eng. Rep. 964, 967-968 (Ex. 1859).
Hidden v. Mutual Life Insurance Company of New York, 217 F.2d 818 (4th Cir. 1954).
Hughes v. Long, 242 F.3d 121 (3d Cir. 2001).
IDC Fin. Pub., Inc. v. BondDesk Grp., LLC, Case No. 15-cv-1085-pp (E.D. Wis. 2017).
In re Detention of Twining, 894 P.2d 1331 (Wash. App. Ct 1995).
Indiana v. Edwards, 554 U.S. 164 (2008).
Insanity Defense Reform Act of 1984, chapter IV of title II of the Comprehensive Crime Control Act of 1984, Pub. L. No. 98-473. https://www.congress.gov/bill/98th-congress/senate-bill/1762/text
Iowa Code § 228.9 (2014).
James v. Brown, 637 S.W.2d 914 (1982).
Jenkins v. United States, 307 F.2d 637 (D.C. Cir. 1962).
J. H. v. Cruz, 2023 U.S. Dist. Lexis 14244 (Tenn. Dist. Ct. 2023).
Johnson v. United States, 547 F.2d 688 (D.C. Cir. 1976).
Johnson v. Zerbst, 304 U.S. 458 (1938).
Joiner v. General Electric Co., 864 F. Supp. 1310 (N.D. Ga. 1994).
Joiner v. General Electric Co., 78 F.3d 524 (11th Cir. 1996)

Kahler v. Kansas, 139 S. Ct. 1318 (2019).
Kahler v. Kansas, 140 S. Ct. 1021, 589 U.S. ___ (2020).
Kansas v. Hendricks, 521 U.S. 346 (1997).
Kan. Stat. Ann § 21-5209 (2011). https://www.ksrevisor.org/statutes/chapters/ch21/021_052_0009.html.
Kumho Tire Co. v. Carmichael, 526 U.S. 137 (1999).
Laney v. United States, 294 F. 412 (D.C. Cir. 1923).
Levine v. Wiss and Co., 97 N.J. 242 (1984).
LLMD of Michigan Inc. v. Jackson-Cross Co., 740 A.2d 186 (Pa. 1999).
Marks v. United States, 430 U.S. 188 (1977).
Marrogi v. Howard, 805 So.2d. 1118 (La. 2002).
Mattco Forge Inc. v. Arthur Young & Co., 60 Cal. Rptr. 2d. 780 (Ct. App. 1997).
Michigan v. Hawthorne, 291 N.W. 205 (Mich. 1940).
Miranda v. Arizona, 384 U.S. 486 (1966).
Murphy v. A.A. Mathews, 841 S.W.2d. 671 (Mo. 1992).
New Mexico Administrative Code § 16.22.2.16 (2018).
North Carolina v. Alford, 400 U.S. 25 (1970).
Padillas v. Stork-Gamco, Inc., 186 F.3d 412 (3d Cir. 1999).
Panetti v. Quarterman, 551 U.S. 930 (2007).
Panitz v. Behrend, 429 Pa. Super. 273 (1993).
Pennsylvania Consolidated Statutes 42 § 5903.
Pennsylvania Rules of Evidence. (2013). 225 Pa. Code Rule 702. https://www.pacodeandbulletin.gov/Display/pacode?file=/secure/pacode/data/225/chapter7/s702.html&d=reduce
Pennsylvania Rules of Evidence. (2013). 225 Pa. Code Rule 705. https://www.pacodeandbulletin.gov/Display/pacode?file=/secure/pacode/data/225/chapter7/s705.html&d=reduce
Penry v. Lynaugh, 492 U.S. 302 (1989).
Plessy v. Ferguson, 163 U.S. 537 (1896).
Pollock v. Panjabi, 781 A.2d 518 (Conn. Super. 2000).
Prince v. Urban, 49 Cal.App.4th 1056 (Cal. Ct. App. 1996).
Protection of Human Subjects, 45 C.F.R. § 46 (2009). https://www.hhs.gov/ohrp/sites/default/files/ohrp/policy/ohrpregulations.pdf
Reilly, Supple & Wischusen, LLC v. Blum, No. A-2618-09T3, 2011 N.J. Super. Unpub. LEXIS 581 (Super. Ct. App. Div. Mar. 9, 2011).
Revised Statutes of Missouri Section 491.280.
Roper v. Simmons, 543 U.S. 551 (2005).
S. Floor Amend. 1 to S.B. 459, 42d Leg., 1st Sess. (N.M. 1995).
Sanborn v. Kaiser, 45 F.R.D. 465 (E.D. Ky. 1968).
Schoenthal v. Irving Trust Co., 287 U.S. 92 (1932).
Taylor v. Erna, 2009 WL 2425839 (D. Mass. 2009).
United States Constitution. Article I, Section 10, Clause 3 https://constitution.congress.gov/browse/essay/artI-S10-C3-3-1/ALDE_00013531/
United States Constitution. Amendment X. https://constitution.congress.gov/constitution/amendment-10/
United States ex rel. Gerald Mayo v. Satan and His Staff, 54 F.R.D. 282 (M.D. Pa. 1971).
United States v. Comstock, 560 U.S. 126 (2010).
United States v. Gissantaner, 990 F.3d 457 (6th Cir. 2021).
United States v. Kwong, 69 F.3d 663 (2nd Cir. 1995).
United States v. Rouse, 100 F.3d 560 (8th Cir. 1996).
Victor v. Nebraska, 511 U.S. 1 (1994).
Virginia Code of Criminal Procedure, Va. Code Ann. § 19.2-169.1 (2023).
Virginia v. Tennessee, 148 U.S. 503 (1893).

Walton v. North Carolina Dept. of Agriculture, 2011 WL 2893622 (E.D. N.C. 2011).
West v. Goodyear Tire & Rubber Co., 167 F.3d 776 (2nd Cir. 1999).
West Virginia v. Driver, 107 S.E. 189 (W. Va. 1921).
Weisgram v. Marley Co., 169 F.3d 514 (8th Cir. 1999).
Weisgram v. Marley Co., 528 U.S. 440 (2000).

Literature

Abrams, Z. (2020, July 1). *How well is telepsychology working?* American Psychological Association. https://www.apa.org/monitor/2020/07/covertelepsychology

Accreditation Council for Graduate Medical Education. (2023, July 1). *ACGME program requirements for graduate medical education in psychiatry.* https://www.acgme.org/globalassets/pfassets/programrequirements/400_psychiatry_2023.pdf

Allen, R. J., & Stein, A. (2013). Evidence, probability, and the burden of proof. *Arizona Law Review, 55*, 557–602.

American Academy of Psychiatry and the Law. (2005). *Ethics guidelines for the practice of forensic psychiatry.* https://www.aapl.org/ethics.htm

American Bar Association. (2022). *How to read a U.S. Supreme Court opinion.* https://www.americanbar.org/groups/public_education/publications/teaching-legal-docs/how-to-read-a-u-s-supreme-court-opinion/

American Bar Association Criminal Justice Section. (2023). *2023 plea bargain task force report.* https://www.americanbar.org/content/dam/aba/publications/criminaljustice/plea-bargain-tf-report.pdf

American Board of Forensic Psychology (n.d.). *About.* https://abfp.com/about/.

American Board of Forensic Psychology. (2021, February 5). *Overview and introduction to ABFP.* https://abpp.org/wp-content/uploads/2022/07/ABFP-Overview-Intro-to-ABFP-2-5-2021.pdf

American Board of Professional Psychology. (2024, April 11). *About ABPP.* https://abpp.org/about-abpp/

American Board of Psychiatry and Neurology. (2023). *2023 annual report.* https://abpn.org/wp-content/uploads/2024/04/ABPN_2023_Annual_Report_WEB.pdf

American Psychiatric Association. (1983). Statement on the insanity defense. *American Journal of Psychiatry, 140*(6), 681–686.

American Psychiatric Association. (2013). *The principles of medical ethics with annotations especially applicable to psychiatry.* https://www.psychiatry.org/getmedia/3fe5eae9-3df9-4561-a070-84a009c6c4a6/2013-APA-Principles-of-Medical-Ethics.pdf

American Psychological Association. (2002). Criteria for practice guideline development and evaluation. *American Psychologist, 57*(12), 1048–1051.

American Psychological Association. (2013). Specialty guidelines for forensic psychology. *American Psychologist, 68*(1), 7–19.

American Psychological Association. (2017). *Ethical principles of psychologists and code of conduct.* https://www.apa.org/ethics/code

American Psychological Association. (2020). *Publication manual of the American Psychological Association* (7th ed.). Author.

American Psychological Association Committee on Legal Issues. (2006). Strategies for private practitioners coping with subpoenas or compelled testimony for client records or test data. *Professional Psychology: Research and Practice, 37*(2), 215–222.

American Psychological Association Committee on Legal Issues. (2016). Strategies for private practitioners coping with subpoenas or compelled testimony for client/patient records or test data or test materials. *Professional Psychology: Research and Practice, 47*(1), 1–11.

American Psychological Association Committee on Psychological Tests and Assessment. (2022). Statement on third party observers in psychological testing and assessment: An updated framework for decision making. https://www.apa.org/science/programs/testing/third-party-observers.pdf

American Psychological Association Practice Organization. (2012). *How to handle subpoenas and depositions.* https://www.apaservices.org/practice/good-practice/subpoenas-depositions.pdf

American Psychological Foundation. *Amicus curiae brief program.* https://www.apa.org/about/offices/ogc/amicus

Association of State and Provincial Psychology Boards. (n.d.). *PSYPACT: Advancing the interjurisdictional practice of psychology.* https://psypact.org/

Association of State and Provincial Psychology Boards. (n.d.). *Maps and states.* https://psypact.org/mpage/psypactmap

Association of State and Provincial Psychology Boards. (2020). *Mobility program policies and procedures v. 12.2020.* https://cdn.ymaws.com/www.asppb.net/resource/resmgr/mobility_/12.2020_asppb_mobility_progr.pdf

Association of State and Provincial Psychology Boards. (2023). *PSYPACT Commission Annual Report 2022.* https://cdn.ymaws.com/psypact.org/resource/resmgr/annual_report_/psypact_commission_annual_re.pdf

Association of State and Provincial Psychology Boards. (2024, April 11). *Exam information.* https://www.asppb.net/

Bartol, C. R., & Bartol, A. M. (2013). History of forensic psychology. In I. M. Weiner & R. K. Otto (Eds.), *The handbook of forensic psychology* (4th ed., pp. 3–34). John Wiley & Sons.

Bartol, C. R., & Bartol, A. M. (2018). *Introduction to forensic psychology: Research and application* (5th ed.). Sage.

Batastini, A. B., Guyton, M. R., Bernhard, P. A., Folk, J. B., Knuth, S. B., Kohutis, E. A., Lugo, A., Stanfill, M. L., & Tussey, C. M. (2023). Recommendations for the use of telepsychology in psychology-law practice and research. *Professional Psychology: Research and Practice, 29*(3), 255–271.

Bernstein, D. E., & Lasker, E. G. (2015). Defending *Daubert*: It's time to amend federal rule of evidence 702. *William and Mary Law Review, 57*(1), 1–48.

Bersoff, D. N. (1986). Psychologists and the judicial system: Broader perspectives. *Law and Human Behavior, 10*(1–2), 151–165.

Bersoff, D. N. (2013). APA's amicus briefs: Informing public policy through the courts. *Monitor on Psychology, 44*(6), 5.

Bersoff, D. N., & Glass, D. J. (1995). The not-so *Weisman*: The supreme court's continuing misuse of social science research. *University of Chicago Law School Roundtable, 2*(1), 279–302.

Billauer, B. P. (2016). Daubert debunked: A history of legal retrogression and the need to reassess "scientific admissibility." *Suffolk Journal of Trial and Appellate Advocacy, 21*(1), 1–57.

Binder, R. L. (2002). Liability for the psychiatrist expert witness. *American Journal of Psychiatry, 159*(11), 1819–1825.

Black, B. (1988). A unified theory of scientific evidence. *Fordham Law Review, 56*(4), 595–695.

Blackstone, W. (1765). *Commentaries on the laws of England.* Oxford.

Bonnie, R. J., & Slobogin, C. (1981). The role of mental health professionals in the criminal process: The case for informed speculation. *Virginia Law Review, 61*(3), 427–452.

Bornmann, L. (2011). Scientific peer review. *Annual Review of Information Science and Technology, 45*(1), 197–245. https://doi.org/10.1002/aris.2011.1440450112

Bornstein, B. H., & Meissner, C. A. (2023). Influencing policy and procedure with law-psychology research: Why, when, where, how, and what. In D. DeMatteo & K. C. Scherr (Eds.), *The Oxford handbook of psychology and law* (pp. 18–35). Oxford University Press.

Brank, E. M. (2019). *The psychology of family law.* New York University Press.

Braswell, A. (1987). Resurrection of the ultimate issue rule Federal Rule of Evidence 704 (b) and the insanity defense. *Cornell Law Review, 70*(3), 620–640.

Brennan, M., Dilenschneider, D., Levin, M., & Robinson, J. (2010). Selecting and retaining an expert. In W. G. Couture (Ed.), *Litigators on experts: Strategies for managing expert witnesses from retention through trial* (pp. 1–65). American Bar Association.

Breyer, S. (2000). The role of science in the courtroom. *Issues in Science and Technology, 16*(4), 52–56.

Brodsky, S. L., Zapf, P. A., & Boccaccini, M. T. (2001). The last competency: An examination of legal, ethical, and professional ambiguities regarding evaluations of competence for execution. *Journal of Forensic Psychology Practice, 1*, 1–25.

Bronstein, D. A. (2012). *Law for the expert witness* (4th ed.). CRC Press.

Budd, K. S., Clark, J., & Connell, M. A. (2011). *Evaluation of parenting capacity in child protection*. Oxford University Press.

Burl, J., Shah, S., Filone, S., Foster, E., & DeMatteo, D. (2012). A survey of graduate training programs and coursework in forensic psychology. *Teaching of Psychology, 39*(1), 48–53.

Bush, S. S., Connell, M. A., & Denney, R. L. (2020). *Ethical practice in forensic psychology: A guide for mental health professionals* (2nd ed.). American Psychological Association.

Bütz, M. R., English, J. V., Meyers, J. E., & Cohen, L. J. (2023). Threats to the integrity of psychological assessment: The misuse of test raw data and materials. *Applied Neuropsychology: Adult*. https://doi.org/10.1080/23279095.2023.2241094

California Board of Psychology. (April 18, 2018). *PSYPACT—Status of PSYPACT and review of board concerns and feedback*. https://www.psychology.ca.gov/about_us/meetings/materials/20180510_27.pdf

Candilis, P. J., Dike, C. C., Meyer, D. J., Myers, W. C., & Weinstock, R. (2014). Should AAPL enforce its ethics? Challenges and solutions. *Journal of the American Academy of Psychiatry and the Law, 42*(3), 322–330.

Chen, D., Salekin, K., Olley, J. G., & Fulero, S. M. (2011). Research with offenders with intellectual disability. In B. Rosenfeld & S. D. Penrod (Eds.), *Research methods in forensic psychology* (pp. 421–432). John Wiley & Sons.

Cheng, E. K., & Yoon, A. H. (2005). Does *Frye* or *Daubert* matter? A study of scientific admissibility standards. *Virginia Law Review, 91*(2), 471–514.

Cicchini, M. D. (2021). The *Daubert* double standard. *Michigan State Law Review, 2021*(3), 705–764.

Clay, R. A. (2021, July 2). *PSYPACT: 26 states have now passed laws allowing interstate practice*. American Psychological Association. https://www.apaservices.org/practice/legal/technology/psypact-interstate-practicetelehealth

Cohen, D. (1988). Punishing the insane: Restriction of expert psychiatric testimony by Federal Rule of Evidence 704(b). *Florida Law Review, 40*(3), 541–561.

Cole, S. A. (2008). Out of the *Daubert* fire and into the *Frye*ing pan? Self-validation, meta-expertise and the admissibility of latent print evidence in *Frye* jurisdictions. *Minnesota Journal of Law, Science, and Technology, 9*(2), 453–542.

Columbia Law Review, Harvard Law Review, University of Pennsylvania Law Review, and Yale Law Journal. (2020). *The bluebook: A uniform system of citation* (21st ed.). Claitors Publication Division.

Committee on National Security Systems. (2010). *National information assurance (IA) glossary*. Retrieved from https://www.cnss.gov/Assets/pdf/cnssi_4009.pdf

Conklin, M. (2020). The *Alford* plea turns fifty: Why it deserves another fifty years. *Creighton Law Review, 54*(1), 1–18.

Constanzo, M., Krauss, D., & Pezdek, K. (Eds.) (2007). *Expert psychological testimony for the courts*. Erlbaum.

Corey, D. M., & Zelig, M. (2020). *Evaluations of police suitability and fitness for duty*. Oxford University Press.

Crumbley, D. L., & Seago, W. E. (2021). Do expert witnesses have immunity from civil liability? *Journal of Forensic and Investigative Accounting, 13*(3), 466–477.

Cunningham, M. D. (2010). *Evaluation for capital sentencing*. Oxford University Press.

Cunningham, M. D. (2016). Forensic psychology evaluations at capital sentencing. In R. Jackson & R. Roesch (Eds.), *Learning forensic assessment: Research and practice* (2nd ed.) (pp. 202–228). Routledge/Taylor & Francis Group.

Curcic, D. (2023, June 1). *Number of academic papers published per year.* WordsRated. https://wordsrated.com/number-of-academic-papers-published-per-year/#:~:text=As%20of%202020%2C%20there%20are,rate%20of%202.56%25%20every%20year

Cutler, B. L. & Kovera, M. B. (2010). *Evaluating eyewitness identification.* Oxford University Press.

Dahir, V. B., Richardson, J. T., Ginsburg, G. P., Gatowski, S. I., Dobbin, S. A., & Merlino, M. L. (2005). Judicial application of *Daubert* to psychological syndrome and profile evidence: A research note. *Psychology, Public Policy, and Law, 11*(1), 62–82.

DeAngelis, T. (2014). Is it time to specialize? *Monitor on Psychology, 45*(2), 50–52.

DeCamp, E., & DeCamp, W. (2022). Racially imbalanced peremptory challenges by the defense as a reactionary process. *Crime and Delinquency, 68*(5), 735–759.

DeMatteo, D., Burl, J., Filone, S., & Heilbrun, K. (2016). Training in forensic assessment and intervention: Implications for principles-based models. In R. Jackson & R. Roesch (Eds.), *Learning forensic assessment: Research and practice* (2nd ed.) (pp. 3–31). Routledge/Taylor & Francis Group.

DeMatteo, D., Fairfax-Columbo, J., & Desai, A. (2020). *Becoming a forensic psychologist.* Routledge/Taylor & Francis Group.

DeMatteo, D., Fishel, S., Jackson, C., & Kudatzky, A. (2024). Judges' *Daubert* decisions. In M. K. Miller, L. A. Yelderman, M. T. Huss, & J. A. Cantone (Eds.), *The Cambridge handbook of psychology and legal decision-making* (pp. 144–158). Cambridge University Press.

DeMatteo, D., Fishel, S., & Tansey, A. (2019). Expert evidence: The (unfulfilled) promise of *Daubert. Psychological Science in the Public Interest, 20*(3), 129–134.

DeMatteo, D., Fishel, S., Wiltsie, K., & Tansey, A. (2023). Legal and ethical issues in mental health assessment and treatment in jails. In V. Barber Rioja, A. Garcia-Mansilla, B. Subedi, & A. Batastini (Eds.), *The Oxford handbook of mental health assessment and treatment in jails* (pp. 272–288). Oxford University Press.

DeMatteo, D., Heilbrun, K., Thornewill, A., & Arnold, S. (2019). *Problem-solving courts and the criminal justice system.* Oxford University Press.

DeMatteo, D., Keesler, M. E., & Strohmaier, H. (2013). Accessing the law and legal literature. In I. B. Weiner & R. K. Otto (Eds.), *The handbook of forensic psychology* (4th ed.) (pp. 57–83). Wiley.

DeMatteo, D., Krauss, D. A., Fishel, S., & Wiltsie, K. (2022). The United States Supreme Court's enduring misunderstanding of insanity. *New Mexico Law Review, 52*(1), 34–69.

DeMatteo, D., Marczyk, G., Krauss, D. A., & Burl, J. (2009). Educational and training models in forensic psychology. *Training and Education in Professional Psychology, 3*(3), 184–191.

DeMatteo, D., Murphy, M., Galloway, M., & Krauss, D. A. (2015). A national survey of United States sexually violent person legislation: Policy, procedures, and practice. *International Journal of Forensic Mental Health, 14*(4), 245–266.

DeMatteo, D., Murrie, D. C., Anumba, N. M., & Keesler, M. E. (2011). *Forensic mental health assessments in death penalty cases.* Oxford University Press.

DeMatteo, D., & Scherr, K. C. (2023). Preface. In D. DeMatteo & K. C. Scherr (Eds.), *The Oxford handbook of psychology and law* (pp. ix–xi). Oxford University Press.

DeMers, S. T., Webb, C., & Horn, J. B. (2014). Psychology licensure and credentialing in the United States and Canada. In W. B. Johnson & N. J. Kaslow (Eds.), *The Oxford handbook of education and training in professional psychology* (pp. 201–213). American Psychological Association.

DeMier, R. L., & Krauss, D. A. (2023). Forensic report writing: Proposing a research agenda. In D. DeMatteo & K. C. Scherr (Eds.), *The Oxford handbook of psychology and law* (pp. 135–149). Oxford University Press.

DeMier, R. L., & Otto, R. K. (2017). Forensic report writing: Principles and challenges. In R. Roesch & A. N. Cook (Eds.), *International perspectives on forensic mental health. Handbook of forensic mental health services* (pp. 216–234). Routledge/Taylor & Francis Group.

Department of Justice. (2014). *Program statement 6010.05.* https://www.bop.gov/policy/progstat/6010_005.pdf

Devers, L. (2011). *Plea and charge bargaining: Research summary.* United States Department of Justice, Bureau of Justice Assistance. https://bja.ojp.gov/sites/g/files/xyckuh186/files/media/document/PleaBargainingResearchSummary.pdf

Dixon, L., & Gill, B. (2001). *Changes in the standards for admitting expert evidence in federal civil cases since the Daubert decision.* RAND Corporation. https://www.rand.org/pubs/monograph_reports/MR1439.html

Dreyer, D. N., Howard, F. B., & Leitch, A. M. (2011). Dancing with the Big Boys: Georgia adopts (most of) the Federal Rules of Evidence. *Mercer Law Review, 63*(1), 1–46.

Drogin, E. Y., & Barrett, C. L. (2010). *Evaluation for guardianship.* Oxford University Press.

Drogin, E. Y., & Barrett, C. L. (2013). Trial consultation. In I. B. Weiner (Series Ed.) & R. K. Otto (Vol. Ed.), *Handbook of psychology, Vol. 11: Forensic psychology* (2nd ed., pp. 648–663). John Wiley & Sons.

Drogin, E. Y., Commons, M. L., Gutheil, T. G., Meyer, D. J., & Norris, D. M. (2012). "Certainty" and expert mental health opinions in legal proceedings. *International Journal of Law and Psychiatry, 35*(5–6), 348–353.

Drogin, E. Y., Dattilio, F. M., Sadoff, R. L., & Gutheil, T. G. (Eds.) (2011). *Handbook of forensic assessment: Psychological and psychiatric perspectives.* John Wiley & Sons.

Drogin, E. Y., & Hagan, L. D. (2023). Trial consultation. In D. DeMatteo & K. C. Scherr (Eds.), *The Oxford handbook of psychology and law* (pp. 365–379). Oxford University Press.

Dvoskin, J., & Guy, L. (2008). On being an expert witness: It's not about you. *Psychiatry, Psychology and Law, 15*(2), 202–212.

Edens, J. F., Smith, S. T., Magyar, M. S., Gingrich, K., Pitta, A., & Petrila, J. (2012). "Hired guns," "charlatans," and their "voodoo psychobabble": Case law references to various forms of perceived bias among mental health expert witnesses. *Psychological Services, 9*(3), 259–271.

Emanuel, A. S. (1989). Guilty but mentally ill verdicts and the death penalty: An eighth amendment analysis. *North Carolina Law Review, 68,* 37–67.

Erickson, S. K., & Ewing, C. P. (2012). Legal contours of expert testimony. In I. B. Weiner & R. K. Otto (Eds). *Handbook of psychology: Forensic psychology* (Vol. 11, 2nd ed., pp. 62–74). John Wiley & Sons.

Ewing, C. P. (2003). Expert testimony: Law and practice. In A. M. Goldstein (Ed.), *Handbook of psychology: Forensic psychology* (Vol. 11, pp. 55–66). John Wiley & Sons.

Faigman, D. (2013). The *Daubert* revolution and the birth of modernity: Managing scientific evidence in the age of science. *University of California at Davis Law Review, 46,* 101–138.

Faigman, D. L., Cheng, E. K., Mnookin, J. L., Murphy, E. E., Sanders, J., & Slobogin, C. (2022). *Modern scientific evidence: The law and science of expert testimony* (Vol. 1). Thomson Reuters.

Faigman, D. L., & Monahan, J. (2009). Standards of legal admissibility and their implications for psychological science. In J. L. Skeem, K. S. Douglas, & S. O. Lilienfeld (Eds.), *Psychological science in the courtroom: Consensus and controversy* (pp. 3–25). Guilford Press.

Faigman, D. L., Porter, E., & Saks, M. J. (1994). Check your crystal ball at the courthouse door, please: Exploring the past, understanding the present, and worrying about the future of scientific evidence. *Cardozo Law Review, 15,* 1799–1835.

Faigman, D. L., Slobogin, C., & Monahan, J. (2016). Gatekeeping science: Using the structure of scientific research to distinguish between admissibility and weight in expert testimony. *Northwestern University Law Review, 110*(4), 859–904.

Fairfax-Columbo, J., Neeser, B., Kudatzky, A., & DeMatteo, D. (2023). Of capital importance: Considerations in capital sentencing contexts. In D. DeMatteo & K. C. Scherr (Eds.), *The Oxford handbook of psychology and law* (pp. 186–203). Oxford University Press.

Federal Judicial Center. (1994). *Reference manual on scientific evidence.* West Publishing.

Fisher, C. B. (2017). *Decoding the ethics code: A practical guide for psychologists* (4th ed.). Sage.

Flanagan, F. X. (2015). Peremptory challenges and jury selection. *The Journal of Law and Economics, 58*(2), 385–416.

Flores, D. M., Richardson, J. T., & Merlino, M. L. (2010). Examining the effects of the *Daubert* trilogy on expert evidence practices in federal civil court: An empirical analysis. *Southern Illinois University Law Journal, 34*(3), 533–564.

Fournier, L. R. (2016). The *Daubert* guidelines: Usefulness, utility, and suggestions for improving quality control. *Journal of Applied Research in Memory and Cognition, 5*, 308–313.

Fox, E., Sreenivsan, S., Weinberger, L., & Lee, A. (2022). Defining reasonable degree of certainty in sexually violent predator evaluations. *Professional Psychology: Research and Practice, 53*(4), 407–414.

Frederick, R. I., Miksell, J. W., Otto, R. K., Boone, K. B., Beattey, R. A., Sweet, J. J., Krauss, D. A., & Scroppo, J. (2024). Ethical considerations for demands for evidence in forensic examinations. *Professional Psychology: Research and Practice, 55*(3), 179–196.

Frierson, R. L. (2020). Examining the past and advocating for the future of forensic psychiatry training. *Journal of the American Academy of Psychiatry and the Law, 48*(1), 16–25.

Fuhrmann, G. S. W., & Zibbell, R. A. (2012). *Evaluation for child custody.* Oxford University Press.

Garrett, B. L., & Fabricant, M. C. (2018). The myth of the reliability test. *Fordham Law Review, 86*(4), 1559–1599.

Gatowski, S. I., Dobbin, S. A., Richardson, J. T., Ginsburg, G. P., Merlino, M. L., & Dahir, V. (2001). Asking the gatekeepers: A national survey of judges on judging expert evidence in a post-*Daubert* world. *Law and Human Behavior, 25*(5), 433–458. https://doi.org/10.1023/a:1012899030937

Giannelli, P. C. (1980). The admissibility of novel scientific evidence: *Frye v. United States*, a half-century later. *Columbia Law Review, 80*(6), 1197–1250.

Gianelli, P. C. (2010). "Reasonable scientific certainty": A phrase in search of a meaning. *Criminal Justice* (Spring): 40–41.

Gibson, B. R., & Phillips, G. (2016). Challenges and opportunities in correctional health care quality: A descriptive analysis of compliance with NCCHC standards. *Journal of Correctional Health Care, 22*(4), 280–289.

Godlee, F., Gales, C. R., & Martyn, C. N. (1998). Effect on the quality of peer review of blinding reviewers and asking them to sign their reports: A randomized controlled trial. *Journal of the American Medical Association, 280*(3), 237–240.

Golan, T. (2008). Revisiting the history of scientific expert testimony. *Brooklyn Law Review 73*(3), 879–942.

Goldstein, A. M., & Goldstein, N. E. S. (2010). *Evaluating capacity to waive Miranda rights.* Oxford University Press.

Goodman-Delahunty, J., & Foote, W. E. (2011). *Evaluation for workplace discrimination and harassment.* Oxford University Press.

Gottesman, M. H. (1994). Admissibility of expert testimony after *Daubert*: The "prestige" factor. *Emory Law Journal, 43*(3), 867–884.

Gould, J. W., & Mulchay, C. (2023). Child custody evaluations. In D. DeMatteo & K. C. Scherr (Eds.), *The Oxford handbook of psychology and law* (pp. 237–257). Oxford University Press.

Graham, M. H. (1994). *Daubert v. Merrell Dow Pharmaceuticals, Inc.*: No *Frye*, now what? *Criminal Law Bulletin, 30*(2), 153–171.

Green, E. D., Nesson C. R., & Murray, P. L. (2017). *Problems, cases, and materials on evidence* (4th ed.). Aspen Publishing.

Greenberg, S. A., & Shuman, D. W. (1997). Irreconcilable conflict between therapeutic and forensic roles. *Professional Psychology: Research and Practice, 28*(1), 50–57.
Greenberg, S. A., & Shuman, D. W. (2007). When worlds collide: Therapeutic and forensic roles. *Professional Psychology: Research and Practice, 38*(2), 129–132.
Greiffenstein, M. F., & Kaufmann, P. J. (2012). Neuropsychology and the law: Principles of productive attorney-neuropsychologist relations. In G. J. Larrabee (Ed.), *Forensic neuropsychology: A scientific approach* (2nd ed., pp. 75–98). Oxford University Press.
Griffith, E. E. H. (Ed.). (2018). *Ethics challenges in forensic psychiatry and psychology practice.* Columbia University Press.
Grisso, T. (1986). *Evaluating competencies: Forensic assessments and instruments.* Plenum Press.
Grisso, T. (2003). *Evaluating competencies: Forensic assessments and instruments* (2nd ed.). Kluwer.
Grisso, T., & Brodsky, S. L. (Eds.) (2018). *The roots of modern psychology and law: A narrative history.* Oxford University Press.
Groscup, J. L., Penrod, S. D., Studebaker, C. A., Huss, M. T., & O'Neil, K. M. (2002). The effects of *Daubert* on the admissibility of expert testimony in state and federal criminal cases. *Psychology, Public Policy, and Law, 8*(4), 339–372.
Haigh, C. (2023). *Guide to graduate programs in forensic and legal psychology: A resource for prospective students* (6th ed.). https://ap-ls.org/resources/training/graduate#guide-to-graduate-programs-in-legal-and-forensic-psychology
Hamilton, R. K. B., Phelan, C. H., Chin, N. A., Wyman, M. F., Lambrou, N., Cobb, N., Kind, A. J. H., Blazel, H., Asthana, S., & Gleason, C. E. (2020). The U-ARE protocol: A pragmatic approach to decisional capacity assessment for clinical research. *Journal of Alzheimer's Disease, 73*(2), 431–442.
Haney, C., Banks, W. C., & Zimbardo, P. G. (1973). A study of prisoners and guards in a simulated prison. *Naval Research Review, 30*, 4–17.
Harlan, E. R., & Routh, J. B. (Eds.) (2016). *Fifty-state survey*: Daubert *v.* Frye*—Admissibility of expert testimony.* American Bar Association.
Harris, A. M. (2006). Two constitutional wrongs do not make right: Double jeopardy and prosecutorial misconduct under the *Brady* Doctrine. *Cardozo Law Review, 28*(2), 931–955.
Harris, E. & Younggren, J. N. (2011). Risk management in the digital world. *Professional Psychology: Research and Practice, 42*(6), 412–418. https://doi.org/10.1037/a0025139
Haug, M., & Baird, E. (2011). Finding the error in *Daubert. Hastings Law Journal, 62*(3), 737–756.
Heilbrun, K. (2001). *Principles of forensic mental health assessment.* Kluwer Academic/Plenum Press.
Heilbrun, K., & Brooks, S. (2010). Forensic psychology and forensic science: A proposed agenda for the next decade. *Psychology, Public Policy, and Law, 16*(3), 219–253.
Heilbrun, K., DeMatteo, D., Brooks Holliday, S., & LaDuke, C. (Eds.) (2014). *Forensic mental health assessment: A casebook* (2nd ed.). Oxford University Press.
Heilbrun, K., DeMatteo, D., & Goldstein, N. E. S. (Eds.) (2016). *APA handbook of psychology and juvenile justice.* American Psychological Association.
Heilbrun, K., DeMatteo, D., King, C., & Filone, S. (2017). *Evaluating juvenile transfer and disposition: Law, science, and practice.* Routledge/Taylor & Francis Group.
Heilbrun, K., Rizzo, M., Wiltsie, K., & Zapotocky, H. (2023). Framework for forensic mental health assessments: Principles, standards of care, and standards of practice. In D. DeMatteo & K. C. Scherr (Eds.), *The Oxford handbook of psychology and law* (pp. 101–115). Oxford University Press.
Herman, M., & Sharer, N. (2013). Trying to summarize state licensure laws for psychologists: Burial by grains of salt. *Training and Education in Professional Psychology, 7*(2), 123–133.

Hilbert, J. (2019). The disappointing history of science in the courtroom: *Frye*, *Daubert*, and the ongoing crisis of "junk science" in criminal trials. *Oklahoma Law Review*, *71*(3), 759–822.

Hitt, J. (2022, July 15). Want to do less time? A prison consultant might be able to help. *New York Times Magazine*. https://www.nytimes.com/2022/06/07/magazine/prison-consultants-fixers.html

Huss, M. T. (2014). *Forensic psychology: Research, clinical practice, and applications* (2nd ed.). John Wiley & Sons.

Igoumenou, A. (Ed.). (2020). *Ethical issues in clinical forensic psychiatry*. Springer.

Imwinkelried, E. (1994). The next step after *Daubert*: Developing a similarity epistemological approach to ensuring reliability of nonscientific expert testimony. *Cardozo Law Review*, *15*, 2271–2294.

Jackson, R., & Roesch, R. (Eds.) (2016). *Learning forensic assessment: Research and practice* (2nd ed.). Routledge/Taylor & Francis Group.

Jefferson, T, Alderson, P., Wager, E., & Davidoff, F. (2002). Effects of editorial peer review: A systematic review. *Journal of the American Medical Association*, *287*(21), 2784–2786.

Jensen, E. G. (1993). When "hired guns" backfire: The witness immunity doctrine and the negligent expert witness. *University of Missouri at Kansas City Law Review*, *62*(1), 185–210.

Joint resolution on the relationship of psychotherapy to medicine. (1954). *Journal of the American Psychoanalytic Association*, *2*(4), 813–816.

Jurs, A., & Devito, S. (2013). The stricter standard: An empirical assessment of *Daubert*'s effect on civil defendants. *Catholic University Law Review*, *62*(3), 675–732.

Jurs, A. W. (2012). Questions from the bench and independent experts: A study of the practices of state court judges. *University of Pittsburgh Law Review*, *74*(1), 47–83.

Jurs, A. W. (2016). Expert prevalence, persuasion and price: What trial participants really think about experts. *Indiana Law Journal*, *91*(2), 353–391.

Kane, A. W., & Dvoskin, J. A. (2011). *Evaluation for personal injury claims*. Oxford University Press.

Kaplow, L. (2012). Burden of proof. *Yale Law Journal*, *121*, 738–859.

Kane, A., Ackerman, M, & Gould, J. (2023). *Update to psychological experts in divorce actions* (7th ed.). Wolters Kluwer Press.

Kavanaugh, A., & Grisso, T. (2021). *Evaluations for sentencing of juveniles in criminal court*. Oxford University Press.

Kaye, D. H. (2010). *The double helix and the law of evidence*. Harvard University Press.

Kaye, D. H., Bernstein, D. E., & Mnookin, J. L. (2010). *The new Wigmore: A treatise on evidence—Expert evidence* (2nd ed.). Aspen Publishers.

Kelley, S. Zelle, H., Brogan, L., & Goldstein, N. E. S. (2018). Review of research and recent case law on understanding and appreciation of *Miranda* warnings. In M. K. Miller & B. H. Bornstein (Eds.), *Advances in psychology and law* (Vol. 3) (pp. 77–117). Springer.

Khaddouma, A. (2023). Which work setting as the most specialists? *On Board with Professional Psychology*, *1*(1), 1–5.

Kilbert, K. K. (2017). Instant replay and interlocutory appeals. *Baylor Law Review*, *69*(2), 267–314.

Kim, S. Y. H. (2010). *Evaluation of capacity to consent to treatment and research*. Oxford University Press.

King, C. M., Grove, L., Hitchcock, S., Gonzalez, K., Palardy, A., & Guevara, N. (2023). Forensic mental health assessments in juvenile justice contexts. In D. DeMatteo & K. C. Scherr (Eds.), *The Oxford handbook of psychology and law* (pp. 273–288). Oxford University Press.

Kovera, M. B., & Austin, J. L. (2015). Expert testimony. In J. D. Wright (Ed.), *International encyclopedia of the social & behavioral sciences* (2nd ed.) (pp. 582–587). Elsevier.

Kovera, M. B., & McAuliff, B. D. (2000). The effects of peer review and evidence quality on judge evaluations of psychological science: Are judges effective gatekeepers? *Journal of Applied Psychology*, *85*(4), 574–586.

Krafka, C., Dunn, M. A., Johnson, M. T., Cecil, J. C., & Miletich, D. (2002). Judge and attorney experiences, practices, and concerns regarding expert testimony in federal civil trials. *Psychology, Public Policy, and Law, 8*(3), 309–332.

Krauss, D. A., Cassar, D., & Strother, A. (2009). The admissibility of expert testimony in the United States, the Commonwealth, and elsewhere. In D. A. Krauss & J. D. Lieberman (Eds.), *Psychological expertise in court: Psychology in the courtroom*, Vol. 2 (pp. 1–24). Ashgate.

Krauss, D. A., Gongola, J., Scurich, N., & Busch, B. (2018). Mental state at the time of offense in the hot tub: An empirical examination of concurrent expert testimony in an insanity case. *Behavioral Sciences and the Law, 36*(3), 358–372.

Krauss, D. A., & Sales, B. D. (2000). Legal standards, expertise, and experts in the resolution of contested child custody cases. *Psychology, Public Policy, and Law, 6*(4), 843–879.

Krauss, D. A., & Sales, B. D. (2001). The effects of clinical and scientific expert testimony on juror decision making in capital sentencing. *Psychology, Public Policy, and Law, 7*(2), 267–310.

Krauss, D. A., & Scurich, N. (2014). The Impact of case factors on jurors' decisions in a sexual violent predator hearing. *Psychology, Public Policy, and Law, 20*(1), 135–145.

Kruh, I., & Grisso, T. (2009). *Evaluation of juveniles' competence to stand trial.* Oxford University Press.

Kuhn, T. S. (1962). *The structure of scientific evolutions.* University of Chicago Press.

Leak, S. R. (2021). Peremptory challenges: Preserving an unequal allocation and the potential promise of progressive prosecution. *The Journal of Criminal Law and Criminology, 111*(1), 275–314.

Lee, C. J., Sugimoto, C. R., Zhang, G., & Cronin, B. (2013). Bias in peer review. *Journal of the American Society for Information Science and Technology, 64*(1), 2–17.

Lewin, J. L. (1998). The genesis and evolution of legal uncertainty about "reasonable medical certainty." *Maryland Law Review, 57*(2), 380–503.

LexisNexis. (2020). Shepard's *signal indicators and treatments.* https://www.lexisnexis.com/pdf/lexis-advance/Shepards-Signal-Indicators-and-analysis-phrases-Final.pdf

Lieberman, J. D., & Olson, J. (2009). The psychology of jury selection. In J. D. Lieberman & D. A. Krauss (Eds.), *Jury psychology: Social aspects of trial processes* (Psychology in the courtroom, Vol. 1) (pp. 97–128). Ashgate.

Lubet, S., & Boals, E. I. (2020). *Expert testimony: A guide for expert witnesses and the lawyers who examine them* (4th ed.). National Institute for Trial Advocacy.

Mabe, M. (2003, July). The growth and number of journals. *Serials, 16*(2), 191–197.

Malone, D. M., & Zwier, P. J. (2014). *Effective expert testimony* (3rd ed.). National Institute for Trial Advocacy.

Marcopulos, B. A., Kaufmann, P., & Patel, A. C. (2024). Forensic neuropsychological assessment, *Behavioral Sciences & the Law, 42*(4), 265–277. https://doi.org/10.1002/bsl.2656

Masterson, L. R. (1998). Witness immunity or malpractice liability for professionals hired as experts? *The Review of Litigation, 17*(2), 393–413.

McAuliff, B. D., & Groscup, J. L. (2009). Daubert and psychological science in court: Judging validity from the bench, bar, and jury box. In J. L. Skeem, K. S. Douglas, & S. O. Lilienfeld (Eds.), *Psychological science in the courtroom: Consensus and controversy* (pp. 26–52). Guilford Press.

McCauliff, C. M. A. (1982). Burdens of proof: Degrees of belief, quanta of evidence, or constitutional guarantees? *Vanderbilt Law Review, 35*(6), 1293–1335.

McCormick, M. (1982). Scientific evidence: defining new approach to admissibility. *Iowa Law Review, 67*(5), 879–916.

McDowell, C. M. (1997). Authorizing the expert witness to assassinate character for profit: A re-examination of the testimonial immunity of the expert witness. *University of Memphis Law Review, 28*(1), 239–269.

McKeever, A. (2020, Sept.). *Why the Supreme Court ended up with nine justices—And how that could change.* https://www.nationalgeographic.com/history/article/why-us-supreme-court-nine-justices.

Meixner, J. B., & Diamond, S. S. (2014). The hidden *Daubert* factor: How judges use error rates in assessing scientific evidence. *Wisconsin Law Review, 2014*(6), 1063–1133.

Melton, G. B., Petrila, J., Poythress, N. G., Slobogin, C., Otto, R. K., Mossman, D., & Condie, L. O. (2018). *Psychological evaluations for the courts* (4th ed.). Guilford Press.

Milgram, S. (1963). Behavioral study of obedience. *Journal of Abnormal and Social Psychology, 67*, 371–378.

Miller, E. (2011). The strongest defense you've never heard of: The Constitution's federal enclave doctrine and its effect on litigants, states, and Congress. *Hofstra Labor and Employment Law Journal, 29*(1), 73–98.

Milroy, C. M. (2017). A brief history of the expert witness. *Academic Forensic Pathology, 7*(4), 516–526.

Monahan, J., & Walker, L. (2022). *Social science in law: Cases and materials* (10th ed.). West Academic Publishing.

Morse, S. (1978). Crazy behavior, morals, and science: An analysis of mental health law. *Southern California. Law Review, 51*(1), 527–654.

Morse, S. J., & Hoffman, M. B. (2008). The uneasy entente between insanity and mens rea: Beyond *Clark v. Arizona. Journal of Law and Criminology, 97*(4), 1071–1150.

Moser, D. J., Arndt, S., Kanz, J. E., Benjamin, M. L., Bayless, J. D., Reese, R. L., Paulsen, J. S., & Flaum, M. A. (2004). Coercion and informed consent in research involving prisoners. *Comprehensive Psychiatry, 45*(1), 1–9.

Moynihan, C. (2004, October 6). Ink expert in Stewart trial found not guilty of perjury. *New York Times.* https://www.nytimes.com/2004/10/06/business/ink-expert-in-stewart-trial-found-not-guilty-of-perjury.html

Münsterberg, H. (1908). *On the witness stand: Essays on psychology and crime.* Doubleday.

Murrie, D. C., & Boccaccini, M. T. (2015). Adversarial allegiance among expert witnesses. *Annual Review of Law and Social Science, 11*, 37–55.

National Center for Interstate Compacts. (n.d.). *Home.* https://compacts.csg.org/

National Commission on Forensic Science. (2016, January 12). Views of the Commission regarding use of the term "reasonable scientific certainty." https://www.justice.gov/archives/ncfs/page/file/831786/download

National Research Council. (in press). *Reference manual on scientific evidence* (4th ed.). National Academies Press.

Neal, T. M. S. (2018). Forensic psychology and correctional psychology: Distinct but related subfields of psychological science and practice. *American Psychologist, 73*(5), 651–662.

Neal, T. M. S., Martire, K., Otto, R., Johan, J. L., & Mathers, E. M. (2022). The law meets psychological expertise: Eight best practices to improve forensic psychological assessment. *Annual Review of Law and Social Science, 18*, 169–192.

Neal, T. M. S., Slobogin, C., Saks, M. J., Faigman, D., & Geisinger, K. F. (2019). Psychological assessments in legal contexts. Are courts keeping "junk science" out of the courtroom? *Psychological Science in the Public Interest, 20*(3), 135–164.

Oswald, M. (1995, March 6). Poll shows legislators don't have many fans. *The New Mexican*, B-1, B2.

Otto, R. K. (1989). Bias and expert testimony of mental health professionals in adversarial proceedings: A preliminary investigation. *Behavioral Sciences & the Law, 7*(2), 267–273.

Otto, R. K. (2009). Meaningful consideration of competence to be executed. In R. F. Schopp, R. L. Wierner, B. H. Bornstein, & S. L. Willborn (Eds.), *Mental disorder and criminal law: Responsibility, punishment, and competence* (pp. 191–204). Springer.

Otto, R. K. (2023). Ethics in forensic psychology practice. In D. DeMatteo & K. Scherr (Eds.), *Oxford handbook of psychology and law* (pp. 116–134). Oxford University Press.

Otto, R. K., DeMier, R. L., & Boccaccini, M. T. (2014). *Forensic reports & testimony: A guide to effective communication for psychologists and psychiatrists.* John Wiley & Sons.

Otto, R. K., Goldstein, A. M., & Heilbrun, K. (2017). *Ethics in forensic psychology practice.* John Wiley & Sons.

Otto, R. K., & Heilbrun, K. (2002). The practice of forensic psychology. *American Psychologist, 57*(1), 5–18.
Otto, R. K., & Krauss, D. A. (2009). Contemplating the presence of third party observes and facilitators in psychological evaluations. *Assessment, 16*(4), 362–372.
Packer, I. K. (2009). *Evaluation of criminal responsibility.* Oxford University Press.
Packer, I. K., & Kois, L. E. (2023). Criminal responsibility evaluations. In D. DeMatteo & K. C. Scherr (Eds.), *The Oxford handbook of psychology and law* (pp. 170–185). Oxford University Press.
Page, C., Stamm, K., Assefa, M., & Khaddouma, A. (2024). Datapoint: The most and least common specialty areas for licensed psychologists. *Monitor on Psychology, 55*(2), 19.
Piechowski, L. D. (2011). *Evaluation of workplace disability.* Oxford University Press.
Piechowski, L. D. (2023). Evaluating workplace disability. In D. DeMatteo & K. C. Scherr (Eds.), *The Oxford handbook of psychology and law* (pp. 223–236). Oxford University Press.
Pinals, D. A., & Mossman, D. (2011). *Evaluation for civil commitment.* Oxford University Press.
Pinta, E. R. (2009). Decisions to breach confidentiality when prisoners report violations of institutional rules. *Journal of the American Academy of Psychiatry and the Law, 37*(2), 150–154.
Pirelli, G., Beatty, R. A., & Zapf, P. A. (Eds.). (2017). *The ethical practice of forensic psychology: A casebook.* Oxford University Press.
Popper, K. (2002a). *Conjectures and refutations.* Routledge.
Popper, K. (2002b). *The logic of scientific discovery.* Routledge.
PSYPACT. (2016). *Psychology Interjurisdictional Compact (PSYPACT).* https://cdn.ymaws.com/psypact.site-ym.com/resource/resmgr/psychology_interjurisdiction.pdf
PSYPACT. (2016). *Psychology Interjurisdictional Compact (PSYPACT)ArtVI(A)(1).* https://cdn.ymaws.com/psypact.site-ym.com/resource/resmgr/psychology_interjurisdiction.pdf
Redlich, A. D. (2016). The validity of pleading guilty. In B. H. Bornstein & M. K. Miller (Eds.), *Advances in psychology and law* (Vol. 2) (pp. 1–26). Springer.
Redlich, A. D., & Özdoğru, A. A. (2009). *Alford* pleas in the age of innocence. *Behavioral Sciences and the Law, 27*(3), 467–488.
Richardson, J. T., Ginsburg, G. P., Gatowski, S., & Dobbin, S. (1995). The problems of applying *Daubert* to psychological syndrome evidence. *Judicature, 79*(1), 10–16.
Riggs Romaine, C. L., Kemp, K., & DeMatteo, D. (2010). Evaluation of juvenile competency to proceed: Applying the *Dusky* standard. *Journal of Forensic Psychology Practice, 10*(1), 1–12.
Risinger, M. D. (2000). Navigating expert reliability: Are criminal standards of certainty being left on the dock? *Albany Law Review, 64*(1), 99–149.
Robertson, C. T. (2010). Blind expertise. *New York University Law Review, 85*(1), 174–257.
Robertson, C. T., & Yokum, D. V. (2012). The effect of blinded experts on juror verdicts. *Journal of Empirical Legal Studies, 9*(4), 765–794.
Rogers, R., & Bender, S. D. (Eds.) (2018). *Clinical assessment of malingering and deception* (4th ed.). Guilford Press.
Rogers, R., Pan, M., & Drogin, E. Y. (2023). Response styles with the forensic context: Conceptual issues and assessment methods. In D. DeMatteo & K. C. Scherr (Eds.), *The Oxford handbook of psychology and law* (pp. 326–342). Oxford University Press.
Rothwell, P. M., & Martyn, C. N. (2000). Reproducibility of peer review in clinical neuroscience: Is agreement between reviewers any greater than would be expected by chance alone? *Brain, 123,* 1964–1969.
Sadoff, R. L. (2015). *The evolution of forensic psychiatry: History, current developments, future directions.* Oxford University Press.
Saks, M. J. (2009). Judging admissibility. *Journal of Corporation Law, 35*(1), 135–158.
Saks, M. J., & Faigman, D. L. (2005). Expert evidence after *Daubert. Annual Review of Law and Social Science, 1,* 105–130.
Schauer, F., & Spellman, B. A. (2013). Is expert evidence really different? *Notre Dame Law Review, 89*(1), 1–26.

Schopp, R. (1991). The psychotherapist's duty to protect the public: The appropriate standard and the foundation in legal theory and empirical premises. *Nebraska Law Review, 70*, 327–360.

Schweitzer, N. J., & Saks, M. J. (2009). The gatekeeper effect: The impact of judges' admissibility decisions on the persuasiveness of expert testimony. *Psychology, Public Policy, and Law, 15*(1), 1–18.

Serota, M. (2011). Stare decisis and the Brady Doctrine. *Harvard Law and Policy Review, 5*(2), 415–432.

Shuman, D., Cunningham, D., Connell, M., & Reid, M. (2003). Interstate forensic psychology consultations: A call for reform and proposal of a model rule. *Professional Psychology: Research and Practice, 34*(3), 233–239.

Simon, R. & Shuman, D. (1999). Conducting forensic examinations on the road: are you practicing your profession without a license? *Journal of American Academy of Psychiatry & Law, 27*(1), 75–82.

Sims, D., Dove, C., & Frederick, R. (2023). Transparency in forensic exams. *Nevada Law Journal, 24*(2), 531–642.

Slobogin, C. (1989). The "ultimate issue" issue. *Behavioral Sciences & the Law, 7*(2), 259–266. https://doi.org/10.1002/bsl.2370070209

Slobogin, C., Hafemeister, T. L., & Mossman, D. (2020). *Law and the mental health system: Civil and criminal aspects* (7th ed.). West Publishing.

Stein, C. T., & Younggren, J. N. (Eds.) (2019). *Forensic psychology in military courts.* American Psychological Association.

Stern, L. H., & Horvitz, S. A. (2002). A test for "general acceptance" under *Daubert. Journal of Forensic Economics, 15*(3), 285–293.

Sung, T. (1981). *The washing away of wrongs* (B. McKnight, Trans.). University of Michigan Center for Chinese Studies.

Taube, D. O., Shapiro, D. L., Harster, K., Cruitt, P., & Maddux, J. (2023). Problems with interjurisdictional regulation of psychological practice. *Professional Psychology: Research and Practice, 54*(6), 389–402.

Thompson Reuters. (n.d.). *Westlaw: KeyCite.* https://legal.thomsonreuters.com/en/products/westlaw/keycite

Trestman, R. L. (2014). Ethics, the law, and prisoners: Protecting society, changing human behavior, and protecting human rights. *Bioethical Inquiry, 11*(3), 311–318.

Tucillo, J., DeFilippis, N., Denney, R. & Dsurney, J. (2002). Licensure requirements for interjurisdictional forensic evaluations. *Professional Psychology: Research and Practice, 33*(4), 377–383.

U.S. Department of Justice, Office of the U.S. Attorney General. (2016, September 16). Memorandum for heads of departments components. Recommendations of the National Commission of Forensic Science. https://www.justice.gov/opa/file/891366/download

Vanderpool, D. (2014). Requests for disclosure of psychological testing information. *Innovations in Clinical Neuroscience, 11*(11–12), 41–44.

Vickers, A. L. (2005). *Daubert*, critique and interpretation: What empirical studies tell us about the application of *Daubert. University of San Francisco Law Review, 40*(1), 109–147.

Walker, L., & Monahan, J. (1987). Social frameworks: A new use of social science in law. *Virginia Law Review, 73*(3), 559–589.

Walker, L. E., & Shapiro, D. (2020). Forensic experts and attorneys: Communication process. In L. E. Walker, D. Shapiro, & S. Akl (Eds.), *Introduction to forensic psychology* (2nd ed., pp. 351–363). Springer.

Weiss, D., & LaPorte, G. (2018). Uncertainty ahead: A shift in how federal scientific experts can testify. *National Institute of Justice Journal, 279*, 1–8.

Weiss, K. J., Watson, C., & Xuan, Y. (2014). *Frye*'s backstory: A tale of murder, a retracted confession, and scientific hubris. *The Journal of the American Academy of Psychiatry and the Law, 42*(2), 226–233.

Wiener, R. L., & Brank, E. M. (Eds.) (2013). *Problem-solving courts: Social science and legal perspectives*. Springer.

Wigmore, J. H. (1909). Professor Muensterberg and the psychology of testimony. *Illinois Law Review, 3*(7), 399–445.

Wiltsie, K., Tansey, A., & DeMatteo, D. (2021, February). Expansion of readily identifiable victims within the scope of the duty to protect. *American Psychology-Law Society Newsletter*. https://ap-ls.org/resources/newsletter/2021/feb2021/

Witt, P. H., & Conroy, M. A. (2009). *Evaluation of sexually violent predators*. Oxford University Press.

Witt, P. H., & DeMatteo, D. (2019). Sexually violent predator laws: Historical development and evolution. In W. T. Donohue & D. S. Bromberg (Eds.), *Sexually violent predators: A clinical science handbook* (pp. 9–20). Springer.

Wolfberg, D. M. (2021, January 13). *Interpretation of PSYPACT re application of state law*. https://cdn.ymaws.com/psypact.siteym.com/resource/resmgr/legal_opinions/psypact_legal_opinion_re_app.pdf

Younggren, J. N., Gottlieb, M. C., & Baker, E. (2022). Navigating the labyrinth of professional regulations: Surviving in a flawed regulatory system. *Professional Psychology: Research and Practice, 53*(4), 333–339.

Your lawmakers at work. (1996, February 1). *The Albuquerque Tribune*, B8.

Zapf, P. A. (2009). Elucidating the contours of competency for execution: The implications of *Ford* and *Panetti* for the assessment of CFE. *Journal of Psychiatry and Law, 37*(2–3), 269–307.

Zapf, P. A. (2016). Competency for execution. In R. Jackson & R. Roesch (Eds.), *Learning forensic assessment: Research and practice* (2nd ed., pp. 229–248). Routledge/Taylor & Francis Group.

Zapf, P. A., Boccaccini, M. T., & Brodsky, S. L. (2003). Assessment of competency for execution: Professional guidelines and an evaluation checklist. *Behavioral Sciences and the Law, 21*(1), 103–120.

Zapf, P. A., & Roesch, R. (2009). *Evaluation of competence to stand trial*. Oxford University Press.

Index

Note: Tables are indicated by an italic t following the page number

For the benefit of digital users, indexed terms that span two pages (e.g., 52–53) may, on occasion, appear on only one of those pages.

Court Cases Index

For the benefit of digital users, indexed terms that span two pages (e.g., 52–53) may, on occasion, appear on only one of those pages.